Delivering Digital Solutions gives Requirements Engineers the practical understanding needed to ensure their specifications translate into effective, high-quality systems that deliver real value after go-live.

Erivan de Sena Ramos CBAP PMP CSM,
Principal Business Analyst, Esri Australia

An essential guide for delivering robust digital solutions at scale. It brings clarity to complex delivery practices and equips professionals across disciplines with actionable insights and structure.

Harpal Lidder, *Vice President, IIBA Toronto*
and Business Analyst, MiWay, City of Mississauga

It is one of the best guides for acquiring a technical background, with all essential pieces of knowledge meticulously curated into a comprehensive learning experience. This book will be invaluable to non-technical roles in software development. As someone who entered this industry from the humanities and had to walk the extra mile to learn the technical aspects, I believe people with similar backgrounds would greatly benefit from reading this book.

Iurii Gomon, *Founder, The Passionate Business Analyst*

Delivering Digital Solutions provides comprehensive and insightful insights into the methodologies, processes, and practical and pragmatic considerations for designing modern, state-of-the-art cloud-based software. This reference guide empowers software architects to reduce time-to-market, streamline operations and turn digital vision into a measurable competitive advantage.

Albert Hui, MSc

This book bridges strategy and execution with clarity. A practical guide for building and delivering effective digital products in fast-moving enterprise environments.

Sibasis Padhi, *Microservices & Cloud Performance*
Optimization Expert, Fintech Solutions

Delivering Digital Solutions offers a concise, comprehensive guide to the methods essential for creating and realising effective digital solutions – a true capstone in this series for digital delivery professionals.

Joris Schut CISA CBAP CGEIT, *Business Advisor,*
BearingPoint

This book is a clear, practical and deeply informed guide to software engineering and deployment. An essential companion for anyone involved in modern digital solution delivery.

Carl Sharman, *Head of Software Development,*
United Learning

Although I have not worked directly in software engineering, testing or deployment, *Delivering Digital Solutions* has served as an excellent reference, enabling me to communicate more effectively with my delivery teams. The coverage of topics is appropriately broad and detailed, allowing readers to consult each section as needed.

Rizwana Qureshi, *Customer Journey Lead,*
Lloyds Banking Group PLC

DELIVERING DIGITAL SOLUTIONS

BCS, THE CHARTERED INSTITUTE FOR IT

BCS, The Chartered Institute for IT, is committed to making IT good for society. We use the power of our network to bring about positive, tangible change. We champion the global IT profession and the interests of individuals, engaged in that profession, for the benefit of all.

Exchanging IT expertise and knowledge
The Institute fosters links between experts from industry, academia and business to promote new thinking, education and knowledge sharing.

Supporting practitioners
Through continuing professional development and a series of respected IT qualifications, the Institute seeks to promote professional practice tuned to the demands of business. It provides practical support and information services to its members and volunteer communities around the world.

Setting standards and frameworks
The Institute collaborates with government, industry and relevant bodies to establish good working practices, codes of conduct, skills frameworks and common standards. It also offers a range of consultancy services to employers to help them adopt best practice.

Become a member
Over 70,000 people including students, teachers, professionals and practitioners enjoy the benefits of BCS membership. These include access to an international community, invitations to a roster of local and national events, career development tools and a quarterly thought-leadership magazine. Visit www.bcs.org to find out more.

Further information
BCS, The Chartered Institute for IT,
3 Newbridge Square,
Swindon, SN1 1BY, United Kingdom.
T +44 (0) 1793 417 417
(Monday to Friday, 09:00 to 17:00 UK time)
bcs.org/contact

shop.bcs.org/
publishing@bcs.uk

bcs.org/qualifications-and-certifications/certifications-for-professionals/

DELIVERING DIGITAL SOLUTIONS
Software engineering, testing and deployment

Peter Thompson

Published by BCS Learning and Development Ltd, a wholly owned subsidiary of BCS, The Chartered Institute for IT, 3 Newbridge Square, Swindon, SN1 1BY, UK.
www.bcs.org

EU GPSR Authorised Representative: LOGOS EUROPE, 9 Rue Nicolas Poussin, 17000 La Rochelle, France.
Contact@logoseurope.eu

Paperback ISBN: 978-1-78017-7113
PDF ISBN: 978-1-78017-7120
ePUB ISBN: 978-1-78017-7137

Ebook available

British Cataloguing in Publication Data.
A CIP catalogue record for this book is available at the British Library.

Publisher's acknowledgements
Reviewers: Holly Cummins, Amanda Chessell, Catherine Plumridge, Maria Papastashi
Publisher: Ian Borthwick
Commissioning editor: Heather Wood
Production manager: Florence Leroy
Project manager: Sunrise Setting Ltd
Copy-editor: Gary Smith
Proofreader: Barbara Eastman
Indexer: David Gaskell
Cover design: Alex Wright
Cover image: iStock/Chunyip Wong
Sales director: Charles Rumball
Typeset by Lapiz Digital Services, Chennai, India

CONTENTS

LIST OF FIGURES AND TABLES

ABOUT THE AUTHOR

Peter Thompson, having graduated from Leicester Polytechnic (now De Montfort University) in 1988 with a bachelor's degree in computer science, has amassed over 35 years' experience working in a variety of business change and solution development roles, including junior programmer, project manager, information systems consultant, systems development manager and managing director of an independent software house. His experience spans a diverse range of industries working with clients from broadcasting, utilities, logistics, financial services, commodities trading, food service, recruitment and leisure hire.

A Fellow of BCS, The Chartered Institute for IT, Peter is currently Learning Services Director at Assist Knowledge Development Ltd, an external examiner for the BCS International Diploma in Business Analysis, chief examiner for the BCS International Diploma in Solution Development and a member of the Leadership Panel for the BCS Business Systems Development certification schemes. He specialises in best practice techniques and standards in business analysis, data analysis and Agile software development, subjects that he continues to teach and practise today.

FOREWORD

When Pete asked me to provide the Foreword to the third book in his Digital Solutions series, it started me pondering about some of the other trilogies that have had an impact on me over the years: Asimov's Foundation, Sartre's Roads to Freedom and Dylan's three 'electric' albums from the 60s. It got me considering what these timeless classics had in common with each other and with this present series of books. More specifically, what the ultimate work in each set added to the full collection. Apart from continuity and seamlessness, they all provided a fitting and complete conclusion to the overall story.

The first book in this specific series, *Defining Digital Solutions*, focussed on making sure that the right solution is built, while the second, *Designing Digital Solutions*, focussed on building the solution right. This final book, *Delivering Digital Solutions*, emphasises that all this application of best practise will have all been in vain if the delivery of the appropriate solution itself is not handled carefully and methodically. This final episode, while building on the foundations previously established also ensures that all the efforts to date are justified and the full benefits achieved.

Our dependence on digital technology is ever increasing In the modern world, The POPIT model (process, organisation, people, information and technology) shows that while the technology aspect of this model is central to any successful solution development, consideration of the interaction between it and the other components is also vital. The significance of this interaction is never forgotten throughout this trilogy.

The three books in this series obviously concentrate on the technology aspects at the centre of the solution, but they are also aware of the relationship between this and the other components of the POPIT model. In fact, they provide the missing piece of the jigsaw by complementing other important BCS publications which focus on the other areas in greater detail, such as business analysis (Debra Paul), information and data (Keith Gordon) and solution architecture (Mark Lovatt). It has been my privilege and honour to have worked with all of these inspirational authors at some point in my own career and with Pete Thompson himself.

Much of what is covered in the three books has been influenced by, and reflected in, the evolution of the syllabus for the BCS Diploma in Solution Development and together they provide an excellent text for those studying for this specific BCS Diploma. In addition to this, they contain a wealth of important guidance for anyone involved in digital solution development. A lot of what is covered in this and the other two books ensures that historic best practices will continue to provide a strong foundation for both current and future generations of developers and will stand the test of time. In addition, it is worth remembering, that in these turbulent times of constant change, where technology both drives and enables transformation, much will always stay the same and the fundamental principles which underlie any discipline should never be taken for granted. This book ensures that we never forget this.

Paul Turner
Life Fellow of the BCS
June 2025

ACKNOWLEDGEMENTS

As is the case with many books, this book owes its existence to many individuals who have helped shape the final product.

First, a special thanks to James Cadle, who conceived, co-authored and edited the predecessor of this series (*Developing Information Systems: Practical Guidance for IT Professionals*). Without his early support and contribution, this book and its siblings (*Defining Digital Solutions* and *Designing Digital Solutions*) would not have been possible.

I would also like to express my heartfelt gratitude to my wife, Sue, for her remarkable patience during the many long hours of working across evenings, weekends and holidays during the writing of all three books. My thanks also to my step-daughter, Sophie, for her constant encouragement and support throughout this project, and special thanks to my son, Alex Bradley-Thompson, who generously contributed his extensive knowledge of data analytics and business intelligence to Book 2, and who has acted as a sounding board, offering both valuable insights and much-needed empathy during the many long hours of writing and rewriting.

I am also extremely grateful to my colleagues at AssistKD for their unwavering support throughout the writing of this book. Their valuable insights, shared through many discussions, have been instrumental in shaping the final work. Special thanks go to Paul Turner for generously writing the foreword, and to Debra Paul and Julian Cox, who authored the forewords for the first two books and, together with Catriona Paul, reviewed early drafts. Collectively, their feedback and suggestions have significantly enhanced the quality of this book, as indeed have the contributions of Andrew Watkinson and his digital content development team at AssistKD – Gina Abdullah, Eduard Cojocaru and Megan Sullivan – whose excellent images have helped illustrate key concepts throughout the series.

Finally, this book could not have been produced without the professional publishing know-how of Ian Borthwick and Heather Wood from BCS – their patience and flexibility as numerous deadlines have been pushed back due to other work commitments is exemplary. I have benefited greatly from their expert advice.

ABBREVIATIONS

AES	Advanced Encryption Standard
AI	artificial intelligence
AOP	aspect-oriented programming
API	application programming interface
AR	augmented reality
ATDD	acceptance test-driven development
AWS	Amazon Web Services
BA	business analyst
BDD	behaviour-driven development
CARE	computer-aided requirements engineering
CASE	computer-aided software engineering
CAST	computer-aided software testing
CD	continuous delivery/continuous deployment
CI	continuous integration
CM	configuration management
CMS	content management system
CPPOLDAT	Customer Product Process Organisation Location Data Application Technology
CPU	central processing unit
CRASH	capabilities, reliability, availability, security, hardware
CRM	customer relationship management
CSS	cascading style sheets
CSV	comma separated values
CVEs	common vulnerabilities and exposures
DBMS	database management system
DNS	Domain Name System
DRY	Don't Repeat Yourself
DSL	domain-specific language
EMF	Eclipse Modeling Framework
ERP	enterprise resource planning

ETL	extract–transform–load
FaaS	function as a service
FAQs	frequently asked questions
GDPR	General Data Protection Regulation
GUI	graphical user interface
HTML	HyperText Markup Language
HTTPS	HyperText Transport Protocol Secure
I/O	input and output
IaaS	infrastructure as a service
IaC	infrastructure as code
IDE	integrated development environment
IEC	International Electrotechnical Commission
IEEE	Institute of Electrical and Electronics Engineers
IoT	Internet of Things
IP	Internet Protocol
ISMS	information security management system
ISO	International Organization for Standardization
ISTQB	International Software Testing Qualifications Board
ITIL	Information Technology Infrastructure Library
ITM	IT manager
ITSM	IT service management
JAC	Java Aspect Components
JDK	Java Development Kit
JSON	JavaScript Object Notation
JWT	JSON web token
KISS	Keep It Simple, Stupid
LOC	lines of code
MCI	Media Control Interface
MDA	model-driven architecture
MDE	model-driven engineering
MFA	multifactor authentication
ML	machine learning
MOF	Meta-Object Facility
MVP	minimum viable product
NCSC	National Cyber Security Centre
NoSQL	not only SQL
OAuth	open authorisation
OMG	Object Management Group
OO	object-oriented

OOP	object-oriented programming
OS	operating system
OWASP	Open Web Application Security Project
PaaS	platform as a service
PID	Project Initiation Document
PIM	platform-independent model
POLP	principle of least privilege
POPIT	People, Organisation, Processes, Information, and Technology
PSM	platform-specific model
QA	quality assurance
QC	quality control
QM	quality management
QMS	quality management system
QVT	Query/View/Transformation
RBAC	role-based access control
RE	Requirements Engineering
SaaS	software as a service
SCCS	source code control system
SDLC	software development life cycle
SEO	search engine optimisation
SLA	service level agreement
SoC	separation of concerns
SOLID	**S**ingle Responsibility Principle
	Open/Closed Principle
	Liskov Substitution Principle
	Interface Segregation Principle
	Dependency Inversion Principle
SQL	Structured Query Language
SRP	Single Responsibility Principle
SSL	Secure Sockets Layer
SVS	Service Value System
TCO	total cost of ownership
TDD	test-driven development
TLS	Transport Layer Security
ToR	terms of reference
UAT	user acceptance testing
UI	user interface
UML	Unified Modeling Language
URI	uniform resource identifier

URL	uniform resource locator
UX	user experience
VC	version control
VCS	version control system
VeriSM	Value-driven, Evolving, Responsive, Integrated Service Management
VR	virtual reality
WCAG	Web Content Accessibility Guidelines
XMI	XML Metadata Interchange
XML	eXtensible Markup Language
XP	Extreme Programming
XSS	cross-site scripting
YAGNI	You Aren't Gonna Need It

PREFACE

Delivering Digital Solutions is the third and final instalment in the *Digital Solutions Collection*, focusing on realising the design of a digital solution into a fully operational system. Building on the foundations laid in its sibling books – *Defining Digital Solutions* and *Designing Digital Solutions* – this volume explores the development, testing, deployment, maintenance and decommissioning stages of the digital solution life cycle.

The journey begins with a recap of the story so far (as told in Books 1 and 2), revisiting the definition, common characteristics and life cycle of a digital solution. It then introduces a structured process for realising a digital solution design as a fully operational system, highlighting the connection between solution delivery and IT service management (ITSM). The remainder of the book is structured into three parts:

- **Part I (Developing the Solution)** introduces the principles of software engineering, coding practices and development methodologies such as Agile, DevOps and no-code/low-code approaches. It discusses different programming paradigms and software construction techniques, before focusing on the importance of creating effective development environments.

- **Part II (Testing the Solution)** delves into software testing fundamentals, including quality assurance and control, the principles and levels of testing and common testing types. It highlights modern testing practices such as test-driven development (TDD), behaviour-driven development (BDD), shift-left testing, and the Agile Test Pyramid, providing a robust framework for achieving high-quality digital solutions.

- **Part III (Deploying the Solution)** covers the various approaches to deploying digital solutions, including on-premises, cloud, hybrid, containerised and serverless models. It outlines critical preparation steps for deployment, explores changeover strategies to ensure smooth transitions and discusses the factors influencing deployment and change decisions. It concludes with guidance on operating and maintaining solutions when they are live, and ultimately decommissioning them.

The book concludes with a detailed exploration of the wide range of software tools available to support digital solution delivery, from collaboration and risk management tools to deployment, DevOps and artificial intelligence (AI)-driven development platforms.

Through a structured, practical approach, this book, supported by an extensive online glossary (bcs.org/books/ddsglossary), equips IT and business professionals with the knowledge and tools necessary to successfully deliver, manage and evolve digital solutions in today's fast-changing technological landscape.

WHO IS THIS BOOK FOR?

When the idea for the *Digital Solutions Collection* was originally conceived, the following categories of reader were envisaged:

- **Business analysts (BAs)**: This book bridges the gap between solution design and delivery, an area where BAs increasingly play a critical role. It provides insights into the software engineering, testing, deployment and post-delivery activities that transform digital solution designs into fully operational systems. By understanding these processes, business analysts can better collaborate with technical teams, contribute to planning and readiness activities, support user adoption and help to ensure that the delivered solutions continue to meet business needs.

- **Project managers and delivery managers**: This book offers project managers and delivery managers a comprehensive understanding of the critical activities involved in successfully delivering digital solutions. It covers the journey from development and testing through deployment and post-delivery operations, providing practical guidance on planning, risk management, readiness assessment and stakeholder coordination. By equipping managers with a clearer view of technical processes and best practices, the book enables them to better oversee delivery timelines, manage dependencies, support cross-functional teams and ensure that digital solutions align with business objectives.

- **Product managers**: This book completes the three-book series that provides a comprehensive view of the processes that transform a digital solution from concept to operational reality. It provides essential insights into development, testing, deployment and post-delivery practices, helping product managers to better align product design with delivery capabilities and timelines. By understanding the technical and operational aspects of solution delivery, product managers can make more informed decisions, manage stakeholder expectations more effectively and ensure that products are launched smoothly and evolve in response to user needs.

- **IT managers (ITMs)**: This book provides a clear and practical understanding of the end-to-end process of delivering digital solutions. It offers detailed insights into development practices, testing strategies, deployment approaches and the post-delivery provision of the solution as an IT service, all of which are crucial for managing technical teams and ensuring the successful implementation of digital initiatives. By bridging the gap between technical execution and the realisation of beneficial business outcomes, the book helps IT managers to better plan resources, manage risks, align IT services with organisational goals and support continuous improvement. It also equips them with strategies for maintaining solution quality, operational stability and adaptability in an evolving digital landscape.

- **Solution developers, testers and technical stakeholders**: This book provides solution developers, testers and technical stakeholders with a comprehensive guide to the full life cycle of digital solution delivery, from development and testing through to deployment and post-implementation support and maintenance. It offers practical insights into modern software engineering practices, testing strategies, deployment models and operational management, helping technical teams to build, test and deliver high-quality solutions more effectively. By linking technical activities to broader business objectives, this book, along with its siblings, enables technical professionals to better understand their role in achieving organisational goals, collaborate more effectively across teams and contribute to the continuous improvement and long-term success of digital solutions.

- **Business stakeholders**: This book offers a clear understanding of how digital solutions are developed, tested, deployed and maintained. It demystifies technical processes and highlights how business readiness, user support and continuous improvement are critical to the success of digital initiatives. By providing insight into the delivery life cycle, the book helps business stakeholders to set realistic expectations, make informed decisions and actively support the adoption and optimisation of new solutions. Ultimately, it empowers them to play a more effective role in ensuring that digital solutions deliver sustained, beneficial business outcomes and align with organisational objectives.

- **Students on university and other courses studying digital business change**: This book, along with its siblings, will be an invaluable resource for students studying digital business change, offering a practical, end-to-end view of how digital solutions are conceived, designed, developed, deployed and maintained within real-world organisations. It bridges the gap between academic theory and industry practice by explaining the technical, operational and business aspects of digital solution delivery in an accessible way. By exploring topics such as software engineering, testing, deployment strategies and ITSM, the book equips students with the knowledge and context needed to understand how digital initiatives succeed and evolve. It provides a strong foundation for students preparing for careers in business analysis, software development, project management, product management, IT management and related fields.

- **Candidates studying for the BCS International Diploma in Solution Development**: This book provides a body of knowledge that covers the breadth of the diploma syllabus and also a range of associated certificates within the diploma scheme.

HOW TO USE THIS BOOK

This book can be used in a number of ways:

- It can be read from cover to cover to provide a good general understanding of the subject, especially for those with little previous exposure to the discipline of digital solution delivery.

- Each chapter also stands alone to provide a detailed reference guide to specific aspects of digital solution delivery, so the reader can choose to dip into the chapters in any order. However, it is recommended that Chapter 1 is read first to provide context for the remaining chapters.

- If more detail is desired after digesting the content of this book, readers can pursue specific topics via the references and further reading sections.

HOW THIS BOOK IS ORGANISED

The book is structured into 12 chapters:

- **Chapter 1: The Context for Delivering Digital Solutions**: This chapter sets the foundation for the book by revisiting the definition, characteristics and life cycle of a digital solution (first introduced in *Defining Digital Solutions*). It provides a recap of the inception, analysis and design stages that were covered in Books 1 and 2 and then introduces a structured approach for realising a digital solution design as a fully operational system, emphasising the crucial role of ITSM in supporting digital solution delivery.

- **Chapter 2: Introduction to Software Engineering**: This chapter introduces the discipline of software engineering, highlighting its evolution into a structured, professional field focused on the systematic development of high-quality software. It explains the software engineering cycle, covering key activities such as coding, compiling, linking, building, testing and debugging. The chapter also explores fundamental software engineering principles – such as modularity, encapsulation and the SOLID principles – and the importance of adhering to recognised standards to ensure software reliability, maintainability and scalability.

- **Chapter 3: Programming Paradigms and Languages**: This chapter examines a variety of programming paradigms – including imperative, procedural, object-oriented and event-driven approaches – that influence how developers structure software and solve problems. It highlights the unique characteristics, benefits and typical use cases of each paradigm, emphasising how the choice of approach impacts code organisation, system behaviour and development efficiency. By understanding these differences, practitioners are better equipped to select the most suitable paradigm (and language) to meet the specific needs of a particular digital solution.

- **Chapter 4: Software Engineering in Practice**: This chapter examines how software engineering practices are applied in real-world development environments. It introduces key development approaches, including TDD, BDD, full stack development, no-code/low-code development and DevOps. It also covers essential practices such as modular programming, secure coding, defensive coding, continuous integration (CI), continuous delivery (CD), Agile development practices and code management techniques such as branching and managing technical debt. Together, these topics highlight how the effective combination of methodologies and best practices can enhance software quality, scalability, security and delivery efficiency.

- **Chapter 5: Development Environments**: This chapter focuses on the different environments used throughout the digital solution development and deployment process. It explains the purpose and setup of key environments, including development, testing, integration, pre-production (or staging) and production environments, highlighting the importance of maintaining separate, well-configured environments to support code quality, reliable testing, smooth integration and successful live deployment. It also emphasises how effective environment management helps to mitigate risks, ensure consistency and streamline the transition from development to operational use.

- **Chapter 6: Introduction to Software Testing**: This chapter lays a strong foundation for understanding the critical role that software testing plays in ensuring the quality, reliability and overall success of digital solutions. It starts by providing a clear definition of software quality, and clarifies the relationship between digital solution design and software quality, distinguishing between quality management, quality assurance and quality control. Consideration is given to the source of software quality issues, with an explanation of the relationship between errors, faults and failures. Having set the scene, it continues with a discussion of the objectives and limitations of testing, and introduces a set of core testing principles. The chapter also explores key testing levels – such as unit, integration, system and acceptance testing – and a broad range of testing types, including functional, non-functional, static, dynamic, black-box and white-box techniques, concluding with an introduction to the fundamental test process and important testing artefacts (e.g. test plans, test procedures and test cases).

- **Chapter 7: Software Testing Practices**: This chapter explores popular software testing practices that enhance the effectiveness and efficiency of quality assurance initiatives, offering practical techniques for building quality into digital solutions from the outset. It introduces the shift-left approach, emphasising the importance of early and continuous testing throughout the development life cycle, and clarifies the distinction between verification and validation. The critical role of continuous testing and test automation in supporting DevOps workflows is discussed along with complementary testing practices such as TDD, BDD and acceptance test-driven development (ATDD). The chapter concludes by exploring Agile testing strategies, including the concept of testing quadrants and the Agile Test Pyramid.

- **Chapter 8: Approaches to Deploying Digital Solutions**: This chapter examines the various approaches to deploying digital solutions, highlighting how deployment strategy impacts performance, scalability, security and operational success. It explores traditional on-premises deployment alongside modern alternatives such as cloud, hybrid, containerised, serverless and edge computing models. The key characteristics, advantages, disadvantages and typical use cases of each approach are discussed along with a range of key factors that influence the choice of approach, including business needs, compliance requirements and operational risks. The chapter concludes by exploring how deployment aligns with frameworks and practices such as the Information Technology Infrastructure Library (ITIL), Value-driven, Evolving, Responsive, Integrated Service Management (VeriSM) and DevOps, particularly CI and CD.

- **Chapter 9: Preparing for Deployment**: This chapter focuses on preparing for the deployment of a digital solution, outlining the critical activities needed to ensure a smooth and successful transition into live operation. It covers release management and the deployment process, including detailed planning, business and technical readiness, data preparation and migration, training, documentation and go-live execution. The chapter concludes with a discussion of post-deployment support, review and optimisation, which are essential for a smooth transition to day-to-day operations, building user confidence and supporting the ongoing adoption and long-term success of the digital solution.

- **Chapter 10: Changeover Strategies**: This chapter explores strategies for transitioning from an old system to a new digital solution, emphasising the importance of managing business change effectively. It introduces Kurt Lewin's three-stage model of organisational change as a foundation for understanding transition dynamics, and then continues to describe various changeover methods, including direct changeover, parallel running, pilot changeover and blue/green deployment, and how hybrid strategies can be employed to balance risk, cost and complexity. A discussion of the various factors that influence the choice of strategy follows, and the chapter concludes with a discussion of risk mitigation techniques for failed changeovers.

- **Chapter 11: Post-Delivery**: This chapter explores the critical activities that take place after the deployment of a digital solution, focusing on its operation, maintenance and eventual decommissioning. It explains how ITSM practices, particularly those based on ITIL, support the ongoing operation of digital solutions through activities such as monitoring, user support and incident management. The chapter also examines different types of maintenance and their role in extending the solution's lifespan and ensuring that it remains current. It concludes by presenting a structured approach to decommissioning outdated solutions, ensuring a smooth and well-managed transition when a system reaches the end of its useful life.

- **Chapter 12: Software Tools to Support Digital Solution Delivery**: This final chapter explores the diverse range of tools that support the development, testing, deployment, maintenance and support of digital solutions, providing a brief description of each category of tool, a summary of their key features and example products. The chapter concludes with a discussion about AI-driven development tools that promise to deliver even greater efficiency, effectiveness and agility throughout digital solution development, testing and delivery workflows.

Peter Thompson
June 2025

1 THE CONTEXT FOR DELIVERING DIGITAL SOLUTIONS

THE STORY SO FAR

Book 1 (*Defining Digital Solutions*) in this three-book series introduces the context for digital solutions, starting with the following definition:

> A way of using computer technology to address a problem, improve a process or provide new capabilities, that leverages software and hardware to make things more efficient, convenient or effective, enhancing user experiences and driving innovation.

It continues to introduce a set of characteristics that digital solutions tend to have in common:

- **Technology-driven**: They rely on digital technologies to target specific challenges, inefficiencies or business opportunities.
- **Problem-solving**: They are designed to solve a particular problem, improve efficiency, enhance user experience or enable new capabilities.
- **Automation and efficiency**: They automate manual processes, reduce time taken to undertake tasks and reduce consumption of non-digital resources.
- **Data-centric**: Many digital solutions are powered by data, utilising analytics, machine learning or artificial intelligence (AI) to provide insights, predictions and optimisation.
- **Scalability**: Digital solutions can often scale easily to accommodate growing user bases, increased data or higher demand.

After exploring the benefits of digital solutions and identifying a range of types of digital solution, with examples, Book 1 presents a life cycle for a digital solution, which is reproduced in Figure 1.1.

In addition to exploring the business context for digital solutions and the various options for acquiring digital solutions, the primary focus of Book 1 is the first two stages of this life cycle:

Figure 1.1 Life cycle of a digital solution

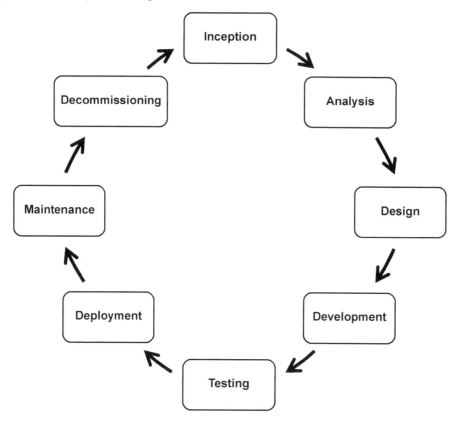

Inception   The inception stage (also known as discovery) is where the business need or opportunity is identified, and the goals for a digital solution are established. This stage often involves conducting market research and feasibility studies, resulting in the development of a business case. If the business case is approved by the relevant business sponsor, inception will also incorporate project initiation.

Project initiation involves the definition of high-level business and project objectives, scope and constraints that restrict the project in some way (e.g. timelines, budget, technology, standards and legislation). This results in the development of a Project Initiation Document (PID) or terms of reference (ToR) document, which also identifies the project authority (project sponsor) for decision-making, as well as available resources. It is also common to produce a high-level plan for the development of the digital solution and to perform a project risk assessment during project initiation.

Analysis   During the analysis stage, detailed solution requirements are elaborated from the high-level business requirements identified during inception. This stage is often the first stage of a digital solution development project, and is the primary focus of Part II of Book 1.

Book 2 (*Designing Digital Solutions*) picks up where Book 1 finishes and concentrates on the third stage of the life cycle:

Design   The design stage translates the solution requirements defined during the analysis stage into a set of design blueprints that specify how the requirements shall be realised during solution development. These blueprints are used by solution developers to build runtime platforms and executable software that comprise the working digital solution.

THE SCOPE OF DIGITAL SOLUTION DELIVERY

This book picks up where Book 2 leaves off, and focuses predominantly on the next three stages of the digital solution life cycle:

Development   The development stage is where software developers translate the design blueprints into working software. Development involves a series of sub-stages where the developer (or software engineer) writes program code using one or more programming languages, and compiles it into a computer readable and executable form. For some technology stacks, this may also involve a process known as linking, to link together a set of executable program modules into the final software system. Development is also referred to as software engineering, which is the subject of Part I of this book.

Testing   During the testing stage the working solution created in the development stage is subjected to a range of different tests to ensure that it works correctly (according to the specifications produced during the design stage), conforms to the functional and non-functional solution requirements (defined during the analysis stage), satisfies the business needs (identified in the inception stage) and meets predefined quality criteria. Upon successful completion of the testing stage, the digital solution is ready for deployment and live operational use. Software testing is the subject of Part II of this book. It should be noted that some forms of testing (such as unit testing) are an integral part of the development stage, as is the case with test-driven development (TDD) (see Chapter 4).

Deployment   The deployment stage is where the digital solution is transferred from the development environment into a production environment, which makes it available to users for live operational use. With the advent of Agile development methods and increasing pressures to deliver digital solutions quickly and continuously, DevOps practices that automate the transition from development to live operation have become commonplace. Deployment is the subject of Part III of this book.

The book concludes the journey through the life cycle of a digital solution with a brief introduction to a range of post-delivery issues that need to be considered during the final two stages:

Maintenance   Maintenance involves making changes to the digital solution after it becomes operational. This stage encompasses the continuous use and optimisation of the solution throughout its life until it is decommissioned. Activities during maintenance include addressing defects identified during live use, modifying the solution's functionality to meet evolving requirements, implementing new features and enhancing usability and performance based on insights from ongoing monitoring. The goal is to ensure the solution remains effective and continues to meet the needs of users and the organisation.

Decommissioning Decommissioning is the final stage in the life cycle of a digital solution, during which the solution is retired from operational use. This occurs when the solution becomes outdated, no longer satisfies the business needs or is replaced by a more suitable alternative. This stage focuses on ensuring a seamless transition away from the existing solution, or to its replacement, while taking all necessary precautions to minimise risks and safeguard critical data.

DIGITAL SOLUTION DELIVERY AND IT SERVICE MANAGEMENT

Once a digital solution is delivered, it becomes an **IT service**, and IT service management (ITSM) steps in to:

- monitor performance;
- fix issues and defects;
- provide support and handle user requests; and
- manage updates and changes.

ITSM is a set of tools and practices used by IT teams to keep services stable, useful and continually improving for users. While digital delivery teams (like DevOps and Agile squads) focus on building and launching solutions, ITSM manages the solution after launch. ITSM practices are explored further in Chapter 11.

REALISING THE DESIGN OF A DIGITAL SOLUTION

Producing a working digital solution from a set of design blueprints (often referred to as the realisation of the digital solution design) involves a structured workflow, summarised in Figure 1.2 and described below. The linear representation of this workflow in Figure 1.2 is to aid understanding, but in modern development (such as development based around an Agile method), these cycles are typically shortened, and a project might iterate through them several times. Additionally, there may be overlap between the stages; for example, front-end and back-end development might be done concurrently, with the use of application programming interface (API) mocking[1] to enable testing on the front-end side.

Figure 1.2 Stages involved in realising the design of a digital solution

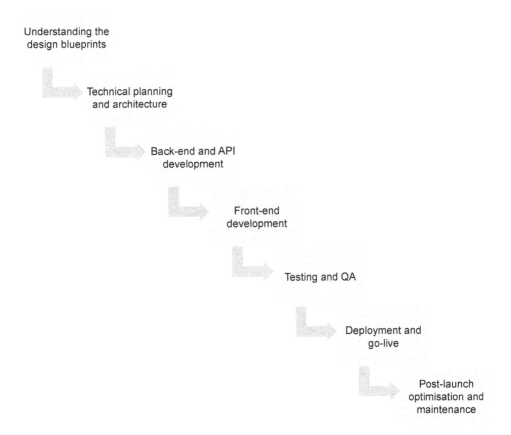

Understanding the
design blueprints

Technical planning
and architecture

Back-end and API
development

Front-end
development

Testing and QA

Deployment and
go-live

Post-launch
optimisation and
maintenance

---

1   API mocking is the practice of simulating the behaviour of a real API by creating fake responses, enabling developers to test and develop applications without relying on the actual API being available or fully implemented.

Understanding the design blueprints	Before development begins, the delivery team reviews the design blueprints to ensure all developers and technical stakeholders fully understand the design, including its technical feasibility and limitations. This involves reviewing user interface/user experience (UI/UX) designs (e.g. wireframes, mock-ups and prototypes), analysing functional and non-functional requirements to identify key features, performance needs and security considerations (among others), and verifying alignment with business goals and user expectations.
Technical planning and architecture	This stage involves the definition of the technology stack and system architecture, by selecting appropriate programming languages, frameworks and databases. This includes planning the front end, back end, APIs, databases and integrations, while setting up the development environment with version control, continuous integration/continuous deployment (CI/CD) pipelines and cloud hosting.
Back-end and API development	During this stage, the core logic, data processing and APIs are implemented, including authentication, data handling and RESTful[2] or GraphQL[3] APIs to facilitate front-end–back-end communication. Security features such as encryption,[4] authentication and authorisation (open authorisation (OAuth) and JSON Web Token (JWT)) are integrated to safeguard data. Additionally, this phase may involve designing and deploying database schemas, such as Structured Query Language or not only SQL (NoSQL).
Front-end development	This stage focuses on the implementation of the user interface as specified in design blueprints, by converting UI designs into code using technologies such as HyperText Markup Language (HTML), cascading style sheets (CSS) and JavaScript frameworks. This stage involves integrating APIs to enable front-end–back-end communication and ensuring the interface is responsive and accessible across different devices, while complying with standards such as Web Content Accessibility Guidelines (WCAG).

---

2 A RESTful API (Representational State Transfer Application Programming Interface) is a type of web API that follows the principles of REST architecture. It enables communication between client and server over the HTTP protocol using standard methods like **GET** (to retrieve data), **POST** (to create data), **PUT** (to update data) and **DELETE** (to remove data).

3 GraphQL is a query language for APIs and a runtime for executing those queries with existing data. It enables clients to request exactly the data they need, making it more efficient and flexible compared to traditional REST APIs.

4 Encryption is the process of converting data into a coded format to prevent unauthorised access, ensuring that only authorised parties can read or understand the information.

Testing and QA	This stage ensures that the solution works correctly and is fit for purpose. This includes functional testing (to ensure that the solution provides the correct functionality as determined by its functional requirements), non-functional testing (to check that the solution has satisfied its non-functional requirements, such as security, usability, accessibility, availability and performance) and acceptance testing (to ensure that it meets the business needs and is fit for purpose).
Deployment and go-live	The objective of this stage is to launch the solution ready for live operational use by setting up the production environment on cloud platforms or local, on-premises infrastructure. CI/CD pipelines automate builds and deployments, while logging and monitoring tools track system performance.
Post-launch optimisation and maintenance	Once the solution is operational, it enters the business as usual stage, which is focused on support and continuous improvement. This includes monitoring performance and user feedback through real-time analytics, logs and service desk[5] requests, and applying regular bug fixes and updates to address security vulnerabilities and optimise performance and usability. The system is also scaled to manage traffic spikes, such as an increase in the number of concurrent users or transaction volume.

The first two stages of this workflow are covered in Books 1 and 2. Stages three and four are covered in Part I of this book; stage five is covered in Part II; and stages six and seven are covered in Part III.

---

5   A service desk is a central point of contact between users and the IT service management team. It is responsible for handling incidents, service requests and communications with users.

PART I
DEVELOPING THE SOLUTION

2   INTRODUCTION TO SOFTWARE ENGINEERING

INTRODUCTION

Although the term **software engineer** was first used by American computing pioneer Margaret Hamilton[6] to describe her work and to emphasise the significance of what previously had been an undervalued field, **software engineering** did not become firmly established as a discipline until the 1980s. In the introduction to their book *Software Development in Practice* (Fishpool and Fishpool, 2020), Bernie and Mark Fishpool reflect on the origins of software engineering as a recognised discipline:

> A push in the late 1980s led the industry to embrace the notion of software engineering principles rather than simply using the term 'programmer' to define development, and this has now become the norm. The profession has become somewhat more formalised, more professional and far less 'wild west' – although, in some development environments, that pioneering spirit still plays a crucial part in thinking outside the proverbial box and creating amazing innovations.

The IEEE defines software engineering in its standard glossary of software engineering terminology (ISO et al., 2017) as:

> The application of a systematic, disciplined, quantifiable approach to the development, operation, and maintenance of software; that is the application of engineering to software.

The IEEE definition reflects the professional and scientific approach to software development that highlights the following important characteristics:

- **Systematic**: Follows a structured, organised process with clear steps and methodologies.
- **Disciplined**: Requires adherence to standards, best practices and rigorous processes to ensure high-quality results.

---

6   Margaret Hamilton's work as a software engineer was critical to the first moon landing on 20 July 1969.

- **Quantifiable**: Emphasises measurement and metrics to track progress, efficiency and quality in software development.

- **Engineering approach**: Applies principles of analysis, design, construction and testing (like other branches of engineering) to develop software solutions.

Based on the IEEE definition, it could be argued that this entire book is about software engineering, but the objective of Part I is to focus on **software construction**.

Software construction is one of the core stages/activities in a software development life cycle (SDLC). It refers to the detailed creation of working, high-quality, reliable, functional and maintainable software components from design specifications, through a combination of coding techniques, tools and best practices. This chapter focuses specifically on software construction activities (the software engineering cycle) and software engineering principles and standards.

THE SOFTWARE ENGINEERING CYCLE

The software engineering cycle (summarised in Figure 2.1 and described below) comprises eight key activities that form a structured workflow, ensuring that the development process is efficient and scalable and results in a reliable software product.

Figure 2.1 The software engineering cycle

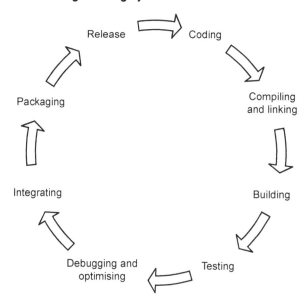

Coding

Coding is the process of transforming the design of a software application or component into source code using computer programming languages. This code implements the required features, addresses problems and fulfils both functional and non-functional requirements defined during Requirements Engineering (RE). It involves selecting suitable programming languages, frameworks and libraries, while following established coding standards and best practices. Different components of an application may be developed in different languages, depending on which is most appropriate for each task. A range of popular programming languages is introduced in Chapter 3.

Source code is often written using a tool called an **integrated development environment (IDE)**, which assists in the coding process and highlights coding errors and potential issues to the developer. Source code may be stored in a source code repository or source code control system (SCCS) and may be subject to version control, which ensures that only the current version is used to build the software for release, while keeping previous versions for traceability, fault diagnosis and potential rollback if necessary. IDEs and related software tools are discussed in Chapter 12.

Compiling and linking

Compiling is the process of translating source code, written in a specific programming language, into object code – an intermediate form of the program that is not yet executable. This task is carried out by a software tool called a **compiler**, with different compilers available for different languages.

During compilation, the compiler checks the source code for correctness, including syntax errors (violations of the programming language's grammatical rules). Once all syntax errors are resolved, the compiler generates an object file for each source file. These object files must then be linked together to produce the final executable program (machine code[7]).

Linking[8] involves combining multiple object files and libraries into a single, final executable file (.exe files in Microsoft Windows, .app files in MacOS or .bin files in Unix-based operating systems), using a software tool known as a **linker**. During the linking process, the linker combines object files produced during compilation, resolves external references – such as function calls to other object files or shared libraries (e.g. .dll files in Microsoft Windows) – and ensures that variable references point to the correct memory locations. It then generates a complete executable program containing all necessary machine code, which can be executed by the computer's operating system.

Building

The purpose of building is to automate the entire process of creating a working software solution, managing all the steps involved. For standalone applications the build process may simply involve compiling and linking. However, building will typically also involve:

---

7   Machine code is the lowest-level programming language, consisting entirely of binary digits (0s and 1s) that a computer's central processing unit (CPU) can execute directly.

8   In languages such as Python, C#, Java and JavaScript, there is no explicit linking stage, as in traditional compiled languages such as C or C++, but there are equivalent mechanisms that serve similar purposes in resolving dependencies and preparing code for execution. Additionally, many modern applications might be distributed as mobile applications or browser-based apps, and therefore will not be deployed as a standalone binary executable.

- using version control systems (such as Git) to manage changes, collaborate with other developers and maintain code history;

- maintaining different versions and branches of the software (see *Code management practices* in Chapter 4);

- packaging the software for deployment, involving the creation of build scripts and pipelines that can handle dependencies, configuration and environment setup for different deployment environments (environments are covered in Chapter 5);

- automating repetitive tasks, such as running tests, and deploying to different environments (see also *Continuous integration* and *Continuous delivery/deployment* in Chapter 4); and

- generating necessary documentation.

Testing

The objective of testing is to find defects, not – as many people believe – to prove the absence of defects. This, among other key principles of testing, is explored further in Chapter 6.

Although testing is shown in Figure 2.1 between 'building' and 'debugging and optimising', in practice there are different types of testing (also explored in Chapter 6) that take place at various points throughout the software engineering cycle.

It is better to find faults as early as possible in the software engineering cycle as this reduces their impact and the cost of correcting them. Therefore, testing usually starts at the coding stage with automated code reviews[9] (using special software tools called **static analysers**) and automated unit testing tools. Static analysers and unit testing tools are often integrated within an IDE (see Chapter 12) and are executed as the developer writes the source code. Code reviews may also be performed by one of the developer's peers, or their supervisor/team leader.

The compiled code of each software module is first tested in isolation (**unit testing**, also known as module testing or component testing), and once multiple modules have been individually tested, they are assembled and tested together (**integration testing**). Unit and integration testing are types of **dynamic testing**.[10]

Once all the individual modules have been integration tested to ensure they work together correctly, the entire application is tested to check that it works correctly as a complete solution, according to its functional and non-functional requirements (using **functional testing** and **non-functional testing**, respectively). This is referred to as **end-to-end testing** or **system testing**. Once the development team is convinced there are no significant faults in the system, it will be subject to further testing by users and other stakeholders (**acceptance testing**).

---

9 Code reviews are a form of static testing, which is a quality review technique where code, documents or other artefacts are examined without executing software.

10 Dynamic testing is a software testing approach that involves executing program code to verify that the software behaves as expected during runtime.

Debugging and optimising

Debugging follows on from the various types of testing identified above. When an individual software module, or the entire application, fails, the developer utilises a special software tool called a debugger to identify the source of the defect(s) in the software that caused the failure. The term 'debugger' refers to the more colloquial name for software defects: bugs. As with static analysers and automated unit testing tools, debuggers are typically incorporated within an IDE.

Debugging involves the developer stepping through the program source code as it is being executed, one line at a time, to identify any problematic program statements that result in the failure of the software (e.g. logic errors that cause performance bottlenecks and unexpected or incorrect behaviour). Debuggers also enable the developer to visualise and analyse the state of the program environment (such as the values of variables, memory usage and processor usage) as the code executes.

Once the developer has identified the defective code, the cycle loops back to coding and the code is modified to fix the problem. The code is then recompiled, linked and tested again to ensure that the defect has been fixed.

Code **optimisation**, while separate to debugging, is often performed alongside, or just after, debugging. The purpose of code optimisation is to improve the performance, efficiency and maintainability of the code, and typically involves refactoring[11] code to:

- improve the code structure and readability;
- reduce the complexity of the code;
- remove any redundant or duplicated code;
- improve resource management (such as memory handling, processor usage and file input and output functions) to enhance efficiency; and
- refine algorithms to improve performance (execution time) or make the code more scalable.

Integrating

The term 'integration' has two meanings in software engineering. First, it refers to the process of combining multiple units of code, or components, into a single cohesive application during software construction; and second, it refers to the **interfacing** of an application with other applications or systems with which it will need to communicate (often referred to as **interoperation**). The former is sometimes referred to as **integration in the small**, as it involves getting small units of code or modules to work together as part of a specific application, and the latter as **integration in the large**, as it involves enabling larger software components, or entire applications, to work together.

---

11 Refactoring is the process of restructuring existing code without changing its external behaviour to improve its readability, maintainability and internal structure.

Both approaches are often essential in modern digital solution development – few, if any, applications work standalone without the need to integrate with other applications or services. Additionally, with the advent of DevOps, integration is often automated with software tools (see *DevOps*, *Continuous integration* and *Continuous delivery/deployment* in Chapter 4).

Development teams often undertake integration incrementally, which can follow either a **top-down** or **bottom-up** approach. With a top-down approach, the higher-level units are developed and tested first, followed by the integration and testing of lower-level ones. This method ensures that the core functionality (typically represented by the top-level units) is tested early, and lower-level (or child) units are integrated progressively. Top-down integration uses special-purpose code known as **stubs**, which act as proxies for any missing units, which may not have been developed yet, or which may not be available to the developer at this stage. With a bottom-up approach, testing begins with the lowest-level units, and then higher-level units are progressively integrated and tested. The goal is to ensure that each low-level unit functions correctly before integrating and testing the higher-level units that depend on them. Since higher-level units may not have been developed or be ready for integration, **drivers** (special-purpose code similar to stubs) are used to simulate the behaviour of higher-level units. Drivers provide the necessary inputs to test the lower-level units. See also *Mocking frameworks* in Chapter 12.

Irrespective of which approach is used, integration typically involves:

- combining different modules or components together into a single cohesive system or application;
- running integration tests to verify that the modules/components work together as expected;
- identifying and resolving conflicts and issues that may not be visible when modules or components are tested individually; and
- ensuring compatibility between different parts of the system.

Packaging

Packaging is the penultimate stage of the software engineering cycle[12] that takes place just prior to release. It involves preparing the software for deployment or distribution by bundling the software's executable files, libraries, configuration files, media files (e.g. images and videos) and documentation into a package (e.g. Media Control Interface (MCI) files and Java Archive (jar) files) that can be installed on a user's machine or server.

Release

Release (also known as deployment) is the final step of the software engineering cycle, when a new application or an update to an existing application is made available

---

12 This is not always the case and different technology stacks have different practices when it comes to packaging. For example, a jar (Java archive) file would need to be produced before handing over to the integration testing team. Additionally, with applications that are delivered as containers, the container is an output of the build process. Containerised deployment is covered in Chapter 8.

to users. This can be done by deploying the software in a production environment or making it available for download or distribution, along with documentation and supporting materials.

The responsibility for software release typically involves multiple roles within a software development team or organisation. The exact roles and responsibilities can vary depending on the company's size, structure and software development methodology. A release management tool may be used to control the process, and there are a range of changeover strategies that can be used (explored further in Chapter 10).

SOFTWARE ENGINEERING PRINCIPLES AND STANDARDS

Software engineering principles and standards are critical to developing high-quality software, promoting modularity, reusability, maintainability and security, while ensuring that best practices and quality benchmarks are consistently applied across projects.

Principles

Software engineering principles provide a foundational framework for creating reliable, efficient and maintainable software. These high-level guidelines help software engineers to make informed decisions throughout the software engineering cycle. When applied consistently, they help development teams to enhance software quality, facilitate collaboration, minimise technical debt[13] and ensure that solutions are scalable, secure and aligned with both user expectations and business objectives. A range of commonly applied principles are described below.

SOLID principles
The SOLID principles, defined by Robert C. Martin (Martin, 2000), are a set of object-oriented (OO) design guidelines that provide a robust foundation for building OO software that is flexible, modular and maintainable, ultimately leading to higher-quality and more resilient code. The acronym **SOLID** stands for:

- **Single Responsibility Principle (SRP)**: This principle states that a class (or component) should have only one reason to change, meaning it should have only one responsibility or purpose.

- **Open/Closed Principle**: This principle states that software entities (classes, modules, functions) should be open for extension but closed for modification. This principle encourages new functionality to be introduced without altering existing code. Once the code has been written and verified, it should remain unchanged. Instead, its behaviour should be extended through mechanisms such as inheritance, interfaces or composition (see *Object-oriented programming* in Chapter 3). This approach promotes stability and maintainability, minimising the risk of defects while supporting ongoing development.

---

13 Technical debt is the implied cost of re-work caused by choosing quick or suboptimal solutions in software development instead of better, often more time-consuming, approaches.

- **Liskov Substitution Principle**: This principle (named after computer scientist Barbara Liskov) states that objects of a superclass should be replaceable with objects of its subclasses without altering the correctness of the program.

- **Interface Segregation Principle**: This principle states that a class should not be forced to implement interfaces it doesn't use. This means that, instead of creating a single broad interface for all possible functionality, the developer should create smaller, more specific interfaces. This way, classes implement only the methods they actually need.

- **Dependency Inversion Principle**: This principle states that high-level modules should not depend on low-level modules – both should depend on abstractions. This principle encourages the use of interfaces or abstract classes to decouple[14] dependencies, enabling higher-level components to remain independent of lower-level implementations.

Don't Repeat Yourself (DRY)
This principle is self-explanatory. It emphasises reducing code duplication, which improves maintainability, reduces the risk of errors and promotes code reuse and the creation of modular, reusable components.

Keep It Simple, Stupid (KISS)
KISS promotes simplicity in design, advocating that software should be as simple as possible, but not simpler. This principle helps to avoid over-engineering and makes code more understandable and easier to debug.

Keeping program code simple may include:

- ensuring that no code is duplicated;

- utilising the fewest possible classes/modules;

- minimising data attributes and arguments;

- utilising the fewest possible methods/operations;

- writing the shortest possible methods/operations; and

- communicating everything through the code itself and any associated unit tests to aid understanding and reduce the need for comments.

You Aren't Gonna Need It (YAGNI)
YAGNI emphasises only implementing features or components when they are actually needed. This principle helps to avoid unnecessary complexity and keeps code lean.

Encapsulation
Encapsulation is an object-oriented programming (OOP) principle that involves bundling an object's data (attributes) and operations (methods/functions) that act on that data into a single unit, typically a class. Encapsulation restricts direct access to some elements of the object (such as some or all of the attributes), which is achieved through

---

14 Decoupling in software refers to designing and developing software modules/components to be as independent of one another as possible, so that changes in one module/component have minimal impact on others.

access modifiers.[15] This concept promotes data protection, modularity and separation of concerns by exposing only necessary parts of an object while hiding its internal details and protecting its state.

Modularity

Modularity is a software design principle that involves dividing software into distinct, self-contained units called **modules**. Each module has a single, well-defined purpose and is responsible for a specific aspect of the functionality provided by the software, thus embracing the design principle of **high cohesion**. Additionally, by interacting through well-defined interfaces, modules promote another important design principle, **loose coupling**, which means that modules are relatively independent of each other. This combination of high cohesion and loose coupling promotes better organisation and reusability in software systems, helping to reduce complexity and making code easier to understand, develop, test and maintain. It also supports more robust and stable code by minimising unintended side effects when changes are made. As a result, developers can work more independently on different parts of the system with greater confidence.

Modular code design exhibits the following key characteristics:

- **Independence**: Modules operate independently of each other, which means that changes in one module have minimal impact on others, enabling parallel development and easier debugging.

- **Single responsibility**: Each module is responsible for a specific task or a closely related set of tasks, which aligns with the SRP (see *SOLID principles* above). This clarity of purpose makes the code easier to understand, debug and maintain.

- **Encapsulation**: As introduced earlier, encapsulation ensures that each module conceals its internal details and reveals only what is needed for interaction – typically through a clearly defined interface – thereby preventing other modules from accessing or unintentionally altering its internal state so that changes can be made safely without affecting other parts of the system.

- **Reusability**: Well-designed modules encapsulate functionality, enabling them to be reused across different parts of a system or even in other projects. This reduces duplication and enhances development efficiency.

- **Interchangeability**: Modular design enables individual modules to be swapped or upgraded independently, provided that they conform to defined interfaces, which enhances the adaptability and extensibility of the software.

Separation of concerns (SoC)

SoC means dividing a program into distinct areas of functionality that overlap as little as possible, as per the SRP. For example, in web development, separating business logic, data access and presentation (user interface) enhances flexibility and maintainability.

---

15 An access modifier is a keyword in programming that defines the visibility or accessibility of a class, method or variable to other parts of the code. The modifiers private, protected and public, are typically available in many languages. Private is used to restrict access to an object's data and/or operations, so that they cannot be accessed by other objects, and are therefore only accessible within the object itself.

Fail fast

This principle advocates that systems should immediately raise an error when an unexpected condition occurs, rather than trying to continue and potentially mask underlying issues. This helps to identify defects early.

Standards

Software engineering standards are specific, detailed rules and conventions that set precise requirements for a software project, development process or methodology. Standards are typically more concrete and measurable than principles, and compliance with standards helps to ensure uniformity and quality, often across an organisation or industry. Standards are often created to facilitate compatibility, regulatory compliance and interoperability.

There is a diverse range of different standards that apply to the discipline of software engineering. Some of the more common ones are explored below.

Coding standards

Coding standards are a set of guidelines or rules that help to ensure that code is consistent, readable and maintainable across projects, teams and even organisations. Well-defined standards ensure that all team members follow the same practices, promoting collaboration and making the codebase easier to understand and maintain.

Some organisations define their own coding standards, but there are also some language-specific standards:

- **Python (PEP 8) Style Guide**: This provides guidelines on naming, indentation, comments and more.
- **Java (Oracle's Code Conventions)**: Oracle's official guidelines cover class structure, naming and file organisation.
- **Google's Java Style Guide**: This includes naming conventions, Javadoc[16] guidelines and code organisation best practices.
- **Airbnb's JavaScript Style Guide**: This is a popular, comprehensive set of rules and best practices aimed at ensuring consistent, readable and maintainable JavaScript code across projects, with guidance on code formatting, naming conventions, use of comments and more.

Common aspects covered by coding standards include:

- **Naming conventions**: A common convention is to use **PascalCase** (where each word is capitalised) for class and type names (e.g. `CustomerAccount` and `TotalCalculator`), **camelCase** (where each word is capitalised except for the first) for variable and function names (e.g. `totalAmount` and `calculateAverage`) and **UPPERCASE_SNAKE_CASE** (where all letters are uppercase and words are separated by underscores) for the names of constants (e.g. `MAX_RETRIES = 3`, `PI = 3.14159`).

---

16 Javadoc is a documentation tool provided as part of the Java Development Kit (JDK). It generates HTML-based API documentation from specially formatted comments within the source code.

- **Indentation and spacing**: Python's PEP 8 guide recommends four spaces for indenting code (avoiding the use of tabs), maintaining a single blank line between functions and limiting the length of lines to 79 characters.

- **Commenting and documentation**: A common standard relates to the use of inline comments. For example, use inline comments sparingly to clarify complex logic, not to explain obvious code such as:

  ```
  # Calculate the average score

  average_score = total_score / num_scores
  ```

- **Error handling**: A widely accepted practice for error handling is to use specific exceptions instead of general catch-all blocks and to include clear, descriptive messages in error logs to simplify debugging.

- **Consistent bracing style**: There are two styles of bracing in popular use: **K&R style** and **Allman style**. K&R style (used with Java, JavaScript and C#) places the open brace at the end of the line:

  ```
  if (condition) {
    // Code
  } else {
    // Code
  }
  ```

  In contrast, Allman style (used with C++) places the open brace on a new line aligned with the corresponding control statement or function definition:

  ```
  if (condition)
  {
    // Code
  }
  else
  {
    // Code
  }
  ```

- **File and directory structure**: A popular standard is to organise code into directories by feature or module, and to keep related classes, scripts and resources together.

- **Use of constants and magic numbers**: Coding standards also incorporate rules about the use of constant values (as opposed to variables). For example, it is better to use named constants (such as `MAX_RETRIES = 3`) instead of 'magic numbers' (unexplained numbers directly in the code). Constants make the code more readable and enable a change to the value (if necessary) in a single line of code rather than at multiple instances.

ISO/IEC standards

The International Organization for Standardization (ISO) and International Electrotechnical Commission (IEC) set widely recognised software engineering standards. For example:

- **ISO/IEC 12207** defines a framework for software life cycle processes.

- **ISO/IEC 25010** specifies software product quality characteristics, including usability, performance and security.

- **ISO/IEC 27001** is an internationally recognised standard for information security management systems (ISMSs) that provides a framework for managing and protecting sensitive company information so that it remains secure. The standard covers processes, policies and controls needed to protect information confidentiality, integrity and availability.

Detailed coverage of these standards is beyond the scope of this book.

IEEE standards

The Institute of Electrical and Electronics Engineers (IEEE) also provides various software engineering standards. For example:

- **IEEE 1016** defines a standard for software design descriptions.

- **IEEE 1063** defines a standard for software user documentation.

Again, detailed coverage of these standards is beyond the scope of this book.

Security standards

Security standards define guidelines and requirements to protect software systems from threats. For example:

- **Open Web Application Security Project (OWASP)** provides guidelines for secure web applications.

- **ISO/IEC 27001** – see *ISO/IEC standards*, above.

Code quality metrics

Code quality metrics are measurable indicators (often calculated using specialist software tools – see Chapter 12) that provide quantitative ways to assess the quality and maintainability of a codebase. While not a standard *per se*, these metrics help developers and development teams to detect potential issues early and make informed decisions about refactoring, so that code remains clean,[17] efficient and easy to understand. Regularly monitoring code quality metrics helps in maintaining high standards and reduces technical debt over time.

The metrics fall into various categories, including complexity, readability, maintainability and performance. Metrics in common use include:

- **Cyclomatic complexity**: This is a measure of the number of linearly independent paths through a program's source code. It is calculated based on the control flow within a program (combinations of sequence, selection and iteration). High complexity indicates that a unit of code is harder to understand, test and maintain, and may indicate a need for refactoring. Values between 1 and 10 are generally considered acceptable.

---

[17] Clean code is program (source) code that is easy to read, understand and maintain, typically characterised by clear structure, meaningful names and adherence to best practices.

- **Lines of code (LOC)**: This is a measure of the total number of lines of code in a program, function or module. It provides a basic measure of size and can give insight into the effort required for testing and maintaining the code. While LOC is easy to measure, it doesn't always correlate directly to quality. More LOC may indicate higher complexity, but fewer lines doesn't necessarily mean better code.

- **Code coverage**: This is a measure of the proportion of code that is executed by automated tests (unit, integration or end-to-end tests), expressed as a percentage of the total LOC. Higher coverage suggests that more of the code is tested, which reduces the risk of undetected defects. Generally, 80 per cent coverage is considered a good benchmark, but the ideal level can vary depending on the project.

- **Technical debt ratio**: This is a measure of the implied cost of additional re-work due to shortcuts or quick fixes in the code, calculated as the estimated time or cost required to refactor the code to meet quality standards, as a percentage of the total development effort or cost of development. This ratio helps teams to understand the future effort required to improve code quality. High technical debt can affect project timelines and budget. A value of 5 per cent or lower is generally considered acceptable; a higher value may indicate a need to focus on reducing technical debt to avoid long-term issues.

- **Duplication**: This is a measure of the percentage (or number of instances) of duplicated code across the codebase. Duplicated code increases maintenance effort and introduces the risk of inconsistencies. Reducing duplication promotes the DRY principle introduced earlier. Ideally, code duplication should be minimised (5–10 per cent or less).

- **Halstead metrics**: These are a suite of metrics that indicate how hard it is to understand and maintain the code, based on the number of operators and operands in the code:

  - **Halstead volume** measures the size of the code.

  - **Halstead difficulty** measures the complexity of the code.

  - **Halstead effort** estimates the effort needed to understand and maintain the code.

- **Maintainability index**: This combines several other factors (e.g. cyclomatic complexity, LOC and Halstead complexity) to assess how easy it is to maintain the code. A higher maintainability index indicates that code is easier to understand, modify and extend. Values range from 0 to 100 and code with an index above 85 is considered highly maintainable.

- **Code churn**: This is a measure of the number of changes (number of lines added, modified or deleted) made to the code over a certain period. Frequent changes in the codebase can indicate instability, so high churn may imply poorly designed code or code that is prone to frequent fixes.

- **Depth of inheritance**: This is a measure of the number of levels in a class inheritance hierarchy. Deep inheritance hierarchies can make code harder to understand and increase coupling, as changes in a base class may affect all derived classes. Ideally, the number of levels should be kept small to simplify code and minimise dependencies.

- **Response for a class**: This is a measure of the number of methods that can potentially be executed in response to a message received by an object of that class. Higher values indicate a more complex class, which may be harder to test and maintain. Values vary, but generally lower values are preferred.

- **Cohesion (lack of cohesion in methods)**: This is a measure of the degree to which methods in a class are related to each other. A high lack of cohesion means that the class does not serve a single, unified purpose. High cohesion is generally desirable, as it indicates that a class has a focused responsibility. Low cohesion often indicates that a class should be decomposed into smaller, more cohesive units.

- **Comment density**: This is a measure of the percentage of comments compared to the total lines of code. Comment density indicates how well documented the code is. Too few comments might make the code hard to understand, while too many could imply overly complex code. A balance is preferred, where the code is clear and comments explain complex or non-obvious logic.

3 PROGRAMMING PARADIGMS AND LANGUAGES

INTRODUCTION

Programming paradigms determine how developers approach problem-solving and writing program code. They represent distinct ways of thinking about, structuring, organising and managing programs. Different paradigms focus on various aspects of programming, such as data, logic, structure and flow.

Each paradigm offers distinct advantages and is suitable for different kinds of problems or development environments. Choosing the right paradigm depends on the specific needs of the project, the problem domain and the preferences of the development team. Some of the more popular paradigms are explored below, along with examples of programming languages that support them.

IMPERATIVE PROGRAMMING

Imperative programming is a paradigm where programs are written as a sequence of instructions (program statements) that change the program's state. These sequences can also include conditional logic, where different branches of an algorithm are followed depending on whether a certain condition is met. They can also incorporate groups of statements that repeat (loops). Therefore, they support the three key programming constructs that were introduced in Book 2: sequence, selection (conditional execution) and iteration (loops).

Programs written in this style focus on how to perform a task step by step. Languages that support this paradigm include C, Fortran, Assembly language and Python (imperative style). Figure 3.1 shows an extract from a program written in Python.

The code in Figure 3.1 starts by creating a variable named `numbers`, which contains a list of numbers. This is followed by the creation of a second variable `total_sum`, which is set to an initial value of 0. The program then continues with a loop that repeats the statement

```
total_sum += number
```

to add each number from the variable `numbers` to the value of `total_sum`. The final value of `total_sum` is then output to the user. The statements prefixed with the # symbol are comments that are ignored by the compiler but help developers to understand what the code is doing and how it works.

Figure 3.1 Example program code written in Python (imperative style)

```
# Initialise a list of numbers
numbers = [1, 2, 3, 4, 5]

# Initialise a variable to store the sum
total_sum = 0

# Loop through the list and add each number to the sum
for number in numbers:
    total_sum += number

# Output the result
print("The sum of the numbers is:", total_sum)
```

In this example:

- **Instructions** are given in a specific sequence (initialise numbers and total_sum, then loop through numbers).

- **State** is updated each time the loop adds the current value of numbers to total_sum. The variable number holds each value in the list numbers as the loop progresses. So the first time the loop executes, the value of number will be 1, the next time 2, and so on.

- The **flow** of execution is clear and controlled step by step.

Imperative programming is typically used for low-level programming such as the development of system software (as opposed to application software) or performance-critical applications that require direct control over the hardware.

PROCEDURAL PROGRAMMING

Procedural programming is an extension of imperative programming that structures the program into reusable procedures or functions that perform specific tasks, and the flow of execution (referred to as control flow) is managed by 'calling' (or invoking) these procedures.

There are two particular benefits of organising the program code in this way:

- Code reuse is encouraged by breaking the program into cohesive functions that can be reused in different programs – cohesion is a key software engineering principle that was introduced in Book 2 and revisited in Chapter 2.

- Debugging of code to identify the source of defects is made more straightforward by isolating the code responsible for a particular task to a specific procedure, rather than having to trace through the entire codebase.

Programs written in this style focus on breaking down a problem into smaller, cohesive procedures (also referred to as modules, functions or subroutines), which is aligned to the process design concept of stepwise refinement introduced in Book 2. Languages that support this paradigm include C, Pascal, ALGOL, COBOL, PL/1, BASIC and Python (procedural style). Figure 3.2 shows a program written in Python that performs the same task as the code in Figure 3.1, but using the procedural style.

Figure 3.2 Example program code written in Python (procedural style)

```python
# Define a function to calculate the sum of a list of numbers
def calculate_sum(numbers):
    total = 0
    for number in numbers:
        total += number
    return total

# Define a function to print the result
def display_result(total):
    print("The sum of the numbers is:", total)

# Main program
numbers = [1, 2, 3, 4, 5]
total_sum = calculate_sum(numbers)
display_result(total_sum)
```

When using Python in procedural style, the program is organised into functions, each with a specific task, and then these functions are called as needed.

The code in Figure 3.2 starts by defining a function (Python's equivalent of a procedure) called calculate_sum, which accepts a parameter (also known as an argument) called numbers. The parameter can be referenced within the function, which also defines its own local variable called total. Parameters are particularly useful for reusability, because the same function can be called from different places with different values (sets of numbers in this case). At the end of the code for the function, the value of the total variable is passed back to the calling module (referred to as Main program in Figure 3.2) using the statement return total. The calculate_sum function is called (invoked) using the statement total_sum = calculate_sum(numbers), which passes the variable numbers, defined in the previous statement, as a parameter and assigns the value returned by the calculate_sum function to a new variable, total_sum. Finally, instead of using the statement print("The sum of the numbers is:", total) in the main program, the code invokes another function (display_result) to perform the task, passing the value held in the variable total_sum as a parameter. This has the advantage of enabling the message displayed to the user to be changed in just one place, rather than everywhere the print statement is used.

In this example:

- The functions calculate_sum and display_result encapsulate specific tasks.

- The main program coordinates these functions to achieve the overall goal.

- Reuse is achieved because each function can be used with different inputs.

Procedural programming is typically used for general-purpose programming, including system-level applications, utilities and scientific computing, especially for larger programs, as it enables code reusability, readability and ease of debugging.

OBJECT-ORIENTED PROGRAMMING

Object-oriented programming is a paradigm that organises program code around objects that interact with each other. Objects encapsulate data (attributes or properties) and behaviour (operations and methods). OOP is based upon the following key concepts:

- **Object**: An object is an entity that combines data (attributes/properties) and behaviour (operations). An object is an instance of a class.

- **Class**: A class is a blueprint or template for defining and creating objects. It defines a set of attributes (data/properties) and behaviours (operations) that the objects created from the class will possess. Classes in OOP enable modular, reusable and organised code. By defining data and functionality in a class, the developer can create multiple objects that follow the same blueprint, making the code more maintainable and scalable.

- **Attribute**: An attribute is an individual item of data (property) that forms part of the definition of a class. When an object is created from the class template, each attribute will contain a value specific to that object.

- **Operation**: An operation is a specific action that can be performed on an object.

- **Method**: A method is the code that implements an operation.

- **Encapsulation**: Encapsulation is the practice of defining an object's data (attributes/properties) along with the methods or operations that act on that data, within the same class. This enables the data to be protected from unexpected or unauthorised access and processing by other program code outside the class definition. Through encapsulation, the developer can provide specific methods to manipulate the data, which enables validation, logging or other logic to be applied whenever data is accessed or modified. It also facilitates hiding of the internal state of an object and exposing only necessary parts through the controlled use of the object's operations.

- **Inheritance**: OOP languages incorporate a mechanism that enables one class to inherit properties from another. This supports a form of abstraction called **generalisation**, where a generic class defines properties common to all types of a given object (such as a `Policy` class in an insurance application), whose attributes and operations are inherited by specific subtypes (such as `MotorPolicy` and `HouseholdPolicy`). The concept of generalisation was introduced in Book 1.

- **Polymorphism**: Polymorphism is the ability to process objects differently based on their class. Polymorphism is enabled by, and builds on, the concepts of generalisation and inheritance. Detailed coverage of polymorphism is beyond the scope of this book.

Languages that support the OOP paradigm include Java, C++, C#, Python (OOP style), R, JavaScript, Ruby, MATLAB and Smalltalk. Figure 3.3 shows a program written in Python that performs the same task as the code in Figure 3.1, but using the OOP style.

Figure 3.3 Example program code written in Python (OOP)

```
# Define a class (TotalCalculator) to calculate the sum of a list of numbers
Class TotalCalculator:

    # code to initialise an instance of the class (object)
    def __init__(self, numbers):
        self.number_list = numbers
        self.total = 0

    # code for calculate_total operation
    def calculate_total(self):
        self.total = 0
        for number in self.number_list:
            self.total += number
        return

    # code for display_result operation
    def display_result(self):
        print("The sum of the numbers is:", self.total)

# Main program
my_total_calculator = TotalCalculator([1, 2, 3, 4, 5])   # create a new object of
                                                         # type (class)
                                                         # TotalCalculator

my_total_calculator.calculate_total()        # invoke the operation to calculate
                                             # the total

my_total_calculator.display_result()         # invoke the operation to display
                                             # the result
```

In the example in Figure 3.3, the class TotalCalculator is defined to provide services that are utilised (invoked) from the main program, but could also be called from other classes or programs. The class definition comprises definitions for three methods: __ init__, calculate_total and display_result, which implement the operations (actions) that can be performed on each object of the class. __init__ is a special method in Python, referred to as a **constructor**. It is used to create a new object (instance) of a particular class, and sets up the initial state of the object by assigning values to the object's attributes. The statement

        my_total_calculator = TotalCalculator([1, 2, 3, 4, 5])

creates a new TotalCalculator object, which invokes the __init__ method, which in turn sets the object's number_list attribute to the list of numbers passed as a parameter.

The calculate_total method defines the code that is used to sum the numbers passed to the object as the parameter numbers. A key difference between the code in Figure 3.3 and that in Figure 3.2 is that the calculate_total method does not need to receive a parameter containing the numbers (unlike the function `calculate_sum` in Figure 3.2), because it can directly access the `number_list` attribute within the object, which contains the list of numbers provided when the object was first created – and similarly for the `display_result` method.

The main program in Figure 3.3 simply comprises the creation of the new `TotalCalculator` object and the invocation of the two methods `calculate_total` and `display_result`, in sequence.

OOP encourages code reuse and modularity (incorporating the design principles of loose coupling and high cohesion). High cohesion is achieved because each type of object (class) has a specific purpose and performs a set of clearly defined services (operations, implemented by methods) on behalf of other objects. Loose coupling is achieved by designing classes that interact with each other in a way that minimises dependencies, enabling changes in one part of the codebase to have minimal or no impact on other parts. This combination of reusability through high cohesion and loose coupling makes OOP particularly suitable for large, complex systems, graphical user interface (GUI) applications, game development and enterprise systems.

DECLARATIVE PROGRAMMING

Declarative programming focuses on what the program should accomplish rather than how to achieve it. Declarative programs 'declare' the required result or problem to solve, leaving the execution details to the underlying platform software. This leads to clear and concise code that focuses on the desired outcome and reduces the complexity of managing state and control flow.

Languages that support this paradigm include SQL (for database queries), HTML (for web pages), CSS, Prolog, Terraform and Ansible (for defining infrastructure as code), as well as certain features of JavaScript (declarative APIs). Figure 3.4 shows a simple database query written in SQL.

Figure 3.4 Simple database query written in SQL

```
SELECT name, dob, start_date FROM employee WHERE start_date >= '2024-01-01'
```

The example in Figure 3.4 shows a SQL `SELECT` statement, which declares to the underlying database platform (e.g. a Microsoft SQL Server database management system (DBMS)) the data required in terms of a list of attributes (`name`, `dob`, `start_date`), the table where the data is stored (`employee`) and a condition that determines which rows in the table to retrieve (`start_date >= '2024-01-01'`). The DBMS then works out how to obtain the required data and packages it up into a new table, known as a ResultSet.

The declarative paradigm is particularly suitable for domain-specific applications like database queries, configuration management, web development (HTML/CSS) and logic programming.

FUNCTIONAL PROGRAMMING

Functional programming is a declarative style of programming in which programs are constructed by applying functions to values and linking them together – for example, by passing a function as the argument to another function, and thus modifying its behaviour. Operations are stateless, and values immutable – meaning data cannot be modified once created; instead of changing existing data, any modification operation results in the creation and return of a new data structure containing the updated values, while the original data remains unchanged. This means that there are no unintended side-effects caused by changes in data, making functions more predictable, easier to test and less prone to defects (by eliminating many common sources of defects related to data changes).

Languages that support this paradigm include Haskell, Lisp, Scala and F#. Many non-functional languages (such as Python, Kotlin and JavaScript) also support programming in a functional style. Figure 3.5 shows an example written in Python that takes a list of numbers and filters out odd numbers, squares the even numbers and then sums the squared even numbers.

Figure 3.5 Example of functional programming written in Python

```
from functools import reduce

# Sample list of numbers
numbers = [1, 2, 3, 4, 5, 6, 7, 8, 9, 10]

# Step 1: Filter out odd numbers
evens = list(filter(lambda x: x % 2 == 0, numbers))

# Step 2: Square the even numbers
squared_evens = list(map(lambda x: x ** 2, evens))

# Step 3: Sum up the squared even numbers
sum_of_squares = reduce(lambda x, y: x + y, squared_evens)

print("Even numbers:", evens) # Outputs: [2, 4, 6, 8, 10]
print("Squared even numbers:", squared_evens) # Outputs: [4, 16, 36, 64, 100]
print("Sum of squared evens:", sum_of_squares) # Outputs: 220
```

In the example in Figure 3.5, the filter function takes another function (lambda) and a sequence (the list of numbers) and returns a new sequence containing only the elements for which the function returns True (the list containing just the even numbers). The map function applies a function (lambda) to each element in a sequence, and returns a new sequence with the transformed elements. Here, map(lambda x: x ** 2, evens) squares each even number. Finally, the reduce function applies a binary function (a function with two arguments) cumulatively to the elements of a sequence, reducing the sequence to a single value. Here, reduce(lambda x, y: x + y, squared_evens) sums up the squared even numbers.

Functional programming is well suited to data transformations, mathematical computations and applications that require parallel processing or high levels of concurrency, such as financial systems and AI.

LOGIC PROGRAMMING

Logic programming is a paradigm based on formal logic, where the developer specifies rules and facts about a problem domain, and the underlying runtime environment derives conclusions based on these rules.

Languages that support this paradigm include Prolog and Datalog, Clingo, Oz/Mozart and Mercury. Figure 3.6 shows an example program written in Prolog.

Figure 3.6 Example of logic programming written in Prolog

```
% Facts
parent(john, mary).     % John is a parent of Mary
parent(john, tom).      % John is a parent of Tom
parent(mary, susan).    % Mary is a parent of Susan
parent(mary, jim).      % Mary is a parent of Jim
parent(susan, bill).    % Susan is a parent of Bill

% Rules

% Sibling relationship: X and Y are siblings if they share a parent
sibling(X, Y) :-
    parent(Z, X),
    parent(Z, Y),
    X \= Y.

% Grandparent relationship: X is a grandparent of Y if X is a parent of Z
% and Z is a parent of Y
grandparent(X, Y) :-
    parent(X, Z),
    parent(Z, Y).

% Ancestor relationship: X is an ancestor of Y if X is a parent of Y
ancestor(X, Y) :-
    parent(X, Y).
% Recursive rule for ancestor: X is an ancestor of Y if X is a parent of Z
% and Z is an ancestor of Y
ancestor(X, Y) :-
    parent(X, Z),
    ancestor(Z, Y).
```

In the example in Figure 3.6, the `parent` facts define the relationships, where the first argument is the parent of the second argument. For instance, `parent(john, mary)` means that John is a parent of Mary. The facts are followed by three rules:

- `sibling(X, Y)`: Two people are siblings if they share a common parent and are not the same person. The `X \= Y` condition ensures that `X` and `Y` are not the same.

- `grandparent(X, Y)`: A person is a grandparent if they have a child who is a parent of someone else.

- `ancestor(X, Y)`: The ancestor rule comprises two separate rules: the first rule states that an ancestor is a direct parent, and the second rule uses recursion, stating that X is an ancestor of Y if X is a parent of Z, and Z is an ancestor of Y.

With this Prolog program, you can ask queries to deduce relationships, such as:

- Who are Mary's siblings?

    ```
    ?- sibling(mary, X).
    ```

    This query will find X values where X is a sibling of Mary.

- Who are the grandparents of Bill?

    ```
    ?- grandparent(X, bill).
    ```

    This query will return X = mary since Mary is the grandparent of Bill.

- Is John an ancestor of Bill?

    ```
    ?- ancestor(john, bill).
    ```

This query checks if there's a path from John to Bill through the ancestor rule, which should return true.

Logic programming is particularly useful in domains requiring formal reasoning, such as AI, knowledge representation, natural language processing, expert systems and database systems, where rule-based logic is critical.

ASPECT-ORIENTED PROGRAMMING

Aspect-oriented programming (AOP) is a programming paradigm that aims to increase modularity by facilitating the separation of cross-cutting concerns[18] (e.g. error handling, logging and security) into aspects, which are reusable modules that can be applied across different parts of a program without duplicating code. Aspects affect multiple parts of a software system but are not easily modularised using traditional programming paradigms.

Languages that support this paradigm include AspectJ (Java), Spring AOP (Java), PostSharp (C#.NET/VB.NET), Java Aspect Components (JAC), JBoss AOP (Java), Python (AspectLib), AspectC++ (C++), Ruby (Aquarium), Perl (Aspect) and JavaScript (MooTools, Meld.js). Figure 3.7 shows an example program written in AspectJ (an extension of Java, and arguably one of the most popular languages that supports AOP) that demonstrates AOP for logging method calls. Figure 3.7 comprises three code extracts:

1. a core Java class (`Account.java`) with two methods for depositing and withdrawing money to and from the account;

2. an aspect (`LoggingAspect.aj`) that logs method calls for this class; and

3. a main program (`Main.java`) to observe the aspect in action.

---

18 Cross-cutting concerns refers to functionality that affects multiple parts of a program but is not central to the business logic of any one module.

33

Figure 3.7 Example of aspect-oriented programming written in AspectJ

```
// Account.java
public class Account {
    private int balance = 0;

    public void deposit(int amount) {
        balance += amount;
        System.out.println("Deposited " + amount + ". Current balance: " + balance);
    }

    public void withdraw(int amount) {
        if (balance >= amount) {
            balance -= amount;
            System.out.println("Withdrew " + amount + ". Current balance: " +
balance);
        } else {
            System.out.println("Insufficient balance.");
        }
    }
}
```

```
// LoggingAspect.aj
import org.aspectj.lang.annotation.Aspect;
import org.aspectj.lang.annotation.Before;
import org.aspecti.lang.annotation.After;
import org.aspectj.lang.JoinPoint;

@Aspect
public class LoggingAspect {

    @Before("execution(* Account.deposit(..)) || execution(* Account.withdraw(..))")
    public void logBefore(JoinPoint joinPoint) {
        System.out.println("Executing: " + joinPoint.getSignature().getName());
    }

    @After("execution(* Account.deposit(..)) || execution(* Account.withdraw(..))")
    public void logAfter(JoinPoint joinPoint) {
        System.out.println("Finished: " + joinPoint.getSignature().getName());
    }
}
```

```
// Main.java
public class Main {
    public static void main(String[] args) {
        Account account = new Account();
        account.deposit(100);
        account.withdraw(50);
    }
}
```

In the example in Figure 3.7, the core Java class (`Account.java`) represents a bank account with methods to deposit and withdraw money. The logging aspect (`LoggingAspect.aj`) intercepts the execution of deposit and withdraw methods and logs the actions. The logging aspect works as follows:

- The `@Aspect` annotation declares the `LoggingAspect` class as an aspect.
- The `@Before` and `@After` annotations define advice to be executed before and after method execution.
- The pointcut[19] `execution(* Account.deposit(..))` defines where the advice should be applied. In this example, the aspect targets the `deposit` and `withdraw` methods in the `Account` class.
- `JoinPoint` provides context information, such as the method name being executed.

The `Main` class in the main program (`Main.java`) creates a new `Account` object and then invokes the `deposit` and `withdraw` operations in turn. The output from executing the program is shown in Figure 3.8.

Figure 3.8 Output from program in Figure 3.7

```
Executing: deposit
Deposited 100. Current balance: 100
Finished: deposit
Executing: withdraw
Withdrew 50. Current balance: 50
Finished: withdraw
```

AOP is particularly useful for managing concerns such as logging (centralised code for logging activities, as demonstrated above), error handling (handling exceptions consistently across the system by applying error-handling logic through aspects), security (checking permissions before certain methods are executed) and transaction management (adding transaction management logic to database operations), without cluttering the core business logic. However, it can add complexity and requires good tooling and design to be used effectively.

CONCURRENT PROGRAMMING

Concurrent programming is a paradigm that focuses on executing multiple tasks simultaneously. This often involves synchronisation mechanisms to prevent conflicts when tasks interact with shared resources.

Languages that support this paradigm include Java (with threads), Go (goroutines), Python (with threads) and Erlang. Figure 3.9 shows an example program written in Python that simulates fetching data from multiple sources concurrently, using Python's `ThreadPoolExecutor` to run tasks concurrently with threads.[20]

---

19 In aspect-oriented programming (AOP), a **join point** is a specific point in a program's execution – such as a method call, object creation or field access – where extra behaviour can be added. A **pointcut** is an expression that selects these join points to specify where an aspect's **advice** (the inserted behaviour) should be applied.

20 A thread is an independent path of execution within a program that can run simultaneously with other threads to perform multiple tasks concurrently.

Figure 3.9 Example of concurrent programming written in Python

```python
import concurrent.futures
import time
import random

# Simulate a task (e.g. fetching data) that takes some time to complete
def fetch_data(source):
    print(f"Fetching data from {source}...")
    # Simulate network delay
    time.sleep(random.uniform(1, 3))
    data = f"Data from {source}"
    print(f"Completed fetching data from {source}")
    return data

# List of data sources
sources = ["Source A", "Source B", "Source C", "Source D"]

# Using ThreadPoolExecutor to fetch data concurrently
def main():
    with concurrent.futures.ThreadPoolExecutor() as executor:
        # Submit tasks to the executor
        futures = [executor.submit(fetch_data, source) for source in sources]

        # Retrieve and print results as they complete
        for future in concurrent.futures.as_completed(futures):
            result = future.result()
            print(result)

if __name__ == "__main__":
    main()
```

In the example in Figure 3.9, the `fetch_data` function simulates a task that fetches data from a source. It uses `time.sleep` to simulate a delay (such as network latency) and returns a message indicating the data source. The `ThreadPoolExecutor` in the `concurrent.futures` module (defined separately and not shown in Figure 3.9) is used to manage a pool of threads. Each call to `executor.submit(fetch_data, source)` submits the `fetch_data` function for execution with a specified data source. The tasks are executed concurrently by the threads in the pool, each fetching data from a different source. The `concurrent.futures.as_completed` function returns results as they complete, enabling the program to process results immediately rather than waiting for all tasks to finish, and the `future.result` function retrieves the result of each completed task.

The output from this program will vary each time it executes because the tasks run concurrently, but a typical example of the likely output is shown in Figure 3.10.

Concurrent programming is particularly useful for applications such as web servers, real-time systems and distributed systems that require concurrency or parallelism.

Figure 3.10 Output from the program in Figure 3.9

```
Fetching data from Source A...
Fetching data from Source B...
Fetching data from Source C...
Fetching data from Source D...
Completed fetching data from Source B
Data from Source B
Completed fetching data from Source A
Data from Source A
Completed fetching data from Source C
Data from Source C
Completed fetching data from Source D
Data from Source D
```

EVENT-DRIVEN PROGRAMMING

Event-driven programming is a paradigm where the flow of the program is determined by events such as user interactions, sensor outputs or messages from other programs. Programs based on this paradigm simplify the handling of user input (such as mouse clicks or key presses) and system events, and enhance responsiveness in interactive applications.

Languages that support this paradigm include: Python, JavaScript (web development), Node.js and C# (with event-driven architecture). Figure 3.11 shows an example program written in Python that creates a basic GUI with a button; when the button is clicked, an event is triggered and a message is displayed.

Figure 3.11 Example of event-driven programming written in Python

```
import tkinter as tk
from tkinter import messagebox

# Event handler function
def on_button_click():
    messagebox.showinfo("Event Triggered", "Button was clicked!")

# Create the main window
root = tk.Tk()
root.title("Event-Driven Programming Example")
root.geometry("300x200")

# Create a button and bind the event handler to it
button = tk.Button(root, text="Click Me", command=on_button_click)
button.pack(pady=50)

# Start the event loop
root.mainloop()
```

In the example in Figure 3.11:

- The `on_button_click` function is defined to act as an event handler. It defines what happens when the button is clicked – in this case, showing a message box.

- A main window (`root`) is created with a title and size, using the `tkinter` library.

- A button widget (`button`) is created (using the `tk.Button` method defined in the `tkinter` library) with the label `Click Me`.

- The `command` argument of the button is set to `on_button_click`, binding this function to the button's click event.

- A call to `root.mainloop()` starts the main event loop, which listens for events like button clicks, and triggers the associated event handler (in this case `on_button_click`) when the button is clicked.

When the program is executed, a window with a 'Click Me' button appears, and when the button is clicked, the `on_button_click` event handler is triggered, displaying a message box that says 'Button was clicked!'

Event-driven programming is particularly useful for applications such as GUIs, games, real-time systems and web applications, where user or system interactions trigger program responses.

4 SOFTWARE ENGINEERING IN PRACTICE

INTRODUCTION

Software engineering is a dynamic and evolving discipline that blends theory, methodologies and best practices to build reliable, scalable, secure and maintainable digital solutions. As technology advances, software engineers must adopt diverse approaches and practices so the solutions they develop continue to meet the needs of the customer, organisation and end-user. By integrating the right approaches and practices, software engineering teams can enhance productivity, improve software quality and accelerate development cycles.

This chapter explores a diverse range of practices from the overall approach to developing the software (e.g. pair programming, test-first development and no-code development) to specific coding practices (e.g. addressing code smells, leveraging design patterns, continuous integration, continuous deployment and managing technical debt).

SOFTWARE ENGINEERING APPROACHES

Software engineering approaches provide structure, consistency and predictability to the effective design, development, testing and deployment of software. Different approaches address a variety of challenges in modern software development, from code quality to speed of development and team collaboration.

This section considers the following popular approaches:

- test-driven development (TDD);
- behaviour-driven development (BDD);
- full stack development;
- no-code and low-code development;
- model-driven architecture (MDA) and model-driven engineering (MDE); and
- DevOps.

Test-driven development

Test-driven development is a software development methodology that originated in the late 1990s as part of Extreme Programming (XP). Kent Beck, the creator of XP, formally introduced TDD in his book *Test-Driven Development: By Example* (Beck, 2003).

TDD encourages developers to begin by defining a small, specific piece of functionality, writing tests for it and then writing the minimum amount of code needed to pass those tests. Once the code passes the tests, the developer refactors it to improve structure and efficiency, ensuring that the functionality remains intact. This process encourages clean, defect-free code, with tests serving as both verification of correctness and documentation of the expected behaviour.

The TDD workflow follows a repetitive cycle known as Red–Green–Refactor:

1. **Red (write a test)**: Developers first write a unit test (unit testing is discussed in Chapter 6) for a new piece of functionality, which initially fails because the functionality has not yet been implemented. This step defines the goal of the next piece of development work.

2. **Green (write just enough code to pass the test)**: The developer writes the simplest possible code to pass the test. The goal here is not to write perfect code, but to have the feature working as quickly as possible.

3. **Refactor (optimise and improve the code)**: When the code passes the test, the developer improves the internal structure of the code without changing its external behaviour. Refactoring focuses on removing duplication, improving readability and ensuring maintainability, all while making sure that tests continue to pass.

This cycle is repeated for each new feature or defect fix, ensuring that every part of the application is continuously tested.

TDD provides a number of benefits:

- **Improved code quality**: Writing tests first forces developers to think about the functionality and design of the software from the outset. This typically leads to cleaner, more maintainable code.

- **Early defect detection**: Since tests are written before the code, developers can catch defects early in the development process, reducing the number of defects found later in the development cycle, when they are often more time-consuming and costly to fix.

- **Test coverage**: TDD encourages writing tests for every piece of functionality, leading to more comprehensive test coverage. This helps to ensure that code behaves as expected in various scenarios.

- **Refactoring confidence**: TDD enables developers to refactor with confidence, knowing that any changes that break functionality will be quickly caught by the tests.

- **Documentation**: Tests serve as documentation and other developers can quickly understand what the code is supposed to do by reading the test cases.

- **Faster feedback**: TDD enables developers to see the effects of their code changes immediately, which supports rapid iteration and helps to improve overall productivity.

Behaviour-driven development

Behaviour-driven development is a software development methodology that bridges the gap between technical teams and business stakeholders, promoting collaboration between developers, testers, business analysts, end users, subject-matter experts, product owners and other business stakeholders. Introduced originally in 2003 by Dan North in various blog posts and discussions, and formally published in 2006 (North, 2006), North proposed BDD as an extension to TDD, building on the principles of TDD but shifting the focus towards describing the behaviour of the software from the end-user's perspective.

By using natural language (a notation called **Gherkin**, described below) to describe how the software should behave from an end-user's perspective, BDD ensures that development and testing are aligned with business goals. In contrast, TDD focuses on writing unit tests (technical tests written by developers) to verify that small units of code function correctly. Moreover, the tests in TDD are often written in programming languages, and may not be understandable by non-technical stakeholders.

Gherkin is an easy-to-understand, structured language that includes keywords such as:

- **Given** – the starting condition or context;
- **When** – the event or action that triggers a behaviour; and
- **Then** – the expected outcome of that behaviour.

For example:

```
Given I have added items to the cart
   And I am on the checkout page
When I enter valid payment details
   And I confirm the purchase
Then I should see a confirmation message "Order placed successfully"
   And the order status should be "Processing"
```

The BDD process works as follows:

1. **Discovery**: Stakeholders come together to discuss and define the desired features and behaviours of the software to be built. The conversation typically revolves around user stories[21] that describe the requirements in a narrative form.

2. **Formulation**: The team refines the user stories into scenarios using the Given–When–Then format, outlining how the software should behave in specific

---

21 First introduced in Book 1, user stories are short, simple descriptions of a feature or requirement told from the perspective of the end-user, typically following the format: 'As a [user] I want [goal] so that [rationale].'

situations. This step helps to ensure that both the technical team and the business stakeholders share a clear understanding of the requirements.

3. **Automation of scenarios**: Once the scenarios are defined, developers and testers use automated testing frameworks (see Chapter 12) to write automated tests based on these scenarios. This ensures that the behaviour described in the scenarios is continually validated throughout the development process.

4. **Development**: The development team writes the code necessary to implement the features and behaviours described in the scenarios. Tests are continuously run to ensure that the code meets the desired behaviour and that no regressions[22] are introduced.

5. **Iteration**: The BDD process is iterative. As new features or changes are introduced, new scenarios are written, automated and tested, ensuring that the software behaves as expected at every stage of development.

BDD provides a number of benefits:

- **Business-driven development**: Development is guided by business requirements, which specify how the software should operate in different scenarios, ensuring consistency between business needs and technical implementation. Gherkin scenarios describe the expected behaviour in a way that directly reflects business objectives and encourages teams to concentrate on the behaviours that are most valuable to the customer, leading to higher customer satisfaction.

- **User-centric**: BDD promotes the use of user stories and real-world scenarios that define, from the end-user's perspective, how the software should work in specific situations. Every feature is designed around how it benefits the end-user.

- **Improved communication**: Requirements are expressed in natural language, making specifications easy for both technical and non-technical stakeholders (e.g. developers, testers, business analysts, product owners and end-users) to understand. This reduces miscommunication and ensures that everyone involved in the software development process shares a clear understanding of the intended behaviour of the system. It also helps to avoid building features that fail to meet business needs.

- **Clarity and completeness of requirements**: By translating high-level requirements into detailed scenarios, BDD helps clarify edge cases,[23] sharpen acceptance criteria and uncover ambiguities early on. This results in a better understanding of requirements, reduces the risk of misinterpretation and ensures that the final product meets expectations.

- **Focus on quality**: Gherkin scenarios include both positive and negative behaviours enabling the software to be tested under a variety of real-world conditions, which enhances overall test coverage. Each scenario is converted into automated tests, which BDD tools execute regularly to help ensure the software continues to meet

---

22 A regression in software engineering is when a previously working feature stops functioning correctly due to changes or updates in the code.

23 An edge case is a situation that occurs at the extreme boundaries of input, conditions or operating parameters, often revealing unexpected behaviour or weaknesses in a system.

expected behaviour as it evolves. Automated testing also enables frequent releases without compromising quality, and provides ongoing feedback, reducing the risk of regression errors[24] and safeguarding existing functionality when new features are added. By defining tests before development, BDD helps to identify any deviation from required behaviour early in the development process. This in turn lowers the cost and effort required to resolve defects, enabling developers to address issues as they arise, and ultimately enhancing software quality.

- **Living documentation**: Gherkin scenarios provide clear, up-to-date documentation of the software's behaviour that can be referred to throughout the development cycle by all team members, not just developers and testers. As the software evolves, the tests and scenarios continue to describe its functionality.

BDD builds on TDD by focusing on ensuring that the software's behaviour aligns with user expectations and is understandable to both technical and non-technical stakeholders. While TDD ensures code quality at the unit level by verifying that individual components work as intended, BDD emphasises delivering valuable features to the business and confirming that the software meets user needs.

Full stack development

Full stack development refers to the practice of a single team or individual developing both the front-end (client-side) and back-end (server-side) components of an application, especially a web application.

The front end is responsible for everything that users see and interact with directly. It focuses on the user experience – the visual layout and user interaction. The back end is the server side of the application, where all the core processing happens. It handles data processing, application logic, authentication and database interactions.

Full stack development is a highly versatile and demanding discipline, requiring developers to be proficient in a range of technologies and skilled in handling all layers of an application, including UI/UX development, database management and deployment.

Full stack development offers a number of benefits:

- **Efficiency**: A full stack developer can bridge the gap between front end and back end, leading to faster development and troubleshooting.

- **Versatility**: Full stack developers can work on any part of an application, making them highly adaptable to different project needs.

- **Enhanced collaboration**: Full stack developers often act as a bridge between teams, facilitating better communication and understanding across disciplines.

- **Cost-effective**: For startups or small teams, a full stack developer can fulfil many roles, reducing the need for multiple individual specialists.

---

24 A regression error in software engineering is a defect that has previously been fixed that reoccurs following a subsequent change to the program code. This is often caused by poor version control of the code.

No-code/low-code development

No-code and low-code development are approaches to software development that aim to simplify and speed up the development process, enabling business change professionals, or even end-users, with limited or no coding skills to build applications. They are designed to make application development accessible to a broader audience, reducing reliance on professional developers and enabling faster development cycles. Consequently, no-code and low-code platforms are valuable tools in modern application development, especially for businesses looking to accelerate digital transformation, empower non-technical staff or quickly prototype new ideas. While both approaches help to reduce development time, lower costs and provide business agility, each approach has its own idiosyncrasies, benefits, challenges and use cases.

No-code development
No-code development platforms enable non-technical stakeholders to create applications without writing any code. They offer a number of features that users can configure to build applications:

- A drag-and-drop interface enables users to add and arrange elements by dragging and dropping them onto an application canvas, making it easy to design user interfaces and workflows.

- Pre-built templates and components provide elements such as forms, tables, buttons and layouts that are ready to use.

- Many no-code platforms have built-in interfaces with popular applications and services (e.g. Google Sheets, Slack and payment gateways) to enrich the offering of bespoke applications.

- Automated workflows enable users to set up workflows and business rules without coding, such as sending automated emails or triggering notifications.

No-code development offers a number of benefits:

- **Accessibility**: Non-technical users are able to create applications, lowering the barrier to entry for developing digital solutions.

- **Speed**: Users can build applications without writing code, which can be very time-consuming, thus supporting rapid prototyping and development.

- **Cost-effective**: No-code development reduces the need for a large development team, which can lower costs for businesses.

Although clearly very beneficial for rapid development of digital solutions, no-code development has its limitations:

- **Limited customisation**: No-code platforms are typically limited to predefined features, which can make it difficult to develop highly customised or complex applications.

- **Scalability issues**: No-code solutions can struggle to scale effectively for high-demand applications.

- **Dependency on a specific platform**: Developers using no-code platforms are often locked into a specific platform, limiting flexibility and control over the application.

Low-code development

In contrast to no-code development, low-code development platforms require some, albeit minimal, programming, enabling the creation of more complex or customised applications than those typically achievable by their no-code counterparts. While they share the visual development features of no-code platforms, low-code applications also enable users to add custom code to achieve more flexibility. These platforms are commonly used by professional developers or semi-technical users who seek to accelerate development while retaining more control over functionality and design than no-code platforms can offer.

Like no-code platforms, low-code platforms feature a drag-and-drop interface and provide pre-built modules or components. However, they offer greater flexibility by enabling developers to modify or extend these components with custom code. This capability enables the addition of unique functionality, integration with external services and the creation of complex workflows or business rules that go beyond what no-code tools can typically handle.

The benefits of low-code development are similar to no-code development, with the following additional benefits:

- Low-code development enables customisations beyond what is possible with no-code platforms, making it suitable for more complex applications.

- Low-code development enables developers to focus on complex tasks while automating repetitive tasks, increasing productivity.

The primary limitation of low-code development is that the platforms are not completely code-free, requiring users to have some programming knowledge for more advanced customisation. Additionally, while low-code is effective for building basic and moderately complex applications, it may still face challenges when managing very large or highly customised projects.

Table 4.1 provides a summary of the key differences between no-code and low-code development.

Further details of tools that support no-code and low-code development are provided in Chapter 12.

Model-driven architecture and model-driven engineering

Model-driven architecture (MDA) and model-driven engineering (MDE) are model-based approaches to software engineering that seek to boost productivity, manage complexity and promote portability. MDA, which closely follows standards such as the Unified Modeling Language (UML), focuses on software architecture by defining platform-independent models (PIMs) that can be transformed into platform-specific models (PSMs) and executable code, aiding portability, interoperability and reusability. Building on the foundation laid by MDA, MDE has evolved into a broader approach that applies modelling techniques and tools across the entire software development life cycle (SDLC) – from requirements and design to testing and deployment – emphasising process standardisation, model consistency and quality improvement.

Table 4.1 Comparison of no-code and low-code development

Aspect	No-code development	Low-code development
Target audience	Non-technical users (citizen developers)	Semi-technical users and developers
Customisation level	Limited	Moderate to high
Development speed	Very fast	Fast
Coding required	No	Minimal
Scalability	Limited	Moderate
Suitability for complex applications	Not suitable	Suitable
Dependency on platform	High	Moderate to high
Use cases	• Straightforward internal tools or dashboards • Marketing or landing pages • Automating workflows between software-as-a-service (SaaS) apps • Straightforward data entry or reporting applications	• Enterprise applications with custom workflows • Mobile applications with moderate complexity • Business process automation • Prototyping complex applications for rapid iteration

Table 4.2 provides a summary of the key differences between MDA and MDE.

Table 4.2 Comparison of model-driven architecture and model-driven engineering

Aspect	MDA	MDE
Scope	Software architecture	Entire software engineering life cycle
Focus	Portability, interoperability, reusability	Productivity, maintainability, quality
Standards	Object Management Group (OMG) standards – UML, Meta-Object Facility (MOF), Query/View/Transformation (QVT)	Flexible – may use domain-specific languages (DSLs), UML, Eclipse Modeling Framework (EMF)
Approach	Platform-independent and platform-specific models	Domain-specific and life cycle-wide modelling
Limitations	Limited domain flexibility, strict standards	Broad scope, complex standardisation

(Continued)

Table 4.2 (Continued)

Aspect	MDA	MDE
Suitability	Suitable for projects that can benefit from consistent, standards-based architecture across different platforms and environments, where portability and interoperability are essential.	Suitable for projects that require domain-specific customisation or where automation across the SDLC can significantly improve productivity and reduce time-to-market.
Primary use cases	Cross-platform software, enterprise applications, legacy system modernisation	Embedded systems, automotive, aerospace (where models represent more than just software and must encompass hardware and system constraints)

DevOps

The term DevOps is widely credited to Patrick Debois, a Belgian IT consultant often referred to as 'the father of DevOps'. In 2009, he organised the first DevOpsDays conference in Ghent, Belgium, to unite software development and IT operations professionals and to explore ways to enhance collaboration and efficiency. He subsequently discussed the principles behind DevOps in an article titled 'DevOps from a Sysadmin Perspective' (Debois, 2011).

DevOps emerged from the need to bridge the gap between development (Dev) and IT operations (Ops) and streamline the software delivery process, addressing the challenges and inefficiencies that arose when these teams operated in silos. The DevOps cycle (Figure 4.1) brings together ideas from the Agile movement, Lean IT[25] and CI and CD practices (see later in this chapter) that emerged in the early to mid-2000s, to create a seamless, automated and efficient software delivery process.

Figure 4.1 shows a continuous, never-ending cycle of development, deployment and operation, which comprises eight stages:

1. **Plan**: This stage involves defining the objectives, requirements and tasks required for the software development project, and prioritising the work.

2. **Code**: This involves writing and reviewing the code (based on the planned requirements), and collaborating on code changes.

3. **Build**: This is where the source code is compiled and linked (if necessary) to produce an executable format, ensuring correct code integration and identifying any basic errors.

---

25 Lean IT is the application of Lean principles to information technology, aiming to maximise value and eliminate waste in IT processes, services and systems.

Figure 4.1 The DevOps cycle

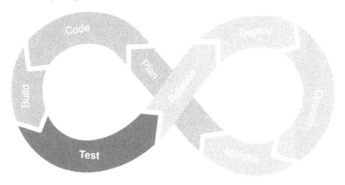

4. **Test**: Both automated and manual tests are conducted to ensure the code meets the specified requirements. This includes running unit tests, integration tests, system tests and acceptance tests.

5. **Release**: During the release stage the software is prepared for deployment to production. This involves scheduling the release, creating release notes and performing final checks, such as securing approvals and completing sign-offs.

6. **Deploy**: During the deploy stage, the executable code is transferred from a development or staging environment to the production environment (see Chapter 5), making it accessible to users. This process includes deploying the code, running scripts[26] and configuring servers.

7. **Operate**: This stage represents the ongoing operation, management and maintenance of the application in the live environment, which ensures the software functions smoothly and meets performance expectations. This stage includes handling infrastructure management, resource scaling and incident response.

8. **Monitor**: Once the software has been deployed, its performance, stability and infrastructure are continuously monitored to identify potential issues early and to ensure high availability and reliability. This stage also provides feedback that helps to enhance and refine future development cycles.

Key characteristics of the DevOps approach include:

- **Collaboration and communication**: DevOps encourages a collaborative culture between development, IT operations and other teams (such as quality assurance (QA) and security), to break down traditional silos and encourage shared responsibility for the software life cycle.

- **Continuous integration (CI) and continuous deployment (CD)**: CI involves regularly merging code changes into a shared repository, followed by automated testing to

---

26 Running scripts refers to executing automated commands or programs – often written in languages such as Bash, Python or PowerShell – to carry out deployment tasks such as configuring environments, installing software, copying files or starting services on target servers.

identify issues early. CD automates the release process, enabling code changes to be deployed to production more frequently and reliably. Together, CI/CD pipelines help teams to deliver updates and new features faster while reducing errors.

- **Automation**: Automation is central to DevOps, from testing and deployment to infrastructure provisioning (see *Infrastructure as code* below). Automated processes minimise manual intervention, reduce errors and speed up workflows, enabling frequent and consistent software releases.

- **Infrastructure as code (IaC)**: IaC involves managing and provisioning infrastructure using program code and automation tools rather than manual processes. This enables consistency, repeatability and version control of infrastructure, enabling environments to be created and modified easily and consistently.

- **Monitoring and logging**: Continuous monitoring and logging of applications and infrastructure helps teams to detect issues early, understand system performance and respond to incidents more effectively. This feedback loop is essential for improving future development cycles and ensuring high availability and reliability.

- **Continuous testing**: Continuous testing during the software development process verifies the functionality of the software and quality of the code, and helps to identify defects before deployment to production. Automated tests (including unit and integration tests) are often embedded within CI/CD pipelines, which facilitates faster and more reliable releases.

- **Security (DevSecOps)**: DevSecOps incorporates security practices within the DevOps pipeline. Rather than treating security as a separate, final stage, security measures are integrated throughout the development life cycle, ensuring vulnerabilities are addressed early and continuously.

DevOps offers a number of benefits:

- **Faster time-to-market**: DevOps enables rapid and frequent releases, enabling businesses to respond quickly to customer needs and market changes.

- **Improved collaboration**: By promoting a culture of shared responsibility, DevOps encourages better collaboration between development, IT operations and other teams.

- **Increased efficiency and reduced costs**: Automation of repetitive tasks, such as testing and deployment, reduces manual effort and operational costs.

- **Higher quality and reliability**: Continuous testing, monitoring and feedback loops help to detect and fix issues early, resulting in more stable and reliable software.

- **Customer satisfaction**: Faster delivery of new features and improvements ensures that customer feedback can be incorporated quickly, improving the overall user experience.

Further details of tools that support DevOps are provided in Chapter 12.

SOFTWARE ENGINEERING PRACTICES

Software engineering embraces a diverse range of practices, some of which are specific to particular methodologies and approaches. This section explores some common practices that are independent of a particular method or approach or are common to different methods and approaches.

Modular programming

Based on the software engineering principle of modularity introduced in Chapter 2, modular programming is a software design strategy that focuses on breaking down a program into independent, self-contained units of code called modules. The primary aim of modular programming is to build an organised, manageable codebase that simplifies understanding, development, testing and maintenance, and uses clear module interfaces to enhance reusability, scalability and separation of concerns.

Secure coding practices

Secure coding practices consist of techniques and strategies that developers implement to avoid vulnerabilities and create robust software. Integrating these practices into the development process is essential for protecting applications from security threats, such as data breaches, unauthorised access and cyberattacks. This approach helps to ensure software can withstand potential threats, reduce risks, safeguard user data and build user confidence.

In his book *Secure Software Design: Safeguarding Your Code Against Cyber Threats* (Carrie, 2024), Saimon Carrie presents five fundamental principles of secure software design:

- **Principle of least privilege (POLP)**: This principle asserts that a user, program or system should have the minimum level of access – or privileges – necessary to perform its functions. By limiting the access and permissions granted to users and software components, the risk of unauthorised actions, whether accidental or malicious, is reduced. For example, a user account that only needs to read data should not have write or execute permissions. Similarly, an application that only needs to access a specific database should not have administrative privileges across the entire system.

- **Defence in depth**: This is a security strategy that layers multiple security measures to protect an asset, which ensures that if one measure fails, others are in place to provide additional protection. By deploying multiple layers of security, organisations create redundancies that help to protect against a wide range of threats and minimise the impact of potential breaches. For example, a web application might implement client-side and server-side input validation, use firewalls and intrusion detection systems, and encrypt sensitive data. If an attacker bypasses one layer, additional layers help to protect the system.

- **Fail-safe defaults**: This principle asserts that access should be denied by default unless explicitly granted. This approach ensures that, in the event of a failure, the system defaults to a secure state, reducing the likelihood of unintentional access or actions. For example, if an access control system experiences an error or fails to retrieve authorisation information, it should deny access rather than allow it.

Similarly, configuration files should only expose essential settings and everything else should be restricted by default.

- **Principle of least astonishment**: This principle asserts that a system should function in a way that reduces unexpected behaviour for users and developers. It should act predictably and align with user expectations and standard practices. Designing systems to be intuitive and consistent helps to lower the risk of user mistakes and misconfigurations that could result in security vulnerabilities. For example, a web application's 'Delete' button should clearly indicate its function, with an appropriate warning message confirming the action. Any deviation from expected behaviour, such as silently deleting records without user confirmation, would violate this principle and could lead to unintended consequences.

- **Separation of concerns (SoC)**: This principle (first introduced in Chapter 2) involves dividing a system into distinct sections, each addressing a separate concern or responsibility. Fundamental to 'modular' design (see *Modular programming* above) SoC ensures that different parts of the system can be developed, tested and secured independently, which improves code security by reducing the impact of vulnerabilities in one module on other parts of the software. For example, in a web application, the presentation layer (UI), business logic layer and data access layer should be separate. This enables security measures, such as input validation (see below) and data encryption, to be implemented and updated independently in the appropriate layers.

Other secure coding practices include:

- **Input validation**: Validation of all inputs to ensure they meet expected criteria before processing. This often includes sanitising user inputs by removing or encoding potentially harmful characters, which helps to prevent common vulnerabilities like SQL injection,[27] cross-site scripting[28] (XSS) and buffer overflows.[29] Whenever possible, whitelist validation (allowing only known safe inputs) should be used rather than blacklist validation, which attempts to block known malicious inputs.

- **Authentication and authorisation**: The use of strong authentication mechanisms, such as multifactor authentication (MFA) and appropriate authorisation checks to verify that users have access only to the resources they are entitled to. Secure password storage methods (such as using a cryptographic hashing algorithm like bcrypt or Argon2) should also be used rather than storing passwords as plain text.

- **Environment variables for sensitive data**: The use of environment variables or secure vaults to safely store and access credentials, API keys[30] and other sensitive information, rather than hard-coding them in the codebase.

---

27 SQL injection is a security vulnerability that allows attackers to manipulate a database query by injecting malicious SQL code through user input, potentially gaining unauthorised access to data or executing unwanted operations.

28 XSS is a security vulnerability that enables attackers to inject malicious scripts into web pages viewed by other users, potentially leading to data theft, session hijacking or other malicious actions.

29 A buffer overflow is a cybersecurity vulnerability where input exceeds a program's memory buffer limit (the fixed amount of memory allocated by a program to temporarily store data – such as user input – during execution), potentially allowing attackers to overwrite memory and execute malicious code.

30 An API key is a unique identifier used to authenticate and authorise a user or application when accessing an API, helping to control and secure usage.

- **Secure communication**: The encryption of data in transit using secure protocols, such as HyperText Transport Protocol Secure (HTTPS), Transport Layer Security (TLS), and Secure Sockets Layer (SSL), to prevent interception, ensure certificate validation and avoid bypassing SSL/TLS checks in production environments.

- **Secure error handling and logging**: Exceptions should be detected and handled without exposing system details – detailed error messages can give attackers information about the system. Additionally, logging of sensitive information (such as passwords and session tokens) in log files should be avoided to prevent unexpected disclosure.

- **Secure session management**: The use of secure session tokens and the storage of session cookies with 'Secure' and 'HttpOnly' flags, to prevent access from client-side scripts. Transmission should only take place over HTTPS, and session expiration mechanisms should be implemented.

- **Limitation of privileges**: The principle of least privilege, introduced above, should always be followed by granting only the minimum access necessary for code execution, and using role-based access controls (RBACs) to manage user permissions and prevent unauthorised actions.

- **Code reviews and static analysis**: Conducting regular code reviews to identify potential security flaws and ensure adherence to secure coding practices, and the use of static code analysis tools (see Chapter 12) to automatically scan for vulnerabilities.

- **Output encoding**: Encoding data (e.g. converting potentially dangerous characters (such as <, >, ", ', and &) into their harmless HTML-encoded equivalents (<, >, ", ', and &) before displaying it in the browser to protect against XSS attacks.

- **Secure libraries and frameworks**: Regularly updating libraries and frameworks to ensure they continue to protect against known vulnerabilities. Libraries should be vetted for security and the use of outdated or untrusted third-party packages should be avoided.

- **Secure data storage**: Sensitive data at rest should be encrypted using strong encryption algorithms like Advanced Encryption Standard (AES). Additionally, access controls for data storage locations should be implemented to prevent unauthorised access.

- **Secure APIs**: Only secure APIs that provide robust authentication, encryption and access controls should be used. Additionally, all data returned from APIs should be validated.

- **Security headers**: The use of HTTP security headers such as 'Content-Security-Policy', 'X-Content-Type-Options', 'X-Frame-Options' and 'Strict-Transport-Security' should be used to add additional layers of protection against common attacks.

Defensive programming

Defensive programming is a software development technique that focuses on creating robust, reliable and secure software by anticipating potential problems and implementing safeguards. It operates on the principle that failures – such as invalid user input, unexpected environmental conditions or defects in other parts of the software – are inevitable. By proactively addressing these possibilities during development, defensive programming helps to prevent crashes, incorrect behaviour and security vulnerabilities. This involves implementing input validation, checks and fallback mechanisms to handle inappropriate inputs and unforeseen scenarios. Ultimately, defensive programming enhances the reliability, security and maintainability of the software by minimising the likelihood of defects and failures.

A number of defensive programming practices have already been covered in the context of secure coding practices. Other practices include:

- **Error handling**: The implementation of robust error handling for exceptions and unexpected conditions. These should ensure that such exceptions are handled gracefully, without crashing the program.

- **Assertions**:[31] Assertions should be used to catch programming errors during development by ensuring certain conditions hold true. Assertions help to identify logical errors early.

- **Fail-safe defaults**: Software should be designed to provide sensible default behaviour when unexpected issues occur. These fail-safe defaults help to maintain system stability and minimise potential damage. For example, a GPS navigation app that loses signal may continue to display the last known route or advise the user to stay on the current road, reducing confusion and preventing incorrect directions. Similarly, a temperature control system in a data centre may switch to maximum cooling if a sensor fails or temperature data becomes unavailable, protecting hardware from overheating despite the lack of accurate input.

- **Defensive copying**: Direct manipulation of input data – especially when it might be modified elsewhere – should be avoided to prevent unexpected changes. Instead, a defensive copy should be made before working with the data. For example, if a program is required to sort a shared to-do list, a defensive copy should first be made to ensure that the changes will not affect the original version that other users or programs may still need.

- **Return values**: The return values of functions should always be checked and possible failure cases appropriately handled. This prevents unexpected behaviour due to ignored or unverified results.

- **Defensive code comments**: Assumptions, edge cases and the purpose of defensive code should be documented using comments to help future maintainers understand why specific checks and safeguards are in place.

- **Minimise assumptions**: Code should be written with minimal assumptions made about how functions will be called or how data will be used. Anticipate potential misuse or incorrect usage.

- **Boundary checks**: Checks should be made for boundary conditions and edge cases to prevent out-of-bounds errors[32] and buffer overflows.

- **Logging and monitoring**: Logging mechanisms should be implemented to record application errors, performance metrics, warnings and unusual behaviour. This

---

31 Assertions are special program statements used by developers to verify assumptions about a program's internal state during execution. They help to catch defects by stopping program execution when unexpected conditions occur.

32 An out-of-bounds error occurs when a program tries to access an element outside the valid range of an array (a data structure that stores a fixed-size, ordered collection of elements accessible by an index number) or some other data structure, leading to unexpected behaviour or system failure.

helps to diagnose issues in production environments after deployment, and provides a trail for troubleshooting.

Continuous integration

Continuous integration (CI) is the practice of frequently merging code changes from multiple developers into a shared repository (usually on a main branch – see *Code branching* later in this chapter). The goal is to detect issues early, reduce integration problems and maintain a healthy, stable codebase using the following practices:

- **Frequent code integration**: Developers push small code changes frequently, ideally several times per day. Each code commit (where changes are saved to a source code repository) triggers an automated build process.

- **Automated testing**: Every integration triggers a set of automated tests (unit tests and integration tests). If any tests fail, the team is alerted and the issue is addressed immediately.

- **Build automation**: The CI server automatically builds the application after each commit. This ensures that the codebase is always in a deployable state.

CI offers the following key benefits:

- **Early defect detection**: Issues are identified early, before they become more difficult and costly to fix.

- **Early feedback**: Developers receive immediate feedback on any code changes they make.

- **Reduced integration problems**: Frequent merging results in fewer code conflicts.

Examples of CI tools can be found in Chapter 12.

Continuous delivery/deployment

Continuous delivery and continuous deployment are both practices that build on top of CI, but they differ in how they handle the final step of transitioning the software into a 'live' production environment.

The primary goals of **continuous delivery** are twofold:

1. To ensure that the codebase of a software application is always in a deployable state, enabling rapid and reliable releases to a production environment at any time.

2. To prepare for deployment quickly and reliably, enabling the organisation to decide when to transition the software into production.

These goals are achieved through the following practices:

- **Automated testing and deployment pipelines**: Automated tests and quality checks (e.g. code linting[33] and security scans) are performed as part of the pipeline. If

---

33 Code linting is the process of automatically analysing source code to identify and flag programming errors, defects, stylistic issues and potential problems.

the tests pass, the changes can be deployed to a staging or pre-production environment for further testing.

- **Manual approval**: While the software is always in a deployable state, actual deployment requires manual approval, especially for production releases.

Continuous deployment goes a step further than continuous delivery. Its primary goal is to achieve a fully automated pipeline where every change that passes tests is automatically deployed to a production environment without the need for manual intervention. Continuous deployment practices are similar to those for continuous delivery, but also include the following:

- **Automated deployment**: Any successful build is automatically deployed to the production environment.

- **Strong monitoring**: Robust monitoring and alerting are critical to catch issues in real time.

- **Feature flags**:[34] Feature flags are used to control the release of new features safely (see also *Code branching* later in this chapter).

Table 4.3 compares the key features and benefits of each practice.

Table 4.3 Comparison of continuous delivery and continuous deployment

Aspect	Continuous delivery	Continuous deployment
Goal	Ensure software is always in a deployable state	Automate the entire release process
Automation	Automated testing and deployment pipeline	Full automation, including production release
Manual intervention involved	Manual approval required for production release	No manual steps; fully automated pipeline
Testing requirements	Extensive automated testing	Even more rigorous automated testing needed than for continuous delivery
Monitoring	Essential for identifying release readiness	Critical for detecting and mitigating issues in production
Risk management	Manual approval step adds a safety layer	Feature flags, canary releases (covered in Chapter 10) and rollback mechanisms
Release frequency	Regular releases, but less frequent than with continuous deployment	Very frequent (could be multiple times per day)
Use cases	Suitable for risk-sensitive environments	Suitable for fast-paced, Agile environments

34 Feature flags are used to enable or disable specific features at runtime, enabling teams to test, release or rollback functionality without deploying new code.

DevOps (discussed earlier in this chapter) uses both continuous delivery and continuous deployment, but the choice depends on the organisation's goals. Continuous delivery is a more cautious approach, enabling manual control over production releases, whereas continuous deployment aligns more closely with the DevOps goal of full automation and rapid iteration, but it requires greater confidence in testing and monitoring.

In many DevOps implementations, continuous delivery is the starting point because it provides a balance of automation and control, and enables the DevOps team to build confidence in the automated pipeline and tests before moving to fully automated deployment. As the team gains experience and confidence in the CI/CD pipeline, they may transition to continuous deployment, which requires a higher level of testing automation, monitoring and incident response capabilities.

A further consideration that may influence the decision as to whether to use continuous delivery or continuous deployment is the nature of the digital solution itself and the organisational context. Continuous delivery is suited to applications where the organisation needs more control over the release process – such as in solutions involving a high degree of regulatory or legislative compliance, or some other risk that needs to be managed. In contrast, continuous deployment works well for companies that release multiple times per day (such as SaaS platforms) and have strong testing and rollback mechanisms.

CI/CD pipelines

The combination of CI and CD working together is core to the DevOps approach. A CI/CD pipeline is an automated workflow that streamlines the process of integrating, testing and delivering/deploying software, in particular, code changes. CI/CD pipelines are designed to:

- deliver software faster and with higher quality;
- streamline the release process;
- minimise manual errors; and
- respond quickly to user feedback and issues.

There are two separate pipelines that work together to form a CI/CD pipeline – a CI pipeline and a CD pipeline (either continuous delivery or continuous deployment):

- **CI pipeline**: This focuses on automating the integration of code changes from multiple developers into a shared repository. Each code change triggers an automated build and test process.
- **Continuous delivery/deployment pipeline**: This extends the CI process by automating the preparation of code for a release to production. The continuous delivery pipeline requires manual approval prior to deployment to production, whereas the continuous deployment pipeline automates the entire process – the software is automatically pushed to production once it passes all automated tests.

An example CI/CD pipeline workflow (for a server-side application built using the Node. js JavaScript runtime environment, and using the GitHub Actions CI/CD tool) is:

1. **Source code**: The developer pushes changes to the 'main' branch on GitHub, triggering the GitHub Actions workflow.

2. **Build**: The GitHub Actions workflow installs dependencies and builds the project.

3. **Test**: Unit tests and integration tests are executed. If any tests fail, the pipeline stops and the team is notified.

4. **Deploy to staging**: If all tests pass, the code is deployed to a staging environment for manual testing.

5. **Approval**: A team member manually approves the release for production (if using continuous delivery).

6. **Deploy to production**: The application is deployed to production, either automatically (continuous deployment) or after manual approval (continuous delivery).

7. **Monitor**: The application is monitored for errors, performance issues or user feedback.

Examples of tools that support CI/CD pipelines can be found in Chapter 12.

Agile development practices

Agile development was introduced in Book 1 (*Defining Digital Solutions*) as a response to traditional, rigid development approaches based around linear software development life cycles (SDLCs) such as the Waterfall model. These approaches often led to delayed projects and unmet user needs.

Agile is an umbrella term that refers to a set of software development practices and methodologies that emphasise collaboration, flexibility, incremental delivery and continuous improvement. Agile approaches prioritise responding to changes and offering value to customers quickly and frequently.

The following Agile development practices and techniques were introduced in Book 1:

- iterations (Sprints);
- daily stand-ups (Scrums);
- iteration reviews (show and tells/Sprint reviews);
- retrospectives;
- backlogs and backlog refinement (Three Amigos session);
- user stories;
- Gherkin scenarios (see *Behaviour-driven development* above);
- MoSCoW prioritisation;
- Planning Poker;
- Agile boards; and
- burndown charts.

Many of these practices are about the definition of the solution or the methodology used to manage the work of an Agile development team. The following practices relate more to the way the team engineer and deliver the software solution.

Iterative development and incremental delivery
Iterative development refers to how the software is built, whereas incremental delivery refers to how the software is delivered to the business for operational use.

Iterative development is a development approach based on the iterative SDLC (introduced in Book 1 and reproduced in Figure 4.2) whereby the overall project is composed of several small, timeboxed developments, called iterations (or Sprints in Scrum) that take place in sequence. Each iteration is essentially a self-contained mini-project composed of activities such as requirements, analysis, design, development and testing, as visualised in Figure 4.2.

Figure 4.2 Iterative development life cycle (© Assist Knowledge Development Ltd)

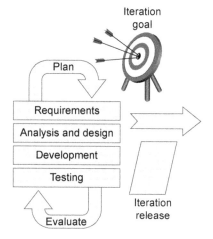

With iterative development, the solution emerges through the construction of a series of evolutionary prototypes (see below) over a series of development iterations, each adding new or enhanced functionality, improved performance or fixes for defects introduced earlier in development. At the end of each iteration, the final version of the prototype is a working, potentially deployable piece of software (shown in Figure 4.2 as the **iteration release**). The full solution develops over time as the users' and developers' understanding of what is required, and how best to deliver the requirements, grows.

A deployment into live operational use may or may not take place at the end of an iteration and it is common for a series of development iterations to be completed before deploying the software into a production environment, as shown in Figure 4.3.

Incremental delivery refers to how the software is delivered into a production environment for 'live' operational use. Traditional approaches, based on linear SDLCs, deliver a complete solution at the end of a development project. However, this 'all or nothing' approach is not workable for many modern businesses because it demands

Figure 4.3 Iterations and releases (© Assist Knowledge Development Ltd)

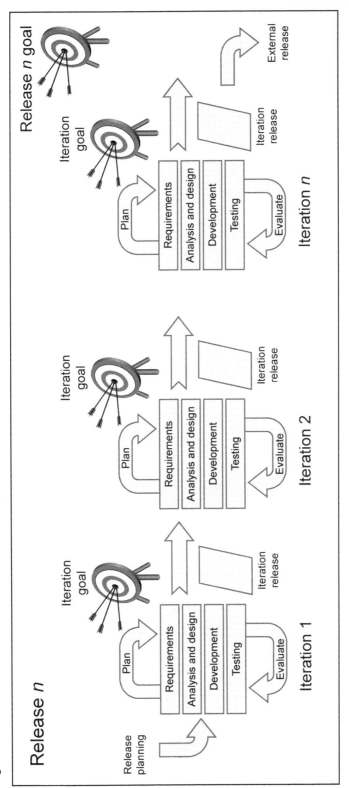

substantial up-front investment with no benefits being realised until the project has been completed. A consequence of this approach is that, if a project is abandoned before completion, the business may have invested significant resources without gaining any real value. To mitigate this risk, development teams in the 1990s began adopting strategies that focused on delivering a partial solution early, followed by additional features in subsequent increments. This incremental delivery model facilitates earlier realisation of benefits, reduces risk by validating the evolving solution against requirements and identifying integration issues sooner, and has become a core practice in Agile development.

For incremental delivery to work in practice, it is important that the user has workarounds in place to mitigate the impact of the missing product features. Moreover, it is imperative that each release provides a viable product that can be used to realise value. This is known as the minimum viable product (MVP), which is essential for setting priorities during both iteration and release planning.

Evolutionary prototyping

Prototyping was first introduced in Book 1 as a qualitative requirements elicitation technique, and again in Book 2, which briefly discussed the use of storyboards and wireframes (types of 'low-fidelity' prototype) in input and output (I/O) and UX design.

The term prototype is defined in ISO 9241-210 (ISO, 2019) as:

> A representation of all or part of an interactive system, that, although limited in some way, can be useful for analysis, design and evaluation.

A prototype demonstrates certain characteristics of a product to be developed. It is typically an early, simplified version or representation of a product that is created to test and validate ideas, concepts, features or designs before investing significant time and resources in full-scale development. It serves as a model that demonstrates how the final product might look and function.

Some practitioners include early sketches of some aspect of a product in this definition, but Nick de Voil disputes this view (De Voil, 2020):

> A sketch is not a prototype! Sketching is an essential part of what designers do. It is a way of developing ideas, which has been described as 'thinking with a pencil'. A sketch is not suitable for using as a prototype. A prototype needs to be something that the user can understand and interact with in some way.

The concept of prototyping dimensions is a useful way of distinguishing between different types and uses of prototyping. One useful dimension is 'fidelity'. Jakob Nielsen introduced the concept of different levels of fidelity in prototyping in his book *Usability Engineering* (Nielsen, 1993). While there is some debate with regard to the distinction between high and low fidelity, common definitions are:

- **Low fidelity** refers to simplified and abstract representations of a product, such as wireframes and paper-based mock-ups. Low-fidelity prototypes tend to focus on the overall concept, layout and basic interactions and are ideal for early-stage exploration and gathering initial feedback.

- **High fidelity** refers to detailed and realistic representations that closely mimic the final product, such as interactive digital mock-ups, coded prototypes or 3D-printed models for physical products. High-fidelity prototypes include visual design, detailed user interface and interactive elements, and are used for usability testing, stakeholder presentations and final user feedback.

A primary goal of prototyping is to gather feedback. Users and other key stakeholders can interact with the prototype and provide valuable insights and suggestions for improvement. Prototypes are often developed iteratively, with feedback leading to refinements and adjustments. The process is focused on continuous improvement.

Two further useful classifications are:

- **Throwaway prototype**: Also referred to as a rapid prototype, a throwaway prototype is created to test a concept or gather requirements and is then discarded after use. The primary goal of a throwaway prototype is to validate ideas (sometimes referred to as a proof of concept) and gather feedback before committing to the full development of the product. For example, a mock-up of a web page created using a virtual whiteboard to demonstrate a new feature or layout idea.

- **Evolutionary prototype**: A working prototype that is continually refined and expanded upon throughout the development process, instead of being discarded after gathering feedback (like a throwaway prototype). An evolutionary prototype is built using the development platform chosen to implement the final software solution and grows incrementally, becoming more detailed and functional with each iteration of the prototyping cycle until it is deemed fit for purpose. The goal is for the prototype to **evolve** into the final product through iterative enhancements.

Throwaway prototypes typically fall into the low-fidelity category, while evolutionary prototypes fall into the high-fidelity category.

Evolutionary prototyping complements iterative development and incremental delivery within Agile software development, where there is often insufficient time to build 'throwaway' prototypes before embarking on the development of the final working product. Once the first evolutionary prototype has been delivered at the end of a development iteration (Sprint), that version becomes the start point for the next evolutionary prototype, which is built during the next iteration, and so on. Each iteration adds more functionality and incorporates feedback from previous iteration reviews (show and tells). Periodically – either after each iteration or after multiple iterations, as illustrated in Figure 4.3 – the final prototype is deployed to the production environment for live operational use.

Pair programming
Pair programming is one of the key practices of the Agile software development method Extreme Programming (XP), where two programmers work together at one workstation to write code. The two programmers perform the following roles:

- **The driver**: This is the person who focuses on solving the problem at hand and writes the code.

- **The navigator**: This is the person who reviews each line of code as it is written, looking for potential issues and suggesting improvements.

The roles are frequently switched between the two programmers to share the workload and knowledge, and to keep them both engaged.

Pair programming can be performed in person, sitting side by side at the same workstation, or remotely, using specialist collaborative tools (see Chapter 12) or generic screen-sharing software such as Zoom or Microsoft Teams.

Pair programming offers the following benefits:

- **Improved code quality**: The navigator acts as a real-time reviewer, catching programming errors and code defects early in the process, resulting in higher-quality code.

- **Knowledge sharing**: Pair programming facilitates the exchange of knowledge and skills between team members. Junior developers can learn from senior developers, and even senior developers can learn new techniques or approaches from junior developers, who may be more up to date with newer frameworks and libraries.

- **Improved problem-solving**: Having two people working on the same problem often leads to faster and more effective solutions. The navigator can provide alternative ideas or help the driver to overcome challenges.

- **Reduced code ownership issues**: By distributing knowledge across the team, the risk of a single developer becoming the sole owner of a specific part of the codebase is reduced.

- **Increased team collaboration**: Pair programming promotes communication and collaboration, helping to build a more cohesive and unified team.

- **Higher focus and fewer distractions**: When working together, both developers tend to stay more focused and avoid distractions, leading to increased productivity.

A potential drawback of pair programming is that these benefits can come at a higher cost in terms of the additional resources required to deliver the same software that could be delivered by a single developer. Consequently, pair programming can be perceived as less efficient in the short term. However, this is often offset by the long-term benefits of reduced defects and improved code quality.

Code reviews

A code review (also known as a peer review) involves one software developer systematically examining another developer's code before it is merged into the main codebase to ensure that it meets quality standards, adheres to coding best practices and aligns with project requirements. The primary goal is to maintain code quality, but within that there are a number of sub-goals:

- **Enforce coding standards**: Verify that the code follows best practices and adheres to the team's coding standards.

- **Detect defects and issues early**: Identify potential defects introduced into the code, including logic errors, performance inefficiencies and security vulnerabilities.

- **Maintain code quality and consistency**: Ensure that the code is readable, maintainable and scalable, and follows a style and structure that is consistent throughout the codebase.

- **Promote knowledge sharing**: Encourage collaboration and knowledge sharing among team members.

- **Facilitate learning and improvement**: Provide constructive feedback to help less experienced developers learn from more experienced ones, improving their coding skills.

The objectives of code reviews are similar in many respects to those for pair programming (see *Pair programming* above). Table 4.4 provides a high-level comparison of the two practices.

Table 4.4 Comparison between code reviews and pair programming

Aspect	Code review	Pair programming
Collaboration	Reviewer and author work separately	High level of collaboration between the author (the driver) and the reviewer (the navigator)
Timing	After the code is written	In real time, during code writing
Feedback	Delayed, after code submission	Immediate, as code is being written
Knowledge sharing	One-time review, limited interaction	Continuous and dynamic
Typical uses	Routine quality checks, all code changes	Complex or critical tasks

Code reviews are a form of static testing (see Chapter 6) and can be automated using specialist static analysis tools (see Chapter 12).

Addressing code smells

When undertaking code reviews, either as part of pair programming or independently, developers look for common patterns in the code that may signal underlying issues, such as poor design choices or deviations from best practices. These so-called 'anti-patterns' or 'code smells' are not defects (they do not typically cause code to fail), but they indicate areas where code could be improved for better readability, maintainability and flexibility. By addressing these smells, teams can create a codebase that is easier to understand, maintain and extend.

Common categories of code smell include:

- **Bloaters**: These indicate the code has become too large, complex or verbose, making it difficult to understand, maintain and modify. Bloaters are typically caused by the gradual accumulation of unnecessary code, repeated patterns or overly complex logic. They are called 'bloaters' because they 'bloat' the codebase, adding unnecessary lines of code and complexity.

- **Couplers**: These indicate excessive coupling[35] between classes. Tight coupling (or high coupling) makes code harder to understand, modify and test, as changes in one class often require cascading changes in other classes.

- **OO abusers**: These occur when developers misuse or fail to leverage object-oriented programming principles effectively, indicating that the code is not taking full advantage of OOP features such as inheritance, polymorphism, encapsulation and abstraction, or that these features are being used incorrectly.

- **Change preventers**: These make it difficult, risky or costly to modify the code. These smells often lead to situations where making even a small change can have unintended consequences, causing defects, increasing development time and reducing the overall maintainability of the codebase.

- **Dispensables**: These refer to pieces of code that are unnecessary and could be removed without affecting the functionality of the application. They are considered 'dispensable' because they do not add value, and their presence often makes the codebase harder to read, understand and maintain. Dispensables are indicators of redundancy, dead code or code that is overly complex without a good reason.

Table 4.5 summarises the high-level categories of code smells described above, and cites some more explicit examples of each. A detailed explanation of these specific code smells is beyond the scope of this book.

Regarding the last example in Table 4.5, comments in code are sometimes seen as code smells, especially where they are used to explain complex logic. This can indicate that the code is too complicated or unclear. Simplifying and refactoring the code can often eliminate the need for excessive commenting.

There are three common ways of addressing code smells:

- **Code reviews**: Code reviews help to identify code smells early and prevent them from accumulating over time.

- **Refactoring**: Regularly refactoring to remove code smells helps to keep code clean and maintainable.

- **Design patterns**: Many code smells can be addressed by applying appropriate design patterns (see below).

---

35 Coupling refers to the degree of interdependence between software modules, with lower coupling indicating more modular, flexible and maintainable code.

Table 4.5 Summary of code smell categories

Category	Description	Main problem	Examples
Bloaters	Code that is too large or complex	Hard to read and maintain	• Long method • Large class • Long parameter list • Primitive obsession
Couplers	Excessive dependency between classes	Tight coupling and reduced modularity	• Inappropriate intimacy • Feature envy • Message chains • Middle man
OO abusers	Misuse of object-oriented principles	Poor extensibility and complex design	• Switch statements • Refused bequest • Temporary field • Alternative classes with different interfaces
Change preventers	Code that makes changes difficult	High risk of defects and costly modifications	• Divergent change • Shotgun surgery • Parallel inheritance hierarchies
Dispensables	Unnecessary or redundant code	Cluttered and hard to maintain code	• Dead code • Duplicate code • Lazy class • Data class • Speculative generality • Comments

Design patterns

Design patterns were introduced in Book 2 as proven solutions to common problems that software developers face during application design. While the concept of a design pattern can be applied at various levels of design, the patterns introduced by the Gang of Four (Erich Gamma, Richard Helm, Ralph Johnson and John Vlissides) in their seminal book *Design Patterns: Elements of Reusable Object-Oriented Software* (Gamma et al., 1994) are particularly relevant to software engineering as they guide the way developers write their code to solve common software engineering challenges and address common code smells. It is good practice to use design patterns as they promote consistency and embody lessons learned from previous solutions.

Configuration management

Configuration management (CM) in software engineering is the process of systematically handling changes to a software system to ensure its integrity, consistency and traceability throughout the SDLC. It involves managing all artefacts (such as source code, documents, requirements and test data) to track and control modifications, avoid conflicts and ensure the software behaves as expected.

Key objectives of configuration management include:

- **Maintain system integrity**: Ensure that changes to the software are implemented correctly and that the system remains stable and functional.

- **Version control**: Keep track of different versions of the software, enabling developers to manage updates, rollback changes and track historical information.

- **Change tracking**: Record and manage all changes made to the software, including who made the change, why it was made and what was changed.

- **Consistency across environments**: Ensure that the software behaves the same way in different environments (see Chapter 5) by managing configuration settings and dependencies.

- **Facilitate collaboration**: Enable multiple developers to work on the same project without one developer's changes conflicting with those of another developer, thus improving team collaboration.

There are four key components of configuration management:

- **Configuration identification**: The items that need to be managed (such as source code, libraries, documentation, configuration files) are uniquely identified and defined. These are known as configuration items. Baselines (the approved version that serves as a reference point) are established for each configuration item.

- **Configuration control**: Configuration items are managed and controlled. This includes the handling of change requests, review processes and approval mechanisms to ensure that changes are necessary and do not introduce errors.

- **Configuration status accounting**: Records are maintained of the status of configuration items, including versions, changes and their current state (such as under development, approved or released). Status accounting provides a history of changes and helps stakeholders to understand the current configuration.

- **Configuration audit**: Verification that the configuration items are correct, complete and conform to the requirements. Audits ensure that the system is built according to the approved configuration and that changes have been implemented correctly.

Configuration management is a critical practice in software engineering that helps to maintain the integrity, consistency and traceability of the software throughout its life cycle. By using version control, automation tools and best practices, teams can manage changes effectively, minimise errors and deliver high-quality software faster.

Further information on configuration management tools and their features is presented in Chapter 12.

Code management practices

Code management practices encompass a set of strategies, tools and processes used by software development teams to effectively organise, control and maintain source code throughout the SDLC. These practices ensure that the codebase remains clean, consistent and manageable, enabling efficient collaboration, reducing the risk of defects and facilitating rapid development.

While other practices are in common use, this section will focus on four specific areas:

- version control;
- code branching;
- software configuration files; and
- managing technical debt.

Version control
Version control (VC) is an important practice in software engineering that tracks changes to files over time, enabling multiple developers to collaborate, maintain a history of changes and manage different versions of a project. It is primarily used for source code management, but it can also be applied to documentation, configuration files and other project assets.

Successful VC requires a software tool called a version control system (VCS), which manages changes to source code over time. The VCS keeps track of individual modifications to the code and enables developers to examine and compare current and earlier versions of the code to help find and eliminate faults and, if necessary, revert to an earlier version (rollback).

Key VC concepts include:

- **Repository**: The storage location for the project's files and their version history. It can be local (on the developer's machine) or remote (on a server).
- **Commit**: A snapshot of changes made to the files in the repository, which is often accompanied by a message describing the changes made.
- **Branch**: See *Code branching* below.
- **Merge**: See *Code branching* below.
- **Conflict**: Occurs when two or more changes are made to the same part of a file prior to a commit. See also *Code branching* below.

Examples of VC tools and their features can be found in Chapter 12.

Code branching

Code branching is a VC technique that involves creating distinct copies of the code, known as branches. Each branch serves as an independent version of the codebase, enabling developers to work on features, defect fixes, experiments or other tasks separately from the main code. This approach enables multiple teams or developers to collaborate on different aspects of a project simultaneously, without disrupting each other's work.

There are a number of key concepts related to the practice of branching:

- **Branch**: A separate version of the codebase where changes can be made independently. It starts as a copy of the main codebase and can diverge as new changes are made. There are a number of different types of branch commonly used:

  - **Main (or master) branch**: This is typically the primary branch where the stable, production-ready code resides. It represents the current release of the software.

  - **Feature branch**: This is created to develop a specific feature or enhancement. Once the feature is complete, it is merged back into the main branch.

  - **Hotfix branch**: This is used for urgent defect fixes that need to be applied directly to the production code. It is merged back into both the main and development branches after the fix is applied to ensure the defect does not return during the next scheduled release, a phenomenon known as a regression error.

  - **Release branch**: This is used to prepare a new version of the software for release. It enables final testing, defect fixing and polishing before merging the new code into the main branch.

- **Merge**: The process of integrating changes from one branch into another. This is often done after a feature is complete or a defect is fixed.

- **Conflict**: A merge conflict occurs when changes in different branches affect the same part of a file. Conflicts must be resolved manually before the merge can proceed.

- **Pull request**: A pull request initiates a collaborative review process, enabling team members to provide feedback, ensure code quality and catch potential issues before the changes are merged from one branch into another.

Development teams use branching for a variety of reasons, including:

- **Parallel development**: Branching enables multiple developers or teams to work on different tasks (such as the development of new features and defect fixes) without affecting the main codebase.

- **Isolation of changes**: Branching enables new code to be developed and tested independently before merging into the main codebase.

- **Safe experimentation**: Branching provides a safe space for experimenting with new ideas or changes without risking the stability of the main branch of code.

- **Code review**: Branching facilitates the code review process by enabling changes to be reviewed in a separate branch before being merged into the main branch.

Feature flags or toggles can be applied to a branch to tag or emphasise code changes within it, linking specific code alterations to a particular feature (although they can be used with any branch type, not just feature branches). These flags or toggles enable features to be turned on or off even after the code is deployed. Additionally, they support the release of two versions of a feature, enabling developers to switch between them to gather live feedback or to test different versions with various user groups to determine which is preferred. This strategy, called A/B testing,[36] involves surveying users to see if they favour version A or B.

Development teams often employ branching strategies (such as Git Flow, GitHub Flow and GitLab Flow) but coverage of these is outside the scope of this book.

Software configuration files
Software configuration files are special-purpose files that specify the settings, preferences and parameters for an application. They provide information on how the software should function and interact with its environment. By keeping configuration data separate from the codebase, configuration files enable developers and users to easily modify application settings and preferences without altering the code itself.

Configuration files play a key role in managing an application's behaviour and deployment environment, enabling software designers and developers to achieve important design goals such as flexibility (configurable), adaptability (portable across different environments), enhanced security and simplified maintenance.

Common uses of configuration files include:

- **Application settings**: These include general settings such as language preferences and UI themes, as well as more technical settings such as database credentials, API endpoints[37] and logging settings.

- **Environment variables**: These store values specific to different environments, such as database credentials, API keys or URLs. This enables different configurations for development, testing and production environments (see Chapter 5).

- **Management of dependencies**: This involves listing required packages, libraries and versions, making it easier to set up the software on different machines.

- **Security**: Configuration files can define access control settings and authorisation and authentication configurations. Using this approach, sensitive information such as API keys and credentials can be stored outside the codebase (often encrypted), reducing the risk of exposure.

- **Feature flags**: Configuration files can be used to store the current settings of feature flags to control the activation of certain features without needing to modify the source code.

---

36 A/B testing is a method of comparing two versions of a feature or web page by showing each to a different group of users to determine which performs better based on specific metrics.

37 An API endpoint is a specific uniform resource locator (URL) or uniform resource identifier (URI) within an API that enables access to a particular resource or function, enabling communication between applications.

- **Network settings**: Configuration files can be used to specify network configurations such as Internet Protocol (IP) addresses, ports and protocols.

- **Infrastructure as code (IaC)**: In virtualised environments like the cloud, infrastructure details, deployment parameters and environment variables for IaC tools can be stored in configuration files, which can be managed alongside an application's source code.

Managing technical debt

Technical debt is an analogy representing the trade-off between the short-term benefit of rapid delivery and long-term value of high-quality code. The analogy is with financial debt – the longer the debt remains unpaid, the more difficult it is to manage.

Technical debt is the accumulated cost of opting for a quicker, or less optimal, solution rather than a more robust, longer-term approach, which can be a common side-effect of Agile software development. It typically results from rushed development, minimal refactoring or inadequate testing, and if left unmanaged it can increase maintenance costs, slow down development and degrade code quality. Properly managing technical debt is vital for maintaining a scalable and maintainable codebase.

Approaches to managing technical debt include:

- **Implementing coding standards and best practices**: Adhering to coding standards and best practices helps to make code easier to read, understand and maintain, and prevents the introduction of new technical debt.

- **Code reviews and peer feedback**: This helps to identify code smells, anti-patterns and quick fixes before they become debt, as well as checking the adherence to coding standards and best practices (see Chapter 2).

- **Regular refactoring**: Refactoring is the process of enhancing the internal structure of code without altering its external behaviour. Regular refactoring – an integral part of TDD – reduces technical debt by improving code readability, clarity, maintainability and scalability.

- **Automated testing and CI**: Comprehensive automated testing and a robust CI pipeline help to reduce the risk of technical debt by detecting defects and issues early, which ensures that changes to the codebase do not introduce new problems.

- **Define and track technical debt**: Defining, documenting and tracking technical debt within the project enables the development team to treat technical debt like any other task or issue in the project management process. It includes detailed descriptions of the debt, its cause and potential consequences in a technical debt backlog, which should be reviewed regularly so that the reduction of technical debt can be balanced with new feature development.

- **Monitoring code quality metrics**: Tracking code quality metrics (see Chapter 2), such as cyclomatic complexity and code churn, helps to identify areas of the code that are prone to technical debt. High complexity often indicates code that is difficult to understand, test and maintain.

- **Using static code analysis tools**: These tools automatically review the code to calculate code quality metrics (see previous item) and identify issues related to complexity, code smells and potential defects, thus helping to identify technical debt early in the development process. Static analysis tools are covered in Chapter 12.

- **Regular codebase audits**: Conducting periodic audits of the codebase helps to identify areas of the code that have accumulated technical debt. Audits involve reviewing the code for potential problems, outdated dependencies and areas needing improvement.

5   DEVELOPMENT ENVIRONMENTS

INTRODUCTION

When developing and deploying digital solutions, project teams use a range of separate environments. These environments are distinct setups where applications are built, tested and deployed. Each of the pre-production environments serves a unique purpose and helps to ensure that the software is functioning as expected before it is finally deployed into a production environment for live operational use.

This chapter discusses the following distinct environments:

- development;
- test;
- integration;
- pre-production/staging; and
- production.

DEVELOPMENT ENVIRONMENT

A development environment is a workspace that provides a sandbox[38] for developers to write, test and debug their code during the early stages of the software engineering cycle. This environment is typically isolated from other environments and provides all the necessary tools and configurations required to build software locally, enabling developers to experiment, make changes and ensure that code works as expected before it moves on to more controlled environments like testing or staging.

Typical components of a development environment include:

- **Source code repository**: This stores all the source code and tracks changes made by developers, typically via an integrated version control system (VCS).
- **Local server**: A local server simulates the application's runtime environment, enabling developers to test their code locally before deploying it to other environments.

---

38 A sandbox is an isolated environment that enables developers to develop and test code or applications safely without affecting the main system or production environment. The name is derived from a physical sandbox where children can play safely within a confined space.

- **Build tools**: Tools to automate tasks such as compiling code, managing dependencies and packaging applications.

- **Package managers**: These help developers to install and manage third-party libraries and dependencies.

- **Environment variables**: These store configuration settings specific to the development environment, such as API keys, database URLs[39] and feature flags.

- **Debugging tools**: These tools enable developers to inspect their code and find issues during development. They help to track down defects, analyse performance and understand application behaviour.

TEST ENVIRONMENT

A test environment is a setup or infrastructure separate from the development environment that is specifically designed for the exclusive purpose of testing software applications before they are released into production. They provide a controlled space where software can be thoroughly evaluated for defects, performance issues, integration issues and user experience problems.

By emulating conditions such as user load, network latency and different data inputs, test environments enable testers and developers to thoroughly assess application behaviour in a range of typical and atypical scenarios that the software could encounter during live operational use.

Typical components of a test environment include:

- **Application code**: The most recent version of the application code, including new features and bug fixes, is deployed to the test environment for evaluation.

- **Database**: A test database, often populated with mock or sanitised production data, is used to replicate real-world scenarios without risking actual user data.

- **Test data**: A set of predefined inputs and conditions designed to evaluate specific aspects of the software; this may include both valid and invalid data to test edge cases.

- **Servers and infrastructure**: The test environment often includes web servers, application servers and network configurations similar to those used in production.

- **Configuration files and environment variables**: These are used in a test environment to define settings – such as database connections, API keys or feature flags – enabling tests to run under controlled, replicable conditions without hardcoding values into the application.

- **Testing tools**: Various testing tools and frameworks (see Chapter 12) are integrated into the test environment.

- **Monitoring and logging**: Logging and monitoring tools are used to capture application behaviour, error messages and performance metrics during testing.

---

39 A database URL is a structured address that specifies the location and connection details of a database, including the type, host, port and database name, enabling applications to connect to it.

INTEGRATION ENVIRONMENT

An integration environment is a special kind of test environment specifically designed to test how different components or systems work together. While general test environments may focus on individual units or features, an integration environment ensures that modules, services or applications interact correctly and reliably as a whole. In the software engineering cycle, the integration environment typically comes after the development environment but before more advanced environments like staging and pre-production. It features a controlled setup or infrastructure where software components and services are integrated and tested together. The goal is to verify the interactions and data exchange between various modules, components or third-party services, ensuring they function as intended and identifying issues early before they escalate in subsequent environments.

While the primary purpose of an integration environment is to identify and resolve issues related to the integration of different components or services, it can also help to ensure that:

- the data passed between components is accurate, and there are no data integrity issues;
- external dependencies such as databases, message queues[40] and third-party services are integrated and tested for correct functionality; and
- changes made to one part of the system do not inadvertently break other parts.

Typical components of an integration environment include:

- **Application code**: The most recent version of the application code, including the latest features and defect fixes, is deployed in the integration environment.
- **Databases**: A dedicated test database is set up, often with mock data or a sanitised subset of production data, to assist in testing data queries, transactions and data consistency across components.
- **API gateways and services**: APIs, microservices[41] and third-party services that the application interacts with to verify that internal and external services work together seamlessly and handle requests, responses and data exchanges correctly.
- **Message queues and event streams**: Special-purpose tools are used for asynchronous communication between services, to test message passing, event-driven architectures and the handling of asynchronous tasks.
- **Mock servers and stubs**: Mock servers, stubs or service fakes simulate the behaviour of third-party APIs or services that are not available during testing, to isolate integration tests from external dependencies and ensure consistent, reliable test results without relying on live third-party services.

---

40 A message queue is a communication system that enables different parts of a software application to send and receive messages asynchronously (the sender and receiver of a message do not need to interact at the same time), helping to manage data flow and decouple components.

41 Microservices (discussed in Book 2, *Designing Digital Solutions*) is a software architecture pattern where an application is structured as a collection of small, independent services that communicate over a network, each responsible for a specific business function.

- **Configuration files and environment variables**: These define system settings – such as service endpoints, authentication credentials and feature toggles – to ensure that integrated components communicate and function correctly under consistent, controlled conditions.

- **CI/CD pipeline**: This automates the process of building, testing and deploying code to the integration environment.

- **Automated testing frameworks**: Tools and frameworks for running automated tests, to validate the integration of different components and to catch issues early in the development cycle.

- **Logging and monitoring tools**: These collect logs and monitor system performance in order to track application behaviour, identify issues and diagnose problems during integration testing.

- **Network infrastructure**: Network setups – including load balancers,[42] proxies[43] and firewall rules[44] – simulate production-like traffic and network conditions to test the application's ability to handle traffic, manage load and ensure that network configurations do not cause issues during integration.

- **Dependency management tools**: Package managers and dependency tools[45] are used to manage and install the necessary dependencies for the application, to ensure that all dependencies are correctly resolved and compatible with the rest of the system.

PRE-PRODUCTION/STAGING ENVIRONMENT

Once mainstream testing has been completed, the software is deployed to a pre-production or staging environment. A pre-production/staging environment is a setup or infrastructure that emulates the production environment as closely as possible in terms of configurations, data, infrastructure and software versions. It serves as a final testing ground where the entire application is deployed and tested before it is deployed into the production environment for live operational use.

In some projects, the terms 'staging' and 'pre-production' are used interchangeably, particularly in smaller teams or straightforward deployment pipelines. However, in larger projects or enterprise environments they often serve distinct purposes:

---

42 Load balancers are systems or devices that distribute incoming network traffic across multiple servers to ensure reliability, improve performance and prevent any single server from becoming overwhelmed.

43 Proxies are intermediary servers that sit between clients and back-end servers to route requests, often used to manage traffic, improve performance, enforce security policies or simulate real-world network conditions during testing.

44 A firewall is a security system that controls incoming and outgoing network traffic based on predefined rules, acting as a barrier between trusted and untrusted networks. These rules determine which data packets are allowed or blocked based on criteria such as IP address, port or protocol.

45 Package managers and dependency tools are software utilities that automate the installation, updating and management of external libraries or packages that a project relies on, ensuring consistent and efficient handling of dependencies.

- **Staging** focuses on simulating the user experience, conducting end-to-end testing and obtaining stakeholder approval. A staging environment is typically used to validate the software's functionality and user experience before release.

- **Pre-production** focuses on final performance testing, infrastructure validation and testing deployment processes under production-like conditions. A pre-production environment is used to conduct extensive load testing, performance checks or validate infrastructure and deployment scripts.

A pre-production/staging environment is used to:

- verify that the software is stable, functional and ready for release;

- replicate the production environment's infrastructure, configurations and dependencies as closely as possible;

- identify any last-minute issues such as remaining defects, performance issues or configuration problems before the software is deployed to production;

- test the deployment scripts, configurations and procedures to ensure a smooth release process; and

- enable stakeholders, product owners and end-users to perform acceptance testing and provide feedback before the final release.

Typical components of a staging environment are similar to an integration environment with the following additional components:

- **Performance testing tools**: For conducting load, stress and endurance testing (see Chapter 6) to simulate real-world traffic and evaluate the application's performance, measuring its speed, stability and scalability under varying load conditions.

- **Security testing tools**: For performing security assessments, such as penetration testing and vulnerability scanning (see Chapters 6 and 7) to identify and fix potential security vulnerabilities before the application is released to production.

- **User acceptance testing (UAT) setup**: A dedicated area within the staging environment where stakeholders and end-users can validate that the application meets their requirements and is ready for release.

- **Disaster recovery and backup systems**: Backup and disaster recovery systems that replicate those in production, including database backups and failover[46] mechanisms, to test backup and restore procedures, ensuring that the application can recover from failures without data loss or service disruption.

---

46 Failover is a backup process in which a system automatically switches to a standby server, system or network if the primary one fails, ensuring continued availability and minimal downtime.

PRODUCTION ENVIRONMENT

A production environment is the live setting where the software application is deployed and accessible to end-users. It represents the final phase for the software, following development, testing, staging and pre-production phases. In this environment, the software is expected to be secure, stable, reliable and efficient, delivering the intended functionality under real-world conditions. Effective management, comprehensive monitoring and stringent security measures are essential to provide a consistent and dependable user experience.

Key characteristics of a production environment include:

- **Real users and live data**: The production environment is the only environment that handles real user traffic and processes live data. It uses actual user inputs and transactions, making stability and reliability critical.

- **High stability and reliability**: The production environment must be stable, with minimal downtime. It is designed for high availability and fault tolerance, ensuring that users experience minimal disruptions.

- **Secure configuration**: Security is a top priority in the production environment. It includes encryption, secure access controls, firewalls and compliance with industry regulations.

- **Performance optimisation**: The production environment is optimised for speed and scalability to handle real-world traffic and user demands. Load balancers, caching[47] and performance monitoring tools are often used to enhance performance.

- **Strict access controls**: Access to the production environment is tightly controlled and restricted to authorised personnel only (e.g. DevOps, site reliability engineers). Changes are carefully managed to avoid disruptions.

Typical components of a production environment are the same as for a pre-production/staging environment.

---

47 Caching is the process of storing frequently accessed data in a temporary location to improve performance and reduce the time needed to retrieve the data.

PART II
TESTING THE SOLUTION

6   INTRODUCTION TO SOFTWARE TESTING

INTRODUCTION

Software testing is a critical part of digital solution development, aimed at verifying that the developed solution meets pre-agreed quality criteria. But what is quality? Why is it so important? What are these pre-agreed criteria? And how does testing ensure the quality of software? This chapter explores these questions and more.

WHAT IS QUALITY?

While there are numerous definitions of quality – the *Oxford English Dictionary* alone lists 35 different definitions – a popular generic definition, courtesy of the *Oxford English Dictionary*, is:

> the standard or nature of something as measured against other things of a similar kind; the degree of excellence of something.

The cost of poor quality can be considerable. For example, a faulty mechanism in an aircraft undercarriage could result in destruction of the aircraft and death of the crew and passengers.

It is always cheaper, and more cost-effective, to build quality into the design and development of a product than it is to correct faults after the product has been built.

What is software quality?

With regard to *software* quality, this typically comes down to characteristics such as fitness for purpose, usability, reliability, maintainability and adherence to requirements and standards. Book 2 introduced a more complete set of quality characteristics (in the form of a set of solution design objectives) based on the ISO/IEC Product Quality Model (ISO, 2023a) and Quality-in-Use Model (ISO, 2023b). The former describes nine product quality characteristics (Table 6.1) and the latter describes three quality-in-use characteristics (Table 6.2).

Table 6.1 Product quality characteristics

Characteristic	Description
Functional suitability	How well the software provides functions that meet stated and implied needs when used under specified conditions.
Performance efficiency	The performance of the software relative to the number of resources used under stated conditions.
Compatibility	The ability of the software to interact with other systems or products without conflict.
Interaction capability (formerly known as usability)	The effectiveness and satisfaction with which specified users achieve specified goals in particular environments.
Reliability	The capability of the software to maintain a specified level of performance when used under specified conditions.
Security	The ability of the software to protect information and data to ensure that individuals or systems have the degree of data access appropriate to their types and levels of authorisation.
Maintainability	The ease with which the software can be modified to correct faults, improve performance or other attributes or adapt to a changed environment.
Flexibility (previously known as portability)	The ability of the software to be transferred from one environment to another.
Safety	The ability of the software to protect against acceptable levels of risk of harm to people, business, software, property or the environment in a specified context of use.

Table 6.2 Quality-in-use characteristics

Characteristic	Description
Effectiveness	The accuracy and completeness with which users achieve specific goals in particular environments.
Efficiency	The resources expended in relation to the accuracy and completeness of goals achieved.
Satisfaction	The degree to which user needs are fulfilled when a product or system is used in a specified context.

Errors, faults, failures and root causes

The *ISTQB Certified Tester Foundation Level Syllabus* (ISTQB, 2023) defines some helpful terminology to better understand the nature of software quality:

Human beings make **errors** (mistakes), which produce **defects** (faults, bugs), which in turn may result in **failures**.

There is a well-known saying 'to err is human' – errors are essentially a very human trait. Humans make errors for various reasons, such as time pressure, complexity of work products, processes, infrastructure or interactions, or simply because they are tired or lack adequate training.

Many people involved in software development use the term bug to refer to a software fault. The term defect refers to faults within documentation (such as a business requirements document or a test script), in source code or in a supporting artefact such as a build file. If undetected, defects in artefacts produced earlier in the software development life cycle (SDLC) often lead to defective artefacts later in the life cycle.

If a defect in code is executed, the software may fail to do what it should do, or do something it should not do, causing a failure. The International Software Testing Qualifications Board (ISTQB) syllabus suggests that:

some defects will always result in a failure if executed, while others will only result in a failure in specific circumstances, and some may never result in a failure.

Defects are not the only cause of failures. Failures can also be caused by environmental conditions, such as when radiation or an electromagnetic field cause defects in firmware.[48]

A root cause is a fundamental reason for the occurrence of a problem (such as a situation that leads to an error). Root causes are identified through root cause analysis, which is typically performed when a failure occurs or a defect is identified. Further similar failures or defects can often be prevented by removing the root cause.

The relationship between digital solution design and software quality

The design of a digital solution plays a critical role in determining its overall quality. A well-structured design ensures alignment with business and user requirements, reducing ambiguity and the risk of defects. By incorporating principles such as modularity, separation of concerns and clear interfaces, good design enhances readability, testability, scalability and maintainability. It also addresses non-functional requirements, including performance, security and usability early in the process, helping to embed quality from the outset. In contrast, poor design often results in tightly coupled, defect-ridden code that increases technical debt and development costs. Ultimately, careful and deliberate design lays the groundwork for attaining high software quality.

---

48 Firmware is a type of low-level software permanently programmed into hardware devices to control their basic functions and enable communication with other software systems.

QUALITY MANAGEMENT, QUALITY ASSURANCE, QUALITY CONTROL AND TESTING

The terms quality management (QM), quality assurance (QA) and quality control (QC) are related but distinct concepts in ensuring that products or services meet certain quality standards.

Quality management

Quality management is a broad concept that focuses on customer satisfaction. Incorporating both QA and QC, along with other aspects of management, it provides a holistic approach to managing quality throughout an entire organisation by promoting continuous improvement in all processes related to product or service delivery, and integrating quality into all business practices.

QM typically involves implementing a quality management system (QMS), such as ISO 9001, which covers leadership, planning, operations, performance evaluation and continuous improvement.

Quality assurance

Quality assurance is the act of giving confidence in advance, of the quality of a product or service. It is proactive and essentially focuses on preventing defects before they occur, by ensuring that the process used to build a product, or deliver a service, is designed in a way that consistently meets predefined quality criteria.

In the context of digital solutions, the ISTQB syllabus defines QA as follows:

> QA is a process-oriented, preventive approach that focuses on the implementation and improvement of processes. It works on the basis that if a good process is followed correctly, then it will generate a good product. QA applies to both the development and testing processes, and is the responsibility of everyone on a project.

Consequently, QA ensures that the software development and testing processes are efficient, well defined and follow best practices to produce high-quality software.

The V model SDLC, introduced in Book 1, is often referred to as the QA life cycle because it explicitly shows various quality-related activities, such as the link between the specification stages of software development and the associated test levels (unit testing, integration testing, system testing and user acceptance testing). An extended version of the V model is shown in Figure 6.1. This version highlights (vertical dashed arrows) how the artefacts produced in each stage on the left-hand side of the model are reviewed against the artefacts produced during the previous stage, to identify possible defects early. It also identifies two different types of testing (static testing and dynamic testing), which are explored later in this chapter.

Figure 6.1 The extended V model SDLC (©Assist Knowledge Development Ltd)

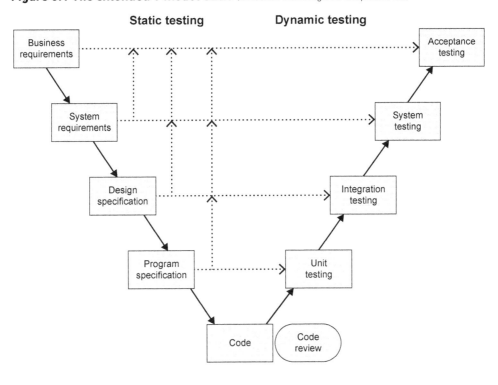

Typically, QA activities in software development include:

- establishing processes, methodologies and standards (such as Requirements Engineering, the software engineering cycle, the fundamental test process, Scrum Agile method and UML modelling standards);

- defining and encouraging the use of guidelines (such as UI style guides);

- designing a workflow for code review to prevent issues in the code early;

- identifying standards (such as UML notation and coding standards) to be met during specific QC activities, and when those QC activities take place within the development process;

- implementing automated testing as part of CI to detect defects during development;

- conducting audits and process reviews;

- training and improving team skills; and

- ensuring the SDLC (V model, iterative, etc.) is followed.

Quality control

Quality control comprises a range of activities that evaluate the quality of a product or service in order to identify defects that may require corrective action. QC is reactive and involves inspecting and checking outputs after development to ensure the product or service meets specific quality standards.

In the context of digital solutions, the ISTQB syllabus defines QC as follows:

> QC is a product-oriented, corrective approach that focuses on those activities supporting the achievement of appropriate levels of quality. Testing is a major form of quality control, while others include formal methods (model checking and proof of correctness), simulation and prototyping.

Therefore, QC concerns the verification and validation of the software product, both during and after development, focusing on identifying and fixing defects to ensure that the software meets the required specifications and is free of defects (subject to the limitations of testing described below).

QC involves a range of activities, including:

- inspections of key artefacts produced during the SDLC, including code reviews;
- performing functional and non-functional testing to ensure that the software works as intended;
- conducting user acceptance testing (UAT) to verify that the software meets the user's needs;
- running automated and manual tests to identify defects and issues; and
- debugging and fixing identified issues.

Testing

As highlighted in the above definition, software testing is a form of quality control that verifies that software meets its defined quality characteristics. Testing takes place at various stages of software development to ensure the final product meets the desired level of quality. According to Thompson et al. (2024):

> Testing does not in itself improve quality, but it does measure the quality and highlights areas where there may be room for improvement ... as a problem reported by those testing may not require corrective action in the software, but needs the so-called failed test to be changed.

The rest of this chapter explores the various aspects of software testing.

THE OBJECTIVES AND LIMITATIONS OF TESTING

The ISTQB syllabus cites the following problems that can result from software that does not work correctly:

- loss of money;
- loss of time;
- loss of business reputation; and
- injury or death.

Book 2 explored a variety of risks associated with the use of digital solutions that can result in the above impacts. Although not all of the risks identified in Book 2 can be avoided or mitigated through testing, the following examples are areas where effective testing can provide significant benefit:

- **Software failures**: A software failure is any malfunction often resulting from defects introduced by human error. Failures can also stem from environmental conditions, such as radiation affecting firmware. Historical examples illustrate the range and impact of software failures – from a TikTok glitch showing users with zero followers, to UK tax return breaches, Federal Aviation Administration system outages, mapping errors and even a rocket self-destructing. The CrowdStrike incident in July 2024 stands out as one of the most severe, where a faulty update crashed millions of devices globally, affecting critical sectors and causing estimated losses of $10 billion (Fraser, 2024). These cases highlight that errors may arise from coding mistakes or from overlooking user behaviour and system context during design, underlining the critical importance of thorough testing to prevent costly software failures.

- **Cyber risks**: Cyber risks represent the potential for malicious actions aimed at damaging or disrupting computer systems, networks or data, often undermining their confidentiality, integrity or availability. When these risks materialise, they result in cyberattacks. Cyberattacks and cybercrime include phishing, identity theft, ransomware, hacking and data breaches, which can impact individuals, organisations and critical infrastructure.[49] These threats are executed through various attack vectors[50] such as malware, brute-force methods, code injections and social engineering tactics. Attacks often exploit vulnerabilities caused by weak policies, technical flaws or human error, leading to significant personal and organisational consequences. The increasing frequency and financial impact of such incidents highlight the critical importance of strong cybersecurity measures, vulnerability scans and penetration testing.

- **Data privacy**: Handling large volumes of data increases the risk of data leaks and breaches, which can compromise sensitive information and violate privacy regulations.

- **System outages**: Technical failures or system outages can disrupt access to digital solutions, impacting business operations or causing inconvenience to users.

- **Integration issues**: Integrating disparate digital solutions can be complex and lead to compatibility problems or unexpected behaviour.

---

49 Critical infrastructure refers to essential systems and assets – such as power grids, water supply, transportation and communication networks – that are vital to a country's security, economy and public health.

50 An attack vector is a method or pathway that cybercriminals use to gain unauthorised access to a system or network.

- **Algorithmic bias**: Algorithms used in some digital solutions can perpetuate biases if not carefully designed and tested. This can lead to unfair or discriminatory outcomes.

- **Compliance risks**: Non-compliance with regulatory standards can result in legal penalties and reputational damage.

The primary objective of software testing is to assess software quality and reduce the likelihood of the above risks occurring. The ISTQB syllabus identifies the following more specific objectives of testing:

- evaluating work products such as requirements, user stories, designs and code;

- triggering failures and finding defects;

- ensuring required coverage of a test object;[51]

- reducing the level of risk of inadequate software quality;

- verifying whether specified requirements have been fulfilled;

- verifying that a test object complies with contractual, legal and regulatory requirements;

- providing information to stakeholders to enable them to make informed decisions;

- building confidence in the quality of the test object; and

- validating whether the test object is complete and works as expected by the stakeholders.

The objectives of a particular instance of testing can vary depending upon the context within which testing is undertaken, including:

- the work product being tested;

- the test level;

- the risks associated with software failure and potential cyberattacks;

- the SDLC being followed; and

- the business context (such as corporate structure, competitive considerations or time-to-market considerations).

A common misconception of testing is that software can be fully tested, and as a consequence is defect-free and works correctly. Unfortunately, complete testing is impossible for several reasons:

- There are too many paths and combinations of paths through the software to test completely.

- The domain of possible inputs is too large.

- User interface issues are too complex.

---

51 A test object is the component, system or part of a system that is being tested.

- There are too many layers of interconnecting hardware and software components and applications to replicate accurately in a test environment.

- The budget, time and resources that are available limit the amount and extent of testing that can be carried out.

Consider, for example, the complexity involved in testing all of the components for an internet-based application running on a mobile phone. The layers of software and hardware include (this list is not exhaustive):

- the software application's processing or workflow logic;

- the mobile phone's operating system;

- the user interface;

- the physical connectivity of key depressions, swipes and screen touch sensitivity;

- connectivity to the local internet access points and routers;

- the hardware, software and operating system on the router; and

- connectivity to the internet service provider, and onward connectivity to the host service provider, and all the associated hardware and software.

The majority of hardware and software components nowadays are developed and tested using software tools. These software tools themselves would have to be tested, but again complete testing of these tools is not possible for the reasons given above.

As a consequence of complete testing being impossible, a digital solution can never be guaranteed to be defect-free. Users' expectations have to be carefully managed, and the testing activity itself has to be focused towards identifying as many defects as possible, or picking up critical defects, within the time and budget available.

PRINCIPLES OF TESTING

The ISTQB syllabus defines seven principles of testing:

1. **Testing shows the presence of defects**: Testing can show that defects exist, but it cannot prove that a digital solution has no defects. Successive testing reduces the probability of defects remaining undetected, but cannot guarantee that all defects have been removed, or the correctness of the test object.

2. **Exhaustive testing is impossible**: Except for trivial cases, testing everything is not feasible. Rather than attempting to test exhaustively, test techniques, test case prioritisation and risk-based testing should be used to focus test efforts.

3. **Early testing saves time and money**: Defects that are removed early in the process will not cause subsequent defects in derived work products. The cost of quality will be reduced since fewer failures will occur later in the SDLC. To find defects early, both static testing and dynamic testing should be started as early as possible. Static and dynamic testing are explored later in this chapter.

4. **Defects cluster together**: A small number of software components usually contain most of the defects discovered, or are responsible for most of the operational failures. This phenomenon is an illustration of the Pareto principle. Predicted defect clusters, and actual defect clusters observed during testing or in operation, are an important input for risk-based testing. Related to this principle is the axiom that defects tend to cluster around areas of complexity, so simplicity is a good objective of software design.

5. **Tests wear out**: If the same tests are repeated many times, they become increasingly ineffective in detecting new defects. To overcome this effect, existing tests and test data may need to be modified, and new tests may need to be written. However, in some cases, repeating the same tests can have a beneficial outcome (such as in automated regression testing, described later in this chapter).

6. **Testing is context-dependent**: There is no single universally applicable approach to testing. Testing is performed differently in different contexts. For example, the approach adopted for testing a company website is likely to be very different to the approach adopted for testing an air traffic control system.

7. **Absence of errors fallacy**: It is a fallacy (or misconception) to expect that software verification will ensure the success of a system. Thoroughly testing all the specified requirements and fixing all the defects found could still produce a system that does not fulfil users' needs and expectations, that does not help in achieving customer's business goals and that is inferior to other competing systems. In addition to verification, validation should also be carried out. Verification and validation in the context of software testing are discussed in Chapter 7.

TEST LEVELS

The term 'test level' is used to refer to the various stages, or phases, in the software testing process, where different kinds of tests are performed, determined by the completeness or readiness of the software. The different test levels ensure that each part of the software is verified at appropriate stages, from the smallest code units to the entire digital solution, including the validation of business and user requirements. Each level addresses different risks and identifies different potential defects, creating a thorough and effective testing process that ensures the software works as intended and meets its business and users' needs. Each level also has its own unique test basis, which provides the foundation for creating test cases and ensuring that the software meets the necessary functional, non-functional and regulatory requirements at that level.

Test levels, and their associated test bases, can be identified from the V model in Figure 6.1. These are listed in Table 6.3 and described below.

Table 6.3 Test levels and their associated test bases

Test level	Test basis
Unit testing	• Source code • Component/module design • Developer specifications • Algorithms/logic descriptions
Integration testing	• Software architecture blueprints • Interface control documents • System/component requirements
System testing	• System requirements specifications • Use cases • Business processes
Acceptance testing	**User acceptance testing** • Business requirements document • User stories • Use cases • Acceptance criteria • Contracts/agreements **Factory acceptance testing** • Functional specifications • System/component design • Operational specifications • Contracts **Site acceptance testing** • Installation guides • Operational requirements • Environmental/safety standards • Contracts **Operational acceptance testing** • Operational requirements • Service level agreements (SLAs) • Maintenance procedures • Security/compliance standards • Business continuity plans

(Continued)

Table 6.3 (Continued)

Test level	Test basis
	Contractual acceptance testing • Contracts • SLAs • Functional specifications • Acceptance criteria • Project Initiation Document **Regulatory acceptance testing** • Regulatory standards • Compliance documentation • Guidelines from regulatory bodies • Industry certifications

Unit testing	Also referred to as component testing or module testing,[52] unit testing is typically performed by developers as they write their program code, and focuses on testing individual units of the software (such as a single function that calculates the total price in an ecommerce application) in isolation from the rest of the system. The purpose of unit testing is to verify that each unit of code behaves as expected. Unit testing often forms part of a test-driven development (TDD) approach, and uses specialist tools that are built into the developer's IDE (see Chapter 12). Testers use a combination of functional and non-functional tests (see below), which are categorised as black-box tests, and also structural (white-box) tests, which check individual paths through the program code. Black-box and white-box testing are also discussed below.
Integration testing	Also referred to as **integration testing in the small** or **component integration testing**, the objective of this test level is to expose defects in the interfaces, interactions and communication between integrated code units, and to ensure that they work together as expected. For example, testing the interaction between a payment gateway module and an order-processing module.

---

52 In this chapter the term 'unit' is used interchangeably with the terms 'component' and 'module'. However, it should be noted that some practitioners differentiate between the testing of small units of code and the testing of larger software components or modules. Ultimately this comes down to the degree of granularity of the unit.

Integration tests need to be planned to match the order in which the units are to be built. This is often referred to as the integration strategy, with two fundamental approaches being used:

- **Big bang integration testing**, where all components are tested together at once.

- **Incremental integration testing**, where components are integrated and tested step by step.

Integration testing can be performed by developers or test engineers, depending on the scope and nature of the testing, and, like unit testing, is often automated. In iterative and incremental development, component integration tests are usually part of the CI process (see Chapter 4).

System testing
The objective of this test level is to validate the entire, fully integrated application as a whole, to ensure that all functionality works together correctly, in accordance with defined solution requirements. For example, testing the entire ecommerce platform, from browsing products to checkout and payment, to verify that the system works as expected.

System testing is typically performed by a team of qualified testers that is independent of the development process, using a dedicated test environment that is representative of the live production environment. Testers use a combination of functional and non-functional tests that are designed to uncover defects that are unlikely to be found using unit and integration testing. Some tests are designed to 'break' the software (see load testing, stress testing and security testing below) as well as to check that it functions correctly.

System testing often produces information that is used by stakeholders to make release decisions, which may include checking that legal or regulatory requirements and standards have been met.

Acceptance testing
The objectives of acceptance testing are three-fold:

1. to validate whether the software meets the business requirements;

2. to provide end-users with confidence that the software will function according to their expectations; and

3. to determine whether the digital solution is ready for release into live operational use.

Acceptance testing, often the final level of testing before software release, is conducted in various commonly used forms:

- **User acceptance testing (UAT)** is performed by end-users or business stakeholders to ensure the software meets their expectations and the business needs. This can include **factory acceptance testing**, where users test the software in a controlled environment at the developer's or vendor's facility to ensure it meets their requirements before it is deployed to their own site.

- **Site acceptance testing** typically follows factory acceptance testing. This is a variant of UAT where users perform acceptance testing at their own site.

- **Operational acceptance testing**, often called operational readiness testing, is a form of testing typically performed by system administrators or IT staff and involves checking that the processes and procedures are in place to enable the software to be used and maintained. This can include checking:

  - backup facilities;

  - installing, uninstalling and upgrading;

  - performance issues;

  - procedures for disaster recovery;

  - user management;

  - maintenance procedures;

  - data load and migration tasks; and

  - security vulnerabilities.

- **Contractual acceptance testing** takes place when software delivery is governed by a formal agreement that defines specific acceptance criteria. Testing is performed to ensure these criteria are met before the software is formally accepted.

- **Regulatory acceptance testing** is required in certain industries, such as defence, banking and pharmaceuticals, where software systems must comply with governmental, legal or safety standards. This type of testing may be witnessed or audited by regulatory authorities to ensure compliance.

- **Alpha testing** and **beta testing**: See *Types of testing* below.

Thompson et al. (2024) define a further test level that sits between system testing and user acceptance testing:

System integration testing	Sometimes referred to as **integration testing in the large**, system integration testing focuses on the interactions and interfaces between standalone software systems rather than between the components of a single software system. It can also cover interactions and interfaces with external organisations. For example, a trading system in an investment bank may interact with the stock exchange to obtain the latest prices for its stocks and shares on the international market.
	Where external organisations are involved, extra challenges for testing present themselves, since the developing organisation will not have control over the interfaces. This can include creating the test environment, defect resolution and so on.

TYPES OF TESTING

There is a diverse range of different test types in current use, with each type playing a crucial role in ensuring the quality, reliability and robustness of software systems. The choice of test types depends on the project's requirements, risks and the stage of the SDLC. Some of the more popular test types (which are not mutually exclusive) are explored in this section.

Functional testing

Functional testing assesses whether a component or application performs its intended functions as specified. Its main goal is to verify the functional completeness, functional correctness and functional appropriateness of the component or system, ensuring the software behaves according to the specified requirements.

Functional testing can be used in all the test levels described above.

Non-functional testing

Non-functional testing evaluates attributes of the test object other than its functional characteristics. It is sometimes described as testing 'how well the software behaves'. The main objective of non-functional testing is to check the non-functional software quality characteristics identified in the ISO/IEC 25010 standard:

- performance efficiency;
- compatibility;
- usability;
- reliability;
- security;
- maintainability; and
- portability.

Many non-functional tests are derived from functional tests as they check that, while performing the function, a non-functional constraint is satisfied (such as checking that a function performs within a specified time).

The late discovery of non-functional defects can pose a serious threat to the success of a project.

Examples of non-functional testing include:

- **Performance testing** tests the overall performance of the software under expected workloads to ensure that it meets specific performance criteria, such as response time, throughput and resource usage (central processing unit (CPU), memory and network bandwidth). Performance testing helps to identify bottlenecks and areas for optimisation, ensuring that the software runs efficiently under typical conditions.

- **Load testing** evaluates the performance of the software under expected peak conditions, ensuring it can handle a high user load without degrading performance, by simulating a growing number of concurrent users or transactions.

- **Stress testing** evaluates the behaviour of the software under extreme conditions that push it beyond its normal operational limits, to see how it reacts when resources are exhausted or performance degrades, and identify how and when it might fail.

- **Endurance testing** (also known as soak testing) evaluates how a system behaves under a sustained workload over an extended period of time. Its goal is to identify issues such as memory leaks, performance degradation or resource exhaustion that may not appear during short-term tests but can affect stability and reliability during prolonged use.

- **Security testing** broadly assesses the security of a system, application or network to identify vulnerabilities, risks and threats. Security testing includes various methods and practices to ensure the software is secure from unauthorised access, data breaches and other cyber threats. It incorporates the following different types of tests:

  - **risk assessment** to evaluate potential security risks;

  - **vulnerability scanning** to identify known weaknesses;

  - **compliance testing** to ensure the software meets security standards; and

  - **penetration (pen) testing**, which involves ethical hackers simulating real-world attacks on the software to identify vulnerabilities that could be exploited by an attacker.

- **Usability testing** assesses how easy and intuitive the software is to use by observing real users interacting with the UI. Its main goal is to evaluate the user experience and identify opportunities to improve satisfaction, efficiency and the overall experience. The following types of usability testing are commonly used:

  - **Moderated usability testing**: A facilitator (moderator) is present, either in person or remotely, guiding the user through the tasks and asking questions to gather feedback.

  - **Unmoderated usability testing**: Users complete the test on their own, without a moderator's guidance, often through automated online tools. This can be more cost-effective but may miss deeper insights from real-time observation.

  - **Remote usability testing**: Usability testing conducted remotely, where users interact with the software in their natural environments rather than in a controlled testing environment. This method can reach a broader range of users.

  - **In-person usability testing**: Users interact with the software in a dedicated usability lab while observers watch and take notes on their behaviour. This enables direct observation and immediate follow-up questions.

- **Compatibility testing** involves testing the software operating across different technical environments (e.g. browsers, devices, operating systems, platforms and hardware configurations) to ensure that it functions correctly and consistently, regardless of the variations in these different environments. Two main types of compatibility test are in common use:

- **Backward compatibility testing** ensures that the software remains compatible with older versions of platform software, operating systems or hardware. This helps to ensure that users who are still using older versions of platform software or devices can still use the software.

- **Forward compatibility testing** ensures that the software is compatible with newer versions of platform software, operating systems or hardware that are expected to be released in the future. This helps to future-proof the software to avoid major issues when new versions of platforms or devices become available.

Static and dynamic testing

Static testing involves reviewing and analysing documentation and other artefacts (such as models, paper-based prototypes and program source code), and does not involve the execution of the software itself. The main objective of static testing is to identify defects early in the development life cycle, when they are less time-consuming and costly to fix. This includes:

- incorrect or ambiguous requirements;
- design specifications that do not fully address the system requirements; and
- inconsistencies or defects in the code that are more difficult to detect using dynamic testing alone.

Static testing is preventive and focuses on identifying and correcting errors (mistakes made by humans), such as in the production of documents, writing of program source code, creation of lists of data and so on.

Three main methods are used to conduct static testing:

- **Reviews**: A team or individual reviews the test object (program code, requirements or design documents). This includes code reviews, peer reviews or walkthroughs.

- **Inspections**: A more formal and structured process where a team of reviewers carefully inspect the test object and agrees a formal outcome: signed-off, deferred (minor changes required) or rejected (significant re-work and further review required).

- **Static code analysis**: Tools are used to analyse the program code for potential defects (e.g. syntax errors, program logic errors, adherence to coding standards and code vulnerabilities), without executing the software. Static analysis tools are explored in Chapter 12.

Dynamic testing refers to any testing that involves executing the program code. The objective of dynamic testing is to validate the functionality and behaviour of the software and detect issues during the execution of the program code by using predefined test data and a range of different test scenarios and/or environments.

Dynamic testing takes place after the source code has been written and continues through different levels of testing, from unit testing and integration testing to system and acceptance testing (see *Test levels* above), using a combination of functional and non-functional testing and black-box and white-box testing (see below).

Typical issues identified during dynamic testing include:

- runtime errors such as system crashes;
- incorrect outputs produced;
- performance bottlenecks; and
- failure of the software to function correctly and realise its requirements.

Black-box and white-box testing

Black-box testing (also known as **specification-based testing**) derives tests from documentation, such as the test bases shown on the V model in Figure 6.1. Its focus is therefore on whether the behaviour of the software meets its requirements and design specifications.

Black-box testing is commonly used for functional testing at various levels, including unit, integration, system and acceptance testing. Its main objective is to validate the software's functionality from the user's perspective, without any knowledge of the internal structure of the program code or control flow logic. Instead, the focus is on whether the software produces the correct output for a given set of inputs.

Popular black-box testing techniques include:

- **Equivalence partitioning**: This is where the input data is divided into different groups that should all result in the same output.
- **Boundary value analysis**: This involves testing at the boundaries of input ranges (e.g. minimum, maximum, just below minimum, just above maximum).
- **Decision table testing**: This uses a decision table to define combinations of inputs and their corresponding expected results.
- **State transition testing**: This focuses on testing how the software behaves as it moves from one state to another.

White-box testing (also known as **clear-box testing**, **glass-box testing** or **structural testing**) is predominantly used for unit and integration testing, and derives tests from the software's internal structure (e.g. code, architecture, workflows and data flows). The main objective of white-box testing is to execute tests to cover the underlying structure of the software to an acceptable level. The tester (either a developer or test engineer) has full knowledge of the internal workings of the software (based on its unit design specification rather than knowledge of the code itself) and designs tests to ensure the code functions correctly according to its specification, and the flow of inputs and outputs through the code covers all (or the most critical) internal paths and conditions.

White-box testing techniques ensure thorough coverage of the control flow, decision points, loops and data usage within the software. Each technique serves a specific purpose in validating the software's internal logic, making white-box testing essential for detecting logical errors, improving code quality and ensuring robustness.

Popular white-box testing techniques include:

- **Path testing**: This tests every possible combination of decision points, loops and execution paths through a unit of program code to ensure that every possible path is executed at least once.

- **Basis path testing**: This tests only the independent execution paths through a unit of program code to achieve maximum code coverage with a minimal number of test cases.

- **Control flow testing**: This evaluates how control flows through the program, especially the execution of loops, branches and conditions, to ensure the correct execution of control structures and logical decisions.

- **Data flow testing**: This monitors how data flows through the code by testing how variables are defined, initialised and updated to ensure they are used correctly throughout program execution. This form of white-box testing helps to detect issues such as unused variables, data leaks and incorrect variable usage.

Confirmation testing and regression testing

Confirmation testing refers to the testing that is undertaken following the fixing of a defect, or when implementing a new feature.

After making the change, the modified code should be retested to confirm that the problem has been successfully removed or the new feature works correctly. This is known as **confirmation testing** and can be achieved by rerunning the test cases that highlighted the problem (in the case of fixing a defect) or adding new tests (in the case of new functionality being introduced). The unchanged code should also be retested to ensure that no additional defects have been introduced as a result of the changes. This is known as **regression testing** (see below).

Confirmation testing and regression testing are particularly prevalent in iterative development projects (such as those following an Agile method) due to the frequency of changes to requirements, or new requirements being added to the product backlog, and the greater need for code refactoring (where a developer makes changes to the code to improve its quality).

Regression testing is performed after modifications have been made to the software – such as fixing defects, adding new features or changing the runtime environment. Unlike confirmation testing, which focuses on verifying the specific changes, regression testing ensures that the rest of the software remains unaffected. Its primary goal is to identify any unintended side effects or issues – such as new defects or disruptions to existing functionality – which may have been introduced as a consequence of making the changes.

There are two main approaches to regression testing:

- **Selective regression**: This involves testing only the parts of the software that are likely to be affected by the recent changes.

- **Complete regression**: This involves retesting the entire software to ensure stability across all features.

Because regression tests are based on the unchanged parts of the software, they lend themselves to being designed and built once, and then used repeatedly. Consequently, regression tests are ideal candidates for automation, using a computer-aided software testing (CAST) tool (see Chapter 12). Automated regression testing is a particular feature of DevOps (see Chapter 4) when automated builds and CI are used.

Sanity testing

Sanity testing is a quick check performed after minor changes or bug fixes to confirm that specific functionality works as intended and that the change hasn't introduced new issues. It targets particular areas of concern to verify that the change has been successful (in the case of bug fixes, that the original defect has been resolved) without causing additional problems.

Smoke testing

Smoke testing is a high-level form of testing that is used to check software after a new build or release, by verifying that the most crucial functions work and that the software is stable enough for further testing.

Exploratory testing

Exploratory testing is an unscripted, dynamic approach to testing that can be highly effective for uncovering unexpected defects, usability issues and design flaws, making it particularly useful in Agile and fast-paced development environments.

Instead of strictly following a scripted test plan, testers leverage their experience, intuition and creativity to actively explore the software in real time, uncovering issues that might not have been anticipated in formal test cases.

Exploratory testing is often used alongside more traditional scripted and automated testing to provide a more thorough evaluation of the software's quality and behaviour.

Alpha and beta testing

Alpha testing is a form of acceptance testing, typically performed at the developer's site or in a controlled environment before the software is released to external customers to undertake beta testing, prior to the final software release. To maintain test independence,[53] it is typically conducted by people outside the developer organisation, although some organisations use their own testing resources, thus reducing the test independence.

---

53 Test independence refers to the separation of testing activities from development tasks to ensure objective evaluation and unbiased identification of defects in the software.

The objective of alpha testing is to improve the stability and reliability of the product by identifying and fixing any residual defects and usability issues after other forms of acceptance testing, before the software is released to a wider audience of beta testers.

In iterative (Agile) development projects, alpha testing and beta testing may occur either after the completion of each iteration or after a series of iterations.

Beta testing (also known as **field testing**) is conducted after alpha testing and is the final testing phase before the official launch of the software. A form of acceptance testing, beta testing involves releasing the software to a group of external users who are representative of the target audience, and who use the software at their own locations. The main objectives of beta testing are to elicit feedback on the performance of the software in a real-world environment and to validate its market readiness prior to final release.

Beta testing generally lasts from a few weeks to a few months and identifies issues related to performance, usability, compatibility or unexpected scenarios encountered in a real-world setting. Beta testers are typically provided with a near-final version of the software and are encouraged to explore the software freely, in their normal environment, on their own devices and within their normal workflows. The development team typically has limited involvement. Feedback is collected via surveys, defect reports or feedback forms, and fixes are implemented before the official release.

There are two common approaches to beta testing:

- **Open beta**: With an open beta the product is made available to a large audience (anyone can participate) to gather a broad range of feedback.

- **Closed beta**: With a closed beta the product is released to a limited group of select users who are invited to participate.

End-to-end testing

End-to-end testing verifies the entire workflow of the application, from start to finish, covering all user interactions and external interfaces, to ensure that the entire application works together as expected. For example, it might involve testing the full ordering process of an e-commerce website – from browsing products to completing the checkout.

Concurrent/parallel testing

Concurrent or parallel testing evaluates how the software performs when multiple users or processes are interacting with it simultaneously (concurrent usage) to ensure that it can handle multiple transactions or interactions correctly. For example, testing an online banking application when multiple users attempt to transfer money at the same time.

Heuristic testing

Heuristic testing is a problem-solving approach that uses heuristics (experience-based techniques, general guidelines or 'rules of thumb') to make decisions about where and how to test areas of the software that are more likely to contain defects. For example, a tester uses heuristics like the 'CRASH' mnemonic (capabilities, reliability, availability, security and hardware) to focus testing on key areas of concern in a web application.

Ad hoc testing

Ad hoc testing is an informal and unstructured approach to testing software, where testers try to find defects or issues without following a predefined plan, test cases or documentation. The key idea behind ad hoc testing is to explore the software freely, often relying on the tester's intuition, experience and understanding of the application. It is typically used when there is limited time for formal testing, or as a complementary testing technique alongside structured methods.

There are different types of ad hoc testing, including:

- **Buddy testing**: This is a collaborative form of ad hoc testing where a developer and a tester work together informally (although not necessarily at the same machine and the same time) to test the application. They share knowledge and identify defects early, usually before formal testing begins.

- **Pair testing**: This is where two testers work together (at the same machine and at the same time) to share ideas and explore the software. One might operate the application, while the other observes and provides feedback or suggestions.

- **Monkey testing**: This is an extreme form of ad hoc testing where testers randomly interact with the software without any goal or strategy, to detect potential failures (crashes or unhandled exceptions) caused by unexpected input or actions.

THE FUNDAMENTAL TEST PROCESS

The fundamental test process (summarised in Table 6.4) provides a structured approach for carrying out software testing activities that outlines the key stages involved in planning, executing and completing testing activities. Each of the five stages plays a crucial role in ensuring that testing is thorough, systematic and aligned with project goals. By following the process, testing teams can maximise test coverage, efficiently identify defects and ensure the software meets the required standards before release.

Table 6.4 Summary of the fundamental test process

Stage	Purpose	Key activities
1. Test planning and control	To define the overall objectives and approach for testing and to monitor and adjust the testing process as needed	**Test planning** • Define the scope (which features and functions will be tested) • Establish the goals of the testing process (e.g. finding defects and verifying functionality) • Develop the test strategy – decide on the overall approach to testing (e.g. manual or automated testing, and types of tests) • Determine the required personnel, tools, test environments and time needed • Define the timeline for the testing process, including deadlines for key activities • Assess potential risks and define mitigation strategies **Test control** • Track the progress of the testing effort against the plan • Analyse any deviations from the plan (e.g. delays or unexpected complications) • Communicate the status of testing to stakeholders • If issues arise (e.g. missed deadlines or resource shortages), adjust the plan accordingly
2. Test analysis and design	To analyse the test basis to identify what needs to be tested and design specific test cases and test data based on the identified test conditions	**Test analysis** • Review the test basis – examine requirements, design documents and other sources of information • Identify test conditions – determine what aspects of the software need to be tested (e.g. specific features, user interactions and performance metrics)

(Continued)

Table 6.4 (Continued)

Stage	Purpose	Key activities
		• Assess testability – identify any gaps or ambiguities in the test basis that may affect the ability to test the software
		Test design
		• Create test cases – define the detailed steps, inputs and expected outcomes for each test
		• Identify the data required to execute the tests (e.g. data files or databases)
		• Establish traceability – link test cases back to the requirements to ensure coverage
3. Test implementation and execution	To prepare everything necessary for executing the test cases and execute the prepared test cases	**Test implementation** • Prepare the test environment – set up the hardware, software and network configurations needed for testing • Develop test scripts – write any automated test scripts needed for execution • Prepare test data – organise the data required for running the test cases **Test execution** • Execute the test cases in the test environment • Compare actual and expected results to verify whether the software behaves as expected • Record results – document the outcomes of each test case (pass/fail status) • Log defects – record any defects or issues encountered during execution

(Continued)

Table 6.4 (Continued)

Stage	Purpose	Key activities
4. Evaluating exit criteria and reporting	• To determine whether the testing objectives have been met and whether the testing process can be considered complete • To provide stakeholders with the results and findings from the testing process	**Evaluating exit criteria** • Assess coverage – determine whether all planned tests have been executed and whether sufficient coverage has been achieved • Evaluate defect status – check whether the number of unresolved defects is within acceptable limits • Check test completion – ensure all required tests have been completed successfully **Reporting** • Create test summary reports summarising the testing results, including key metrics (e.g. test case pass rates, defect counts and coverage) • Present the test results to stakeholders (e.g. project managers, developers and customers) • Provide recommendations based on the results (e.g. whether the software is ready for release or requires further testing)
5. Test closure	To wrap up the testing effort and bring the testing project to a close	• Finalise and archive test deliverables – ensure that all required documents (e.g. test plans, test cases and test reports) are completed and stored for future reference or audits, along with the test data • Close defects – ensure that any remaining defects are documented, assigned and closed or deferred as needed • Review lessons learned – conduct a post-mortem review of the testing process to identify what worked well and what could be improved • Release resources – release the testing team, hardware, software and tools that were used during testing so that they can be utilised on other projects

TEST PLANS, TEST PROCEDURES AND TEST CASES

Test plans, test procedures and test cases are key artefacts produced to support the fundamental test process. They provide a structured, systematic, efficient and reliable approach to testing that ensures software meets desired quality standards.

Test plans provide the big picture of the testing strategy, aligning with project goals and ensuring adequate resources are available and risks are managed. Test procedures and test cases, on the other hand, guide the execution of tests in a consistent and repeatable manner, ensuring all necessary steps are followed and results are clearly documented.

Test plan

A test plan (often produced as part of the project planning process) is a high-level document that outlines the overall strategy, approach, objectives, resources, schedule and scope of testing activities. It is a comprehensive document that defines what will be tested, when, how and who will perform the tests.

The purpose of a test plan is two-fold:

1. To provide a clear roadmap for the testing effort, communicating the testing approach to stakeholders – including management, developers and customers.
2. To ensure that the testing process aligns with project goals and requirements.

The key components of a test plan are summarised in Table 6.5.

Table 6.5 Key components of a test plan

Item	Description
Test scope	Identifies which features, functionality or components will be tested.
Objectives	Defines the goals of testing (e.g. verifying functionality and identifying defects).
Test strategy	Describes the overall approach to testing, including test levels, types of tests and methods to be used (e.g. manual and/or automated).
Test environment	Provides details of the hardware, software, network(s) and tools required for testing.
Resources and roles	Identifies the personnel involved in testing (e.g. test engineers and/or developers) and their responsibilities.
Schedule and milestones	Defines the timeline for testing activities and where key deliverables are produced.
Test deliverables	Describes the documents, reports and other artefacts that will be produced during testing.
Risks and contingencies	Identifies any potential risks that might affect testing, and defines any associated mitigation plans.
Entry and exit criteria	Specifies the conditions that must be met before testing can begin (entry criteria) and end (exit criteria).

Test procedure

A test procedure is a detailed document that focuses on the execution of tests by providing step-by-step guidelines for testers to follow during the execution of a specific test case or set of test cases. Its primary purpose is to ensure consistency and accuracy in the testing process. The key components of a test procedure are summarised in Table 6.6.

Table 6.6 Key components of a test procedure

Item	Description
Test steps	Lists the specific, sequential actions to be performed, such as navigating to a page, entering data or clicking a button.
Test data	Defines the inputs required for executing the test steps, such as user credentials and product IDs.
Pre-conditions	Describes any conditions or setups that must be in place before executing the test, such as specific configurations or data creation.
Expected results	Describes the expected behaviour or output after each step, which helps testers to determine whether the test has passed or failed.
Actual results	Records the observed behaviour when the test steps are executed.
Post-conditions	Describes the state of the software after the test has been executed.

Test cases

A test case is a detailed document that serves as a guide for testers to systematically validate that the software meets its requirements, helping to identify defects and ensuring that software behaves as intended, and meets the required level of quality.

Test cases offer several benefits:

- They serve as formal documentation of what has been tested and how the software is expected to behave.
- They help to ensure that all aspects of the application are tested, leaving no gaps in the testing process.
- They provide a clear reference to specific requirements, making it easier to trace which tests verify which functionality.
- Well-written test cases can be reused in future testing cycles, especially in regression testing or when new versions of the software are released.
- They provide a consistent framework for testing, ensuring that tests are performed the same way every time, reducing variability in results.
- They provide a structured way to identify defects, making it easier to pinpoint issues and their root causes.

There are a variety of different types of test case:

- **Functional test cases** focus on verifying that a particular function offered by the software (e.g. logging in or adding a product to a shopping basket) works as specified. See *Functional testing* above.

- **Non-functional test cases** focus on verifying qualities of the software such as performance, usability, reliability, scalability or security. See *Non-functional testing* above.

- **Positive test cases** test scenarios with valid and expected inputs to confirm the software behaves as intended.

- **Negative test cases** test scenarios with invalid inputs or conditions to ensure the software handles errors or unexpected or illegal behaviour correctly (e.g. entering an invalid email format or attempting to break a business rule or legal constraint).

- **Boundary test cases** test the software with boundary values, such as the minimum and maximum input limits, to ensure it handles edge cases correctly.

- **Regression test cases** ensure that new changes to the codebase have not introduced new defects in previously working functionality.

The key components of a test case are summarised in Table 6.7.

Table 6.7 Key components of a test case

Item	Description
Test case ID	A unique identifier assigned to each test case for easy reference and tracking.
Description	A brief description of the functionality or feature being tested, explaining the purpose of the test case.
Pre-conditions	Any conditions or setup that must be in place before the test case can be executed.
Test steps	A series of actions or steps that need to be performed to execute the test. These are written in a clear step-by-step format so testers know exactly how to replicate the test.
Test data	The input data required to execute the test case.
Expected result	The expected outcome or behaviour of the software after performing the test steps. This is based on the solution requirements or design specifications and is used to determine whether the test passes or fails.
Actual result	The actual behaviour or output of the software observed when the test case is executed. This is compared against the expected result to determine if the test passes or fails.
Post-conditions	The state of the software after the test case has been executed. This includes any changes made to the software during testing, such as database updates or UI changes.

(Continued)

Table 6.7 (Continued)

Item	Description
Pass/fail	An indication of whether the test case passed or failed, based on the comparison between the expected and actual results.
Test environment	Details about the environment in which the test is executed, such as the hardware, software, network and other relevant settings.
Priority/severity	An indication of the importance or criticality of the test case. Some test cases may have higher priority due to their impact on the core functionality of the application.
Author	The name of the person who created the test case to identify who to consult if there are any queries relating to the test case.

Figure 6.2 shows an example of a test case for testing a login facility.

Figure 6.2 Example test case

Test case ID	TC-001
Description	Verify login functionality for valid users.
Pre-conditions	User is registered in the system.
Test steps	1. Open the login page. 2. Enter valid username and password. 3. Click the "Login" button.
Test data	Username: testuser Password: password123
Expected result	User is successfully logged in and redirected to the dashboard.
Actual result	User is logged in and taken to the dashboard.
Post-conditions	User session is active in the system.
Pass/fail	Pass
Test environment	Microsoft Windows 11, version 24H2 Google Chrome, version 128.0.6613.84
Priority/severity	High
Author	Toby Bradley-Thompson

7 SOFTWARE TESTING PRACTICES

INTRODUCTION

Modern software testing practices have evolved significantly to accommodate new development paradigms such as Agile, continuous integration/continuous delivery (CI/CD) and DevOps. This chapter provides a brief summary of some of the more popular practices and how they contribute to the quality of software.

SHIFT-LEFT APPROACH

The shift-left approach refers to the practice of performing testing activities earlier in the software development life cycle (SDLC), referring specifically to the left-hand side of the V model life cycle (Figure 6.1), which focuses on the specification stages of development. This aligns to testing principle 3, *Early testing saves time and money*, described in Chapter 6.

Traditionally, testing occurred after the development phase was completed, as shown on the right side of the V model. However, in the shift-left approach testing is moved to the left, meaning it starts earlier, during the Requirements Engineering (analysis), design and coding stages.

The shift-left approach typically incorporates the following concepts:

- **Test early and often**: The main principle of shift-left testing is to detect and prevent defects as early as possible in the development process. Since fixing defects early is much cheaper and easier, this approach helps to improve software quality and reduce development costs.

- **Involve quality assurance (QA) from the start**: In shift-left testing, the QA team is involved in the initial stages of the project, such as requirements definition and design discussions, rather than waiting until after the development phase to start testing.

- **Continuous testing**: In many shift-left implementations, testing is performed continuously, using automated testing tools integrated with the development pipeline (e.g. in CI/CD pipelines). This ensures that code is tested frequently and immediately whenever the code changes.

- **Collaboration between teams**: The shift-left approach encourages closer collaboration between developers, test engineers, business analysts (BAs) and other stakeholders early in the SDLC. This helps to identify potential issues in requirements, design or code before they become costly to fix.

The ISTQB syllabus identifies the following practices associated with the shift-left approach:

- Review the specification from the perspective of testing. These review activities on specifications often find potential defects, such as ambiguities, incompleteness and inconsistencies.

- Write test cases before the code is written and have the code run in a test harness[54] during code implementation.

- Use CI and CD as these provide rapid feedback and automated component tests to accompany source code when it is submitted to the code repository.

- Complete static analysis of source code prior to dynamic testing, or as part of an automated process.

- Perform non-functional testing starting at the component test level, where possible. This is a form of shift-left as these non-functional test types tend to be performed later in the SDLC, when a complete system and a representative test environment are available.

VERIFICATION VERSUS VALIDATION

Verification and validation, cited in principle 7, *Absence of errors fallacy*, are two distinct but complementary activities that ensure the quality of a software product. Both are critical to producing reliable, functional software, but they focus on different aspects of the software development process. Table 7.1 provides a comparison of the two concepts.

Table 7.1 Comparison of verification and validation in testing

Aspect	Verification	Validation
Focus	Process-oriented (focuses on ensuring the process is followed correctly)	Product-oriented (focuses on ensuring the final product meets user needs)
Objective	Ensures the product is built correctly according to the specifications	Ensures the correct product is built and works as expected
Timing	Ongoing throughout the development process	Occurs after the product is developed or during the final stages
Question addressed	Are we building the product right?	Are we building the right product?
Activities	Reviews, inspections, walkthroughs, code analysis	Testing, user acceptance testing (UAT), performance testing
Examples	Code reviews, design reviews, requirements analysis	Functional testing, performance testing, UAT

---

54 A test harness is a collection of tools and code used to automate the execution of tests and evaluate the output of a software component, helping to validate its correctness in a controlled environment.

AUTOMATED TESTING

Automated software testing refers to the process of using software tools to execute test cases automatically, without manual intervention. It is an essential element of modern software development and QA practices, especially Agile and DevOps, where rapid development cycles demand faster, more reliable testing.

Typical benefits of automated testing include:

- **Speed and efficiency**: Automated tests can be executed much faster than manual tests, making it feasible to run thousands of tests in a short period. This is especially beneficial for regression testing, where the same tests are run repeatedly after changes are made to the code. This also enables more comprehensive test coverage than manual testing can realistically achieve.

- **Accuracy and consistency**: Automated tests reduce the risk of human error, ensuring that the same steps are followed exactly, every time. This improves test reliability and provides consistent results, especially for repetitive tasks.

- **Cost-effectiveness**: Although the initial setup of automated tests requires effort, over time it becomes cost-effective. Once automated tests are set up, they can be run repeatedly without additional costs, unlike manual testing, which requires ongoing human resources.

- **Frequent feedback**: Automated tests provide rapid feedback to developers, enabling them to identify and address defects earlier in the development cycle. This supports CI/CD pipelines, where testing is integrated into the development process.

- **Scalability**: Automated testing enables parallel execution, meaning multiple tests can be run simultaneously across different environments, platforms and configurations. This increases scalability, making it suitable for large-scale applications.

Automated testing can be used for a wide range of testing activities, including:

- unit testing;
- integration testing;
- functional testing;
- regression testing;
- performance testing; and
- acceptance testing.

Some of the more popular automated testing tools (also known as CAST – computer-aided software testing – tools) are explored in Chapter 12.

TEST-DRIVEN DEVELOPMENT

Test-driven development (TDD) was introduced in Chapter 4 as a software development methodology in which tests are written before the code. It plays a significant role in improving both software quality and testing practices, by enforcing good development practices, such as early testing, comprehensive test coverage and continuous verification.

TDD also helps developers to produce cleaner, more reliable code while reducing defects and improving the overall design of the software. By focusing on writing tests before writing code, TDD strengthens the software's foundation, leading to more maintainable, scalable and defect-free applications over time.

Specific benefits from a software quality and testing perspective include:

- early defect detection;
- improved code quality;
- continuous testing;
- comprehensive test coverage;
- refactoring, leading to cleaner, more efficient code;
- better alignment with requirements; and
- reduction in defects identified when the solution is live.

BEHAVIOUR-DRIVEN DEVELOPMENT

Behaviour-driven development (BDD) was introduced in Chapter 4 as a collaborative development approach that extends TDD by focusing on user-centric behaviours and automating the validation of those behaviours. BDD improves software quality and testing by aligning development with business goals (ensuring that the software meets both business and technical expectations), promoting collaboration, clarifying requirements and ensuring comprehensive test coverage through scenario-based, automated testing, which results in higher-quality products.

As BDD is an extension of TDD, the benefits overlap with TDD. Specific benefits from a software quality and testing perspective include:

- BDD scenarios, written in Gherkin syntax, directly reflect business goals, ensuring that development efforts remain aligned with the underlying business needs they encapsulate.

- BDD scenarios provide clear, up-to-date documentation of the system's behaviour that can be easily understood by both technical and non-technical stakeholders (developers, testers, BAs, product owners and end-users) throughout the SDLC, thus reducing miscommunication.

- Software tools support the automated testing of BDD scenarios, enabling tests to be executed regularly (e.g. in a CI/CD pipeline), which results in software that consistently behaves as expected as it evolves.

- BDD scenarios describe both positive and negative behaviours, thus providing broader test coverage, which results in more robust and reliable software.

- Automated testing enables frequent releases without compromising quality, and provides continuous feedback, which reduces the chances of regression errors, and ensures that new features do not break existing functionality.

- The process of translating high-level requirements (in the form of user stories) into concrete scenarios helps to clarify edge cases, refine acceptance criteria and identify ambiguities before development begins. This leads to a clearer understanding of requirements, reduces the likelihood of misinterpretation and ensures that the final product behaves as expected.

- BDD helps to identify potential issues during the early stages of development. As scenarios are implemented as automated tests, any deviation from the expected behaviour is flagged early.

- Early detection of defects reduces the cost and effort involved in fixing them. Developers can address issues as soon as they are introduced, improving overall software quality.

- BDD encourages teams to focus on the behaviour that is most valuable to the customer. By ensuring that development is always based on customer-facing scenarios, the team prioritises functionality that directly benefits the end-user, which results in higher customer satisfaction.

ACCEPTANCE TEST-DRIVEN DEVELOPMENT

Acceptance test-driven development (ATDD) is an extension to TDD. Where TDD focuses on improving code quality at the technical level (ensuring small pieces of code work as expected), ATDD is broader and focuses on ensuring that the software meets business requirements and user expectations, and is validated against acceptance criteria before development.

ATDD significantly improves software quality by ensuring that development is requirements-driven, user-focused and collaborative. By writing acceptance tests early, teams can prevent defects, ensure alignment with business goals and build software that consistently meets user expectations. Additionally, the automation of acceptance tests facilitates continuous validation, reducing the likelihood of regression errors and ensuring that software quality is maintained throughout the SDLC.

Specific benefits from a software quality and testing perspective are similar to those cited above for BDD, and include:

- ATDD ensures alignment with business goals by focusing on user acceptance criteria from the start.

- ATDD provides clear, testable requirements that guide development.

- Acceptance tests serve as 'living documentation' that describes the system's expected behaviour in real-world terms.

DEVOPS AND TESTING

DevOps was introduced in Chapter 4 as an organisational approach to uniting the disciplines of software development and IT operations, enabling them to work together seamlessly. In the DevOps paradigm, software testing plays a critical role in ensuring that CI/CD processes are smooth, efficient and reliable.

The integration of testing into DevOps is often referred to as continuous testing, which aligns with the DevOps principles of automation, collaboration and speed. By automating testing and integrating it into the CI/CD pipeline, DevOps ensures faster, higher-quality releases with fewer defects, but, although DevOps involves a high level of automated testing, manual testing – especially from the user's perspective – is still necessary.

From the testing perspective, DevOps offers significant benefits:

- Continuous testing is integrated into the CI and CD pipelines, and therefore automated tests are run every time code is changed or integrated. This ensures every new feature, bug fix or configuration change is verified immediately, providing faster feedback to developers (e.g. whether changes adversely affect existing code) and enabling new issues to be identified quickly, improving code quality and reducing time-to-market.

- Automated processes like CI/CD facilitate establishing stable test environments and reduce the need for repetitive manual testing. Test automation is used for unit, integration, performance, security and regression testing, which enables rapid execution of tests at scale, and ensures that feedback is provided to developers in real time. This is essential in fast-paced software development environments, where the goal is to release software frequently and reliably. Additionally, automated regression testing minimises the risk of reintroducing errors (regression errors).

- DevOps integrates performance testing with real-time monitoring of the live system in the production environment, which enables teams to proactively identify and fix performance bottlenecks, leading to more reliable software in production environments.

- Security testing is embedded into the development process through a practice known as DevSecOps. Security tests, such as vulnerability scanning and penetration testing, are automated and included in the CI/CD pipeline, which ensures that security vulnerabilities are identified and addressed early in the SDLC, rather than being left to the end, reducing the risk of security breaches in production.

- Testing in DevOps breaks down silos between development, testing and operations teams, encouraging cross-functional collaboration. Test engineers work closely with developers and operations teams throughout the entire SDLC, which ensures that tests are designed with operational considerations in mind (such as scalability and performance under load) and that developers can build testable software from the outset.

TESTING QUADRANTS

First introduced in a blog post by Brian Marick and later expanded by Lisa Crispin and Janet Gregory in their book on Agile testing practices (Crispin and Gregory, 2009), the testing quadrants are a framework that helps teams to understand the different types of tests needed in software development, particularly when using Agile methodologies.

Testing types are sorted into four categories (quadrants) on a grid (as shown in Figure 7.1), which categorise tests based on their purpose (e.g. supporting the team or critiquing the product) and their focus (technology-facing versus business-facing). The quadrants provide a balanced view of testing that ensures coverage across various testing types, from unit tests to exploratory testing, helping to balance automated tests, manual tests, functional tests and non-functional tests throughout the development cycle. They help Agile teams plan for comprehensive testing, ensuring that quality is built into the process rather than added at the end. By covering both business-facing and technology-facing tests, teams can ensure that the product is not only built right, but also meets the needs of users and performs well in real-world scenarios.

Figure 7.1 Testing quadrants (Source: Adapted from Crispin and Gregory, 2009)

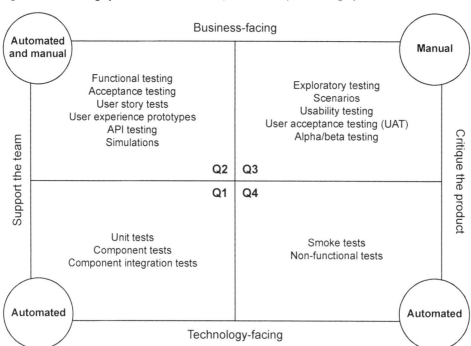

Q1 (technology-facing, support the team)

These are automated tests that support the development team by ensuring that the code behaves as expected. Q1 tests are used to verify functionality at the unit and component levels, helping developers to catch issues early in the development cycle. They enable fast feedback on code quality and correctness.

- **Automated unit tests** verify that small units of code (such as methods or functions) work correctly.
- **Component and component integration tests** test larger modules or components of the software system and ensure they integrate correctly.

Q2 (business-facing, support the team)

These tests are also supportive but focus on validating business-facing functionality, from the user's perspective. Q2 tests ensure the software meets business requirements and behaves correctly in terms of user interaction. They help the team to understand if they are building the right product by validating functionality against user stories or specifications. These tests check the acceptance criteria and can be manual or automated.

- **Functional testing** ensures features and workflows behave as intended from the end-user's perspective.
- **Automated acceptance testing** is written in collaboration with business stakeholders using frameworks such as Cucumber or SpecFlow (see Chapter 12 for further details regarding testing tools).

Q3 (business-facing, critique the product)

These are manual tests, or exploratory tests, aimed at discovering issues that automated tests may not capture. They focus on business-facing concerns, such as user experience and acceptance. Q3 tests help to identify unexpected behaviours, usability issues or missing features from the user's perspective. These tests focus on critically assessing whether the product provides value and works for the end-user.

- **Exploratory testing** actively explores the system without predefined scripts to find defects or usability issues.
- **User acceptance testing** involves real users or stakeholders testing the system to ensure it meets their needs.

Q4 (technology-facing, critique the product)

These are smoke tests and non-functional tests (except usability tests) that are typically automated. They examine the product's technical qualities against non-functional requirements, such as system robustness, performance, security and scalability. Q4 tests help to ensure that the software performs well under different conditions and can handle external threats or large-scale usage.

- **Performance testing** tests the system's ability to handle high loads or stress.
- **Security testing** identifies vulnerabilities or weaknesses in the system.
- **Load testing** checks how the system performs under various workloads.

AGILE TESTING PRACTICES

Testing is an integral part of an Agile software development process, which considers testing to be a continuous activity that is embedded throughout the development life cycle rather than a separate phase. Agile methodologies, such as Scrum and Kanban, promote the idea of testing early and often, promoting collaboration between developers, test engineers and business stakeholders.

By embedding testing early and frequently into every stage of development, Agile teams can produce higher-quality software, reduce risk and ensure faster delivery of features that meet both technical and business requirements. With the combination of automated and manual testing practices, Agile teams maintain flexibility while ensuring comprehensive test coverage.

Popular practices used in Agile software development include:

- **Continuous testing**: Agile teams integrate testing (using automated and manual tests) into every iteration or Sprint (often as part of a CI/CD pipeline), which means that testing starts from day one and continues until the final product is delivered. This helps in identifying and fixing defects early, which reduces the cost and time required for fixes. By testing frequently, Agile teams ensure that the product is always in a potentially shippable state at the end of each iteration.

- **Test automation**: The use of automated testing ensures that frequent code changes do not introduce new defects. Automating repetitive tests (such as regression testing) reduces manual effort, ensures faster feedback for developers and supports continuous integration practices, which are crucial in Agile environments. Automated unit tests, integration tests and acceptance tests are executed in every build cycle.

- **Shift-left testing**: Agile promotes the concept of shift-left testing, where testing activities are performed as early as possible in the development process. Test engineers collaborate with developers and business stakeholders from the very beginning to define the acceptance criteria and prepare test cases before coding begins. This approach ensures early identification of issues, reduces the chances of costly defects later in the development cycle and enhances communication and understanding between testers and developers.

- **Collaboration and cross-functional teams**: In Agile development projects, test engineers, developers, business analysts and business stakeholders work closely together throughout the project. This collaboration ensures that everyone has a shared understanding of the project's goals, and testers are involved in requirements discussions, story development and iteration (Sprint) planning. Collaboration leads to faster feedback loops, improved communication and more effective problem-solving. It also ensures that testing is aligned with business goals.

- **Exploratory testing and Agile testing quadrants**: Alongside automation, exploratory testing plays a vital role in Agile projects. Testers are encouraged to actively explore the software, identify edge cases and usability issues and detect defects that automated tests may miss. Additionally, Agile testing quadrants (introduced above) help teams to balance different types of testing across both functional and non-functional requirements.

- **ATDD and BDD**: Agile teams often use methodologies like ATDD and BDD (see pp. 113–114), which involve writing tests before development starts. Acceptance tests and behaviour scenarios are created collaboratively by business analysts, developers, test engineers and business stakeholders, using natural language to define the expected behaviour of the system. This improves communication and reduces misunderstandings, while ensuring the system meets predefined acceptance criteria and user expectations – helping to align Agile development with business goals.

- **Regression testing**: The iterative nature of Agile development means that new features are frequently added to the software. Therefore, regression testing becomes essential to ensure that newly introduced changes do not break existing functionality. Automated regression tests ensure that the product remains stable as it evolves, and enables faster, more reliable releases.

The Agile Test Pyramid

The Agile Test Pyramid, originally conceptualised by Mike Cohn (2009), provides an alternative visual tool to the testing quadrants described above. Designed to ensure comprehensive test coverage, it proposes a structured approach to testing in Agile environments that helps teams adopting Agile or DevOps practices to optimise their testing efforts by balancing different types of tests across different layers of the software, and promoting test automation and cost-effective, fast and reliable feedback loops, resulting in early defect detection.

By following the pyramid's principles, teams can create a robust, fast and scalable testing strategy that supports CI/CD while maintaining high software quality and minimising testing costs and execution times.

The pyramid consists of three primary layers, each representing a different type of testing, with a focus on varying levels of the software system, as shown in Figure 7.2.

Figure 7.2 The Agile Test Pyramid (Source: Adapted from Cohn, 2009)

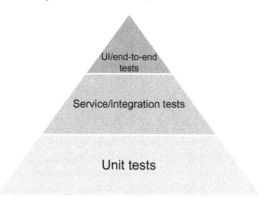

Unit tests   These are the foundation of the pyramid and are designed to test individual components or functions of the code, typically in isolation. Unit tests verify that each small piece of code works correctly, provide quick feedback to developers and catch defects early in the development process, leading to more stable software.

Typical characteristics of these tests include:

- high volume of tests;
- fast to execute;
- automated; and
- focus on testing logic, boundaries and edge cases within individual units of code.

Service/ integration tests   These tests focus on the interactions between components, systems or services to ensure they work together as expected. Service tests verify whether different parts of the system (e.g. APIs and databases) communicate properly and behave correctly under various conditions. They detect integration issues early, ensuring that modules or services work well together, and reduce the risk of functional defects in the combined system.

Typical characteristics of these tests include:

- moderate volume of tests;
- slower than unit tests, but still faster than full system tests;
- automated; and
- ensure that individual components integrate correctly in a production-like environment.

UI/end-to-end tests	These tests validate the system's functionality from the end-user's perspective, testing how the entire system works together, typically via the user interface (UI). UI tests simulate how a user interacts with the system, testing end-to-end workflows, including interactions between services, components and external systems. UI and end-to-end tests ensure that the application behaves correctly from the user's standpoint, providing confidence that key workflows are functioning as expected.

Typical characteristics of these tests include:

- low volume (due to their complexity and cost);
- slow to execute;
- often harder to automate and maintain; and
- test the application in its entirety, focusing on critical paths and user journeys.

While Cohn's Agile Test Pyramid still provides a useful framework, some authors have challenged its logic today, especially with the increased adoption of automated testing tools for end-to-end and UI testing, enabling more extensive testing of this type. In an online article, Maria Homann discusses the evolution of the testing pyramid (Leapwork, 2024):

Running end-to-end tests isn't necessarily as complex and time-consuming as it used to be ... In 2018, most test automation tools on the market were open source and code-based, and required at least some level of programming experience to use. This meant that your developers or specialized test automation engineers would have to get involved in the end-to-end layer of the testing pyramid ... What's more, tests at this time would tend to fail a lot more because of things like dynamic elements in the DOM,[55] or timing issues ... Today, however, in the age of AI, self-healing capabilities are becoming more common in test automation tools. Combine this with a wide range of in-built intelligence mechanisms and general technology advancements, and you have businesses who are now able to build highly stable and robust UI-based test automation.

---

55 'dynamic elements in the DOM' (document object model) means parts of the web page that are added, removed or changed dynamically (often by JavaScript), which can make automated tests unreliable if the elements aren't yet available or behave unpredictably.

PART III
DEPLOYING THE SOLUTION

8 APPROACHES TO DEPLOYING DIGITAL SOLUTIONS

INTRODUCTION

Many digital solution development projects prioritise building the solution, often treating deployment as a secondary concern. However, choosing the right deployment approach is crucial, as it directly impacts the solution's performance, security, scalability, cost efficiency and overall success. A well-thought-out deployment strategy ensures that the solution aligns with business objectives, compliance requirements and system integration needs, while also optimising the user experience.

Organisations can select from a variety of deployment options, with the most suitable choice depending on factors such as business needs, security considerations, budget, scalability and operational control.

The most popular digital solution deployment approaches are:

- on-premises deployment;
- cloud deployment;
- hybrid deployment;
- containerised deployment;
- serverless deployment; and
- edge computing.

The approaches listed above are not mutually exclusive. For example, both containerised and serverless deployments can be on-premises or cloud.

In recent years, cloud-based deployment has become the most popular approach for digital solutions. According to the *2024 State of the Cloud Report* by Flexera, multi-cloud adoption has continued to rise, with enterprises increasingly siloing applications into specific clouds and selecting best-fit services and vendors for each.

This chapter will consider each of these in turn and take a deeper look at the factors affecting the choice of approach.

ON-PREMISES DEPLOYMENT

On-premises (sometimes called *on-prem*) deployment refers to a digital solution hosting model where all software, applications and data infrastructure are installed and managed within an organisation's own physical servers or data centres. Unlike cloud-based deployments (see *Cloud deployment* below), which rely on third-party providers, on-premises deployment gives organisations full control over their IT environment.

On-premises deployments exhibit the following key characteristics:

- **Hosted on local infrastructure**: All servers, databases and software run on hardware owned by the organisation.
- **Full control and customisation**: Organisations manage security, system configurations and updates without external dependencies.
- **Higher up-front costs**: On-premises deployment requires significant investment in hardware, networking and platform technologies, with ongoing costs associated with maintenance and the IT personnel to manage the necessary infrastructure.
- **Strict security and compliance**: On-premises deployment is suitable for businesses with high security requirements, such as banking, healthcare and government.
- **Limited scalability**: Unlike cloud deployments, scaling resources requires physical upgrades and additional infrastructure.

Advantages and disadvantages of on-premises deployment

On-premises deployment offers the following benefits:

- **Greater data security and privacy**: Sensitive data remains within the organisation's infrastructure.
- **Compliance and regulatory control**: The on-premises model meets industry regulations requiring strict data sovereignty.[56]
- **Lower/more controllable costs**: Comparing costs between on-premises and cloud deployments is complex. On-premises setups typically avoid recurring subscription fees, unlike cloud solutions. However, cloud costs – especially with multi-year reserved capacity contracts for large accounts – are often more consistent and predictable. In contrast, on-premises costs can fluctuate due to factors such as staff costs and electricity rates. When capacity needs are stable and deployment is large-scale, cost savings often motivate repatriation from cloud to on-premises. A related but distinct advantage of on-premises is the reduced risk of uncontrolled consumption – an issue in cloud environments where open credit lines can lead to unexpected, and sometimes catastrophic, expenses (e.g. runaway scripts – automated code or instructions written to perform tasks that consume excessive cloud resources unintentionally, often due to a defect, misconfiguration or lack of effective limits – causing massive bills). This cost control can be especially critical for smaller organisations.

---

56 Data sovereignty refers to data being subject to the laws and regulations of the country or region where it is collected, stored or processed.

- **Better performance and low latency**: Local hosting (via a local area network as opposed to a wide area network – the internet) ensures faster data access for internal applications.

However, on-premises deployment does suffer from the following disadvantages:

- **High initial investment**: On-premises deployment has significant up-front costs for purchasing hardware, software licences, infrastructure setup and ongoing maintenance.
- **Requires IT expertise**: Organisations must manage security patches, updates and infrastructure maintenance.
- **Limited flexibility and scalability**: Expanding resources requires additional hardware purchases.
- **Disaster recovery risks**: On-premises systems need dedicated, off-site failover solutions to prevent data loss.

On-premises deployment is favoured by industries with stringent security, compliance and performance requirements, such as banks (handling sensitive financial data), government and defence organisations (ensuring data sovereignty and compliance with national security policies), healthcare institutions (protecting patient records) and manufacturing companies (running mission-critical, low-latency applications).

While offering greater control, security and regulatory compliance, on-premises deployment also entails higher costs and maintenance responsibilities. Organisations must carefully evaluate these factors against cloud or hybrid models to determine the most efficient solution for their needs.

CLOUD DEPLOYMENT

Cloud deployment refers to the process of hosting, managing and delivering digital solutions through cloud computing infrastructure instead of traditional on-premises servers. In this approach, applications, services and data storage are provided by cloud service providers such as Amazon Web Services (AWS), Microsoft Azure, Google Cloud Platform and IBM Cloud.

Cloud deployments exhibit the following key characteristics:

- **Managed infrastructure**: The infrastructure that the solution depends on is managed by a cloud provider, so the user organisation does not need to maintain physical servers or data centres.
- **Scalability and elasticity**: Cloud deployments provide the ability to dynamically adjust computing resources based on demand, enabling systems to scale up to handle increased workloads or scale down to optimise cost and efficiency.
- **Automatic updates and maintenance**: The cloud provider manages regular software updates, security patches and infrastructure upgrades, reducing downtime, minimising security risks and eliminating the need for manual intervention.

Cloud deployment models

Cloud deployment models define how cloud resources are structured, managed and accessed, impacting the way businesses deploy and operate their digital solutions. Each model offers distinct advantages and trade-offs depending on factors such as data sensitivity, regulatory compliance, infrastructure control and workload distribution. The primary cloud deployment models are described below, and a comparison between the models is provided in Table 8.1.

Public cloud   Public cloud is a cloud computing model where computing resources (e.g. servers, storage and networking) are owned and managed by third-party providers (e.g. AWS, Microsoft Azure, Google Cloud Platform and IBM Cloud) and made available to **multiple organisations** over the internet.

Private cloud   Private cloud is a cloud computing model in which infrastructure and resources are dedicated to a **single organisation**, offering greater control, security and customisation compared to public cloud services. It can be hosted on-premises within an organisation's data centre or managed by a third-party provider while maintaining a private environment. Private cloud is ideal for businesses with strict regulatory requirements, sensitive data or specialised workloads that demand high performance and security.

Multi-cloud   Multi-cloud is a cloud computing model in which an organisation utilises services from multiple cloud providers to optimise performance, cost and redundancy. By distributing workloads across different cloud platforms, businesses can avoid vendor lock-in, enhance reliability and tailor cloud services to specific operational needs. Multi-cloud architectures also improve disaster recovery capabilities and enable organisations to comply with regional data regulations by leveraging providers that meet specific compliance standards. While offering flexibility and resilience, multi-cloud deployments require robust management and integration strategies to handle complexities such as interoperability, security and data governance.

Hybrid cloud   Hybrid cloud is a cloud computing model that integrates both public and private cloud environments, enabling organisations to seamlessly share data and applications between them for greater flexibility, scalability and security. This approach enables businesses to leverage the cost-effectiveness and scalability of public cloud services while maintaining critical workloads or sensitive data in a private cloud for enhanced control and compliance. Hybrid cloud solutions are ideal for organisations with dynamic workloads, regulatory requirements or a need for disaster recovery, offering a balanced approach that optimises performance, cost and operational efficiency.

Table 8.1 Cloud deployment models comparison

Model	Benefits	Use cases
Public cloud	• Cost-effective • Scalable • Easy to deploy • High availability • Minimal maintenance	• Web applications • SaaS platforms • Big data analytics • Artificial intelligence (AI)/ machine learning (ML) workloads • Startups and enterprises seeking agility
Private cloud	• Greater security and control • Regulatory compliance • Customisation • Dedicated resources	• Highly regulated industries (finance, healthcare, government) • Organisations with sensitive data and strict security requirements
Multi-cloud	• Avoids vendor lock-in • Optimised performance and cost • Redundancy • Regulatory compliance	• Enterprises requiring diverse cloud services • Multinational organisations managing compliance across regions • Optimising cost and performance
Hybrid cloud	• Flexibility • Balanced cost and control • Scalability • Disaster recovery • Workload optimisation	• Businesses needing a mix of public and private cloud • Disaster recovery • Legacy system integration • Scalability with security control

Cloud services (the cloud stack)

The cloud stack refers to the layered architecture of cloud computing, comprising various components that work together to deliver cloud services. It is typically divided into three main layers: infrastructure as a service (IaaS), platform as a service (PaaS) and software as a service (SaaS). Each layer is described below and plays a crucial role in enabling organisations to build, deploy and manage cloud-based solutions efficiently. Understanding the cloud stack helps businesses and developers to select the right services, optimise resource usage and align cloud strategies with their operational and technological needs.

Software as a service
SaaS is a cloud computing model that delivers software applications over the internet on a subscription basis, eliminating the need for users to install, maintain or update software on their local devices. SaaS solutions are hosted and managed by third-party providers, ensuring automatic updates, scalability and accessibility from any internet-connected device. This model is widely used for business applications such as customer

relationship management (CRM), enterprise resource planning (ERP), collaboration tools and productivity suites. SaaS enables organisations to reduce IT overhead, improve operational efficiency and rapidly deploy software solutions without the complexities of traditional software management.

Platform as a service

PaaS is a cloud computing model that provides a comprehensive development and deployment environment, offering developers the tools, frameworks and infrastructure needed to build, test and deploy applications without managing the underlying hardware or operating systems. PaaS solutions include preconfigured environments with runtime libraries, databases and development tools, enabling faster development cycles and improved collaboration. This model is widely used for web and mobile application development, AI and big data analytics. By eliminating the need to manage underlying infrastructure, PaaS enables businesses to concentrate on innovation, enhance development workflows and efficiently scale applications.

Infrastructure as a service

IaaS is a cloud computing model that provides virtualised computing resources, such as servers, storage, networking and operating systems, on a pay-as-you-go basis. It eliminates the need for organisations to invest in and maintain physical hardware, enabling them to scale resources dynamically based on demand. IaaS is widely used for hosting websites, running enterprise applications, big data processing and disaster recovery solutions. By offering high flexibility, cost efficiency and automation, IaaS enables businesses to focus on their core operations while leveraging reliable and scalable cloud infrastructure.

Advantages and disadvantages of cloud deployment

Cloud deployment offers the following benefits:

- **Faster deployment and time-to-market**: Applications can be rapidly deployed without the need for hardware setup, as cloud computing offers on-demand resources, automated provisioning[57] and scalable infrastructure, enabling businesses to efficiently develop, test and launch applications without the delays associated with traditional IT environments.

- **Reduced IT maintenance**: Cloud deployments reduce IT maintenance by shifting infrastructure management, updates and security responsibilities to cloud providers, minimising the need for in-house IT resources and reducing operational overhead.

- **High availability and disaster recovery**: Cloud deployments provide high availability and disaster recovery by utilising distributed data centres, automated backups and failover mechanisms, reducing downtime and ensuring business continuity during failures or disruptions. Integrated redundancy[58] ensures continuous access to data and applications.

---

57 Provisioning is the process of setting up and allocating cloud resources and services, such as virtual machines, storage and networks, to make them ready for use.

58 Redundancy refers to the duplication of critical components or functions of a system to ensure high availability and reliability in case of failure.

- **Remote accessibility**: Applications, data and services can be securely accessed from any location with an internet connection, facilitating seamless collaboration and operational flexibility.

- **Cost-effectiveness**: With cloud deployments, up-front infrastructure costs and operational expenses are reduced by offering pay-as-you-go pricing, resource optimisation and scalability, ensuring that organisations only pay for what they use.

Typical challenges associated with cloud deployment include:

- **Security and compliance risks**: Cloud deployments present security and compliance challenges due to risks such as data breaches, unauthorised access and complex regulatory requirements, necessitating robust security measures and adherence to industry standards. Organisations must ensure that sensitive data stored in the cloud complies with relevant regulations.

- **Vendor lock-in risk**: Cloud deployments can lead to vendor lock-in if businesses become reliant on a specific provider's services, making it difficult to migrate workloads, integrate with other platforms or switch providers without incurring significant costs, technical challenges or service disruptions.

- **Ongoing operating costs**: Cloud deployments can lead to accumulating expenses over time due to pay-as-you-go pricing, data transfer fees and scaling demands, making cost monitoring and resource optimisation essential to avoid unexpected charges. In the long run, cloud costs may surpass those of on-premises infrastructure.

Cloud deployment is a versatile, cost-effective and scalable solution applied across multiple industries, including web and mobile applications (such as SaaS platforms and ecommerce websites), big data and AI workloads (for analytics and machine learning), disaster recovery and backup (to ensure business continuity) and Internet of Things (IoT) (for processing device-generated data). It provides businesses with high availability, minimised infrastructure management and the flexibility to meet performance, security and compliance demands.

HYBRID DEPLOYMENT

Hybrid deployment integrates on-premises infrastructure with cloud-based services, enabling organisations to take advantage of both approaches. With this model, organisations can keep sensitive or mission-critical data on-premises while leveraging the cloud's scalability and flexibility for less-sensitive workloads.

Hybrid deployments exhibit the following key characteristics:

- **Combination of on-premises and cloud resources**: In a hybrid deployment, some components of the digital solution run on local servers while others are hosted in the cloud. This approach combines on-premises infrastructure with cloud resources, enabling organisations to maintain security, control and compliance while benefiting from the scalability, flexibility and cost efficiency of cloud computing.

- **Seamless integration**: Hybrid deployments offer smooth interoperability between on-premises infrastructure and cloud environments, enabling data, applications and workflows to function cohesively without disruption.

Advantages and disadvantages of hybrid deployment

Hybrid deployment offers the following benefits:

- **Better control over data**: Hybrid deployments provide better control over data by enabling organisations to store and manage sensitive, regulated or critical information on-premises, while utilising cloud resources for less-sensitive operations, ensuring compliance, security and operational flexibility.

- **Cost optimisation**: Hybrid deployments enable organisations to optimise costs by strategically distributing workloads between on-premises infrastructure and cloud services. This minimises cloud expenses by leveraging resources only when needed, while ensuring that essential business functions are managed to balance performance and resilience with carefully controlled spending, avoiding unnecessary costs without compromising effectiveness.

- **Enhanced security and compliance**: Hybrid deployments enhance security and compliance by enabling organisations to keep sensitive data and critical workloads on-premises for greater control, regulatory adherence and robust data protection.

- **Improved scalability, performance and flexibility**: Hybrid deployments enhance scalability and flexibility by enabling organisations to allocate workloads between on-premises infrastructure and the cloud, with efficient resource management and seamless scaling to meet changing demands while minimising overheads for peak workloads. Organisations can scale cloud resources as needed while retaining critical workloads on-premises for improved control and security.

- **Business continuity and disaster recovery**: Hybrid deployments strengthen business continuity and disaster recovery by keeping critical workloads running on-premises while utilising cloud services for automated backups, failover mechanisms and rapid recovery in the event of disruptions or failures.

- **Legacy system integration**: Hybrid deployments support legacy system integration by enabling organisations to modernise their IT infrastructure incrementally, ensuring smooth connectivity between on-premises systems and cloud services without the need for a full-scale replacement.

Despite seemingly offering the best of both worlds (on-premises and cloud), hybrid deployment does have its challenges:

- **Complex to manage**: Hybrid deployments can be complex to manage due to the need for seamless integration, data synchronisation, security enforcement and workload distribution across both on-premises and cloud environments, requiring advanced management tools and expertise.

- **Data synchronisation issues**: Data synchronisation issues in hybrid deployments stem from inconsistencies, latency[59] and integration complexities when handling data across on-premises and cloud environments, necessitating strong synchronisation mechanisms to maintain accuracy. Achieving real-time data consistency between both environments can be particularly challenging.

- **Security risks**: Hybrid deployments introduce security risks as data must be safeguarded across both on-premises and cloud environments, complicating access control, encryption and compliance management while increasing exposure to potential threats. Implementing strong encryption and access controls is essential to secure data transfers between cloud and on-premises systems.

- **Integration costs**: Due to the need to ensure seamless connectivity, data synchronisation and security across on-premises and cloud environments, hybrid deployments require specialised tools, custom configurations and continuous maintenance, which incur additional integration costs. Establishing connections between different platforms may also necessitate custom APIs and middleware[60] solutions.

Hybrid deployment is a strategic deployment approach that balances control, security and scalability by integrating on-premises infrastructure with cloud resources. It is widely used across industries such as:

- **finance and healthcare**, where sensitive data remains on-premises while AI-driven analytics run in the cloud;

- **retail and ecommerce**, where cloud-based customer insights complement on-premises transaction processing;

- **manufacturing and IoT**, where factory sensors handle local data processing and cloud services perform predictive analytics; and

- **enterprises with legacy systems** that gradually migrate critical workloads without full cloud adoption.

By combining both environments, organisations can optimise costs, enhance security and improve performance, making hybrid deployment a popular option.

CONTAINERISED DEPLOYMENT

Containerised deployment packages software applications and their dependencies into lightweight, portable containers using orchestration[61] and containerisation tools to ensure consistency and scalability across different environments. These containers encapsulate everything required for an application to run, including code, runtime

---

59 Latency is the delay in data transmission or processing that occurs when data is transferred between on-premises and cloud environments, which can lead to timing mismatches and inconsistencies in synchronised data.

60 Middleware is software that acts as a bridge between different applications, services or operating systems, enabling them to communicate and exchange data.

61 Orchestration is the automated management, coordination and scaling of containers to ensure efficient operation, availability and resource utilisation across environments.

libraries and configurations, ensuring uniform execution regardless of the underlying infrastructure. Containerisation supports CI/CD, making it essential for enhancing portability and efficiency, particularly in microservices-based architectures.

Containerised deployments exhibit the following key characteristics:

- **Portability**: Containers encapsulate all necessary application dependencies, ensuring seamless deployment and consistent performance across various environments, from development and testing to production, without compatibility issues.

- **Isolation**: Each container runs independently, with its own resources, dependencies and runtime environment, preventing conflicts between applications and improving security, stability and resource management.

- **Efficiency**: Containers share the host operating system (OS) kernel,[62] making them lighter and faster than traditional virtual machines.[63]

- **Scalability**: Supports application scaling (up or down) by dynamically provisioning or decommissioning containers based on demand, maintaining optimal resource utilisation and performance.

- **Automation-friendly**: Containerised deployment seamlessly integrates with CI/CD pipelines, orchestration tools and infrastructure-as-code (IaC) practices, enabling automated deployment, scaling and management of applications.

Advantages and disadvantages of containerised deployment

Containerised deployment offers the following benefits:

- **Cross-platform compatibility**: By encapsulating all necessary application dependencies, containers ensure consistent execution across various environments, including on-premises, cloud and hybrid systems, enhancing flexibility, scalability and resource efficiency while broadening deployment possibilities. This approach also eliminates compatibility issues by providing a standardised runtime environment, enabling applications to run seamlessly across different operating systems and platforms.

- **Faster deployment and scaling**: By integrating with CI/CD pipelines, containerisation facilitates rapid application rollouts and dynamic resource allocation. Additionally, containers can be quickly and easily created, replicated or removed as needed, ensuring optimal efficiency and responsiveness.

- **Improved resource efficiency**: Multiple containers share the same host OS kernel while using only necessary resources, reducing overhead and maximising computing power utilisation. Containerised deployments typically use fewer resources than traditional virtual machines, leading to increased performance.

---

62 The kernel is the core component of an operating system that manages system resources and facilitates communication between hardware and software.

63 A virtual machine is a software-based emulation of a physical computer that runs an operating system and applications independently on shared hardware.

- **Easier DevOps and CI/CD integration**: Containerised deployment streamlines DevOps and CI/CD integration by providing consistent environments, seamless automation and efficient orchestration, enabling faster development, testing and deployment cycles with minimal manual effort. It also supports automated deployments, rollback mechanisms and CI for improved workflow efficiency.

- **Fault isolation**: Issues in one container do not affect others, which enhances application stability, improves security and enables faster troubleshooting and recovery.

Containerised deployment also has some challenges:

- **Security risks**: Vulnerabilities such as container escapes,[64] insecure images and misconfigurations require strong security policies and robust security measures (e.g. access controls), along with regular updates and patches to address infrastructure vulnerabilities and newly discovered common vulnerabilities and exposures (CVEs)[65] to mitigate threats. Note that regular security patching is also an issue with other deployment approaches.

- **Orchestration complexity**: Managing multiple containers, along with networking, scaling and security, requires advanced orchestration tools such as Kubernetes, and skilled expertise to configure and operate them efficiently.

- **Networking and storage management**: Managing networking and storage in containerised deployment is complex due to requirements such as dynamic IP allocation (automatic assignment of IP addresses to devices on a network), service discovery (the automatic detection of devices or services on a network, enabling applications to locate and communicate with each other without hardcoded configurations), persistent storage and data consistency across distributed environments. This necessitates specialised tools and configurations to enable smooth inter-container communication.

- **Learning curve**: Implementing and managing containerised deployments requires skilled DevOps engineers, and the learning curve can be steep (due to the need to master container orchestration, networking, security and management tools such as Docker and Kubernetes), necessitating specialised training and expertise.

Containerisation plays a crucial role in DevOps and cloud computing, and containerised deployment is a flexible and efficient solution for modern applications, especially those based on microservices architectures. It promotes scalable, modular applications by running services in separate containers that integrate easily with cloud platforms such as AWS, Microsoft Azure, Google Cloud Platform and IBM Cloud.

SERVERLESS DEPLOYMENT

Serverless deployment is a cloud computing model (although it differs from cloud deployment introduced above) that enables applications to run without requiring

---

64 Container escapes occur when a process running inside a container breaks out of its isolated environment and gains unauthorised access to the host system or other containers, potentially leading to security breaches or system compromise.

65 CVEs – publicly disclosed security flaws assigned a unique CVE ID (e.g. CVE-2024-12345). CVE IDs are globally managed by MITRE Corporation in the US and monitored by the National Cyber Security Centre (NCSC) in the UK.

developers to manage servers. Instead of provisioning or maintaining infrastructure, developers simply write and deploy code, while the cloud provider takes care of server allocation, scaling and maintenance automatically. This approach eliminates infrastructure management by executing code in response to events, significantly reducing operational overhead. Resources are assigned dynamically when needed and billing is based on actual execution time rather than pre-allocated infrastructure, making serverless computing a cost-efficient, scalable and developer-friendly solution.

Serverless deployments exhibit the following key characteristics:

- **No server management**: Cloud providers handle server provisioning, scaling and maintenance.

- **Event-driven execution**: Applications run in response to specific triggers (e.g. API requests, database updates and file uploads).

- **Pay-as-you-go pricing**: Charges are based on actual usage (execution time, memory and number of requests) rather than pre-allocated server resources.

- **Automatic scaling**: The cloud provider dynamically scales resources up or down based on demand.

- **Microservices and function-based**: Applications are often built using microservices or **function as a service (FaaS)**, where microservices encapsulate specific business functionality as independently deployable services, and FaaS executes small, stateless functions in response to events for more granular and short-lived processing.

Advantages and disadvantages of serverless deployment

Serverless deployment offers the following benefits:

- **Cost efficiency**: As a consequence of pay-as-you-go pricing, customer organisations pay only for actual usage, eliminating costs for idle resources.

- **Automatic scaling**: Applications dynamically adjust resources based on demand, ensuring optimal performance and cost efficiency without manual intervention.

- **Reduced operational overhead**: By eliminating the need to manage servers, infrastructure and maintenance, serverless deployment enables developers to focus solely on writing and deploying code.

- **Faster time-to-market**: By eliminating infrastructure management (server provisioning or maintenance), serverless deployment enables developers to quickly build, deploy and scale applications.

- **Built-in fault tolerance**: Serverless deployment ensures high availability and resilience by leveraging cloud providers' automatic failover mechanisms, redundant infrastructure and distributed execution.

- **Improved developer productivity**: Serverless deployment helps to streamline application development by enabling developers to focus on writing code and automating deployments, thereby accelerating the development and delivery of high quality software.

- **Seamless integration**: Serverless deployment works well with cloud-native services such as databases, storage and APIs.

Serverless deployment also has some challenges:

- **Cold-start latency**: Cold-start latency occurs when a function experiences a delay in execution due to the time required to initialise a new instance[66] after being idle, impacting application performance and response times.

- **Vendor lock-in**: Applications become highly dependent on a specific cloud provider's proprietary services, making migration, interoperability and switching providers costly and complex.

- **Limited execution time**: Serverless functions often have execution time limits, making them unsuitable for long-running tasks.

- **Debugging and monitoring complexity**: Troubleshooting can be more difficult than other deployment approaches due to the lack of direct server access, and distributed execution.

- **Security and compliance risks**: Multi-tenant[67] cloud environments limit control over the underlying infrastructure and may introduce vulnerabilities in provider services, necessitating strong security measures and strict compliance with regulatory standards.

- **Resource limitations**: Predefined constraints on memory, execution time, request limits and concurrency set by cloud providers can restrict performance and make serverless deployment unsuitable for resource-intensive or long-running applications.

- **Higher latency for stateful applications**: Serverless functions are inherently stateless,[68] requiring frequent access to external storage or databases, which introduces additional delays in processing and response times.

EDGE COMPUTING

Edge computing is a strategic deployment approach aimed at optimising performance, cost efficiency, responsiveness and compliance. It involves distributing computational resources and data processing closer to where data originates – such as near end-users, sensors or IoT devices. It is particularly beneficial as a deployment model for digital solutions when:

- low latency and real-time responsiveness are critical;
- applications must handle high volumes of localised data efficiently;

---

66 New instance refers to a new execution environment that a cloud provider must initialise when a serverless function is invoked after a period of inactivity. This involves allocating resources, loading dependencies and setting up the runtime environment.

67 Multi-tenant refers to a cloud computing model where multiple users or organisations share the same underlying infrastructure, resources and services, while the cloud provider ensures isolation, security and performance for each tenant.

68 Stateless means that each function runs independently without remembering previous activity, so any data must be stored externally. In contrast, a stateful application keeps data or session information between uses, enabling it to remember and maintain continuity over time.

- bandwidth limitations make transmitting large data volumes to centralised locations impractical or expensive; or

- compliance and security concerns require local data processing and storage.

Edge computing deployments exhibit the following key characteristics:

- **Proximity to data sources**: Computing resources are positioned close to data sources or end-users to significantly reduce latency, enabling rapid data processing and real-time decision-making.

- **Bandwidth optimisation**: Network traffic and bandwidth usage is minimised by processing data locally, which reduces transmission volumes and associated costs.

- **Scalability and distributed architecture**: Edge computing infrastructure is geographically distributed near data-collection points, enabling flexible expansion and decentralised placement of computing resources to efficiently manage increasing data volumes and workloads.

Advantages and disadvantages of edge computing

Edge computing offers the following benefits:

- **Improved reliability and availability**: Edge computing enhances resilience, enabling digital solutions to remain operational and responsive even during disruptions or intermittent connectivity with centralised servers or cloud environments.

- **Low latency**: Positioning computing resources close to the data source or end-users minimises the delay in data processing and communication, enabling rapid and real-time responses.

- **Reduced network traffic**: Processing data locally minimises the volume of data transmitted across networks, resulting in lower bandwidth consumption, cost savings and improved performance.

- **Enhanced security and privacy**: Processing and storing sensitive data locally reduces exposure during transmission, enabling organisations to meet strict regulatory obligations and data sovereignty requirements more effectively.

- **Reduced operational costs**: Lower bandwidth and cloud usage result in cost savings for data-intensive operations.

- **Flexibility and scalability**: Edge computing provides a flexible and decentralised infrastructure that can efficiently handle increasing data volumes and workloads, enabling organisations to easily scale and adapt resources across distributed locations as business needs evolve.

Edge computing also has some challenges:

- **Complexity of management**: Managing a distributed infrastructure can increase complexity and maintenance demands, as it requires continuous monitoring, security management and coordination across multiple locations.

- **Higher initial costs**: Edge computing requires a significant up-front investment in distributed hardware and infrastructure across multiple locations, leading to higher initial costs compared to centralised cloud solutions.

- **Limited computing resources**: Edge devices typically have limited processing power, storage and capacity compared to centralised cloud data centres, which can affect performance for resource-intensive applications.

- **Security challenges**: The increased number of distributed endpoints in edge computing increases the potential attack surface,[69] making robust security measures essential to safeguard data, devices and networks from potential threats.

- **Integration effort**: Integrating edge solutions with existing IT infrastructure, cloud services and legacy systems can be complex, often requiring significant effort, expertise and the use of middleware, APIs and specialised configurations.

FACTORS AFFECTING THE CHOICE OF DEPLOYMENT APPROACH

Selecting an appropriate deployment approach depends on multiple factors, including business requirements, technical constraints and operational goals. This choice typically involves balancing cost, security, scalability, performance, compliance and ease of maintenance.

Hybrid deployments are popular because they offer flexibility and control by combining the strengths of cloud-based and on-premises solutions. However, the growing adoption of cloud-based, serverless and containerised solutions highlights an industry-wide shift towards more agile and efficient deployment methodologies. Despite this trend, on-premises deployments remain highly relevant, particularly for industries with strict security and compliance needs.

Organisations should carefully evaluate the following factors to ensure their deployment strategy aligns effectively with their business objectives and technical capabilities:

Scalability and performance	Consideration should be given to whether the solution requires dynamic scaling or needs to handle high traffic loads. Cloud-based, containerised and serverless deployments provide 'elastic' scalability, making them ideal for variable workloads. In contrast, on-premises solutions offer controlled scalability but typically require manual intervention to scale resources.
Geographical and latency considerations	Edge computing is particularly beneficial for low-latency applications, such as IoT devices and gaming, due to its proximity to end-users and rapid processing capabilities. Similarly, cloud-based content delivery networks effectively reduce latency for globally distributed users. On-premises deployments are best suited for localised processing, especially where strict data residency regulations[70] apply. Applications demanding low latency and high-speed processing typically gain the greatest advantage from edge computing or on-premises hosting rather than cloud-based solutions.

---

69 An attack surface is the total set of points in a system – such as software, hardware or network interfaces – where an attacker could try to gain unauthorised access or extract data.

70 Data residency regulations are laws that require certain data to be stored and processed within specific geographic or national boundaries.

Security and compliance	Industries with strict regulatory and compliance requirements, such as healthcare, finance and government, must carefully consider data residency and sovereignty laws when choosing a deployment approach. On-premises or hybrid deployments often provide greater control over sensitive data, ensuring compliance with security and privacy regulations. While cloud providers offer robust security measures and compliance certifications, organisations must verify encryption, access controls and regulatory adherence to mitigate risks. Hybrid and multi-cloud strategies offer flexibility but require careful integration to maintain compliance across environments. In some cases, data sovereignty laws may limit cloud adoption, making on-premises or hybrid solutions the preferred choice for ensuring legal and regulatory alignment.
Reliability, uptime and disaster recovery	Cloud-based deployments typically include built-in redundancy, failover capabilities and backup features, enabling effective disaster recovery without additional infrastructure. In contrast, on-premises deployments generally require dedicated backup systems and explicit disaster recovery plans to achieve similar resilience. Multi-cloud or hybrid approaches further enhance reliability by distributing workloads across multiple environments, reducing dependence on any single platform.
Integration with existing systems	Consideration should be given to how well the deployment approach integrates with legacy systems and third-party tools. Hybrid cloud deployments are particularly advantageous, enabling organisations to transition gradually by connecting cloud capabilities with existing on-premises infrastructure. Achieving seamless integration often requires APIs and middleware to ensure compatibility and efficient communication between new and legacy systems.
Development and deployment speed	Containerised architectures and serverless solutions facilitate rapid deployment and seamless integration with CI/CD pipelines, especially in cloud-based, DevOps-enabled environments. Conversely, on-premises deployments often involve longer set-up periods and manual configurations, making them less optimal when rapid deployment and CI/CD automation are high priorities. Therefore, organisations prioritising speed, automation and DevOps compatibility typically benefit most from cloud-based or containerised deployments.
Maintenance and IT expertise	Organisations with mature IT teams are typically well equipped to manage on-premises deployments effectively, whereas those with limited in-house expertise often prefer cloud-based or managed services, as these offload maintenance tasks to cloud providers. Serverless solutions go further by eliminating infrastructure management entirely, enabling organisations to focus solely on development. Consequently, enterprises with dedicated IT resources may choose on-premises or hybrid deployments, leveraging internal expertise, while others benefit from the reduced operational overhead offered by cloud-based and serverless options.

Customisation and control	When selecting a deployment approach, organisations must balance customisation needs with control over infrastructure and data. On-premises and private cloud deployments offer maximum control, enabling tailored configurations, security policies and compliance adherence, but require significant management effort. Similarly, containerised solutions provide flexibility while maintaining control. In contrast, public cloud and serverless solutions reduce maintenance and offer scalability but may impose vendor constraints that limit customisation. Hybrid and multi-cloud models strike a balance, enabling organisations to manage critical workloads while benefiting from cloud flexibility. Ultimately, the choice depends on customisation requirements, regulatory obligations and the organisation's capacity to manage infrastructure effectively.
Vendor lock-in and flexibility	Cloud-native services like AWS Lambda and Azure Functions can lead to vendor lock-in due to their proprietary nature. In contrast, hybrid and multi-cloud strategies offer greater flexibility and reduce reliance on a single provider but require additional integration and management efforts. Open-source solutions provide maximum independence but demand in-house management and maintenance, adding to operational complexity.
Future growth and technology roadmap	An important consideration, often overlooked when choosing a deployment approach, is future growth and technological advancements to ensure long-term scalability and adaptability. Cloud-based and containerised solutions offer flexibility for integrating emerging technologies such as AI, big data and IoT, while on-premises deployments may require significant upgrades to support these capabilities. A scalable architecture is essential for handling increasing workloads efficiently, and hybrid or multi-cloud strategies provide agility for gradual transitions and innovation. Ultimately, the deployment model should align with the organisation's evolving technology needs, supporting modernisation and long-term sustainability.
Cost and budget constraints	Consideration of the total cost of ownership (TCO), including infrastructure, licensing, maintenance and operational expenses is essential when selecting the most appropriate deployment option. On-premises deployments require significant up-front investment in hardware and infrastructure, while cloud-based and serverless solutions operate on a pay-as-you-go basis, reducing initial costs but potentially leading to variable expenses. Hybrid and multi-cloud strategies can help to balance cost efficiency by combining on-premises control with cloud scalability. Additional factors such as licensing fees, data transfer costs and operational overhead must also be considered. Ultimately, the chosen approach should align with budget constraints while supporting long-term technological needs.

DEPLOYMENT APPROACHES AND ITIL

The deployment approaches discussed above align with the Information Technology Infrastructure Library (ITIL)[71] by supporting key IT service management (ITSM) principles, including service management, efficiency and continual improvement. Each deployment model impacts ITIL processes differently:

- **On-premises deployment** provides greater control and aligns with ITIL's focus on governance and security.
- **Cloud and hybrid deployments** enhance service agility, scalability and cost management.
- **Containerised deployment** supports ITIL's principles of automation, CD and service resilience.
- **Serverless deployment** accelerates service delivery by minimising operational overhead and enabling dynamic resource allocation.

By integrating ITIL best practices, organisations can ensure that their chosen deployment model aligns with ITIL concepts such as the Service Value System (SVS), the Four Dimensions Model, and key practices like Service Design, Change Enablement, Service Operations, and Continual Improvement – resulting in better ITSM, enhanced user experience and efficient resource utilisation. ITIL is discussed further in Chapter 11.

DEPLOYMENT APPROACHES AND VERISM

The deployment approaches introduced above also align with VeriSM[72] by supporting its focus on flexible, value-driven and service-oriented IT management. VeriSM emphasises a holistic approach to service management, integrating different technologies and methodologies to meet business objectives:

- **On-premises deployment** aligns with VeriSM's emphasis on governance and risk management.
- **Cloud and hybrid deployments** support agility, scalability and service optimisation.
- **Containerised deployment** enhances automation, DevOps practices and rapid service delivery.
- **Serverless deployment** streamlines service management by reducing infrastructure complexity and enabling dynamic resource scaling.

By leveraging VeriSM's management mesh, organisations can select and combine the most suitable deployment models to drive innovation, efficiency and continual improvement, ensuring IT services align with business goals and customer expectations.

---

71 ITIL is a globally recognised framework for ITSM that provides best practices for delivering efficient, reliable and customer-centric IT services while aligning with business objectives.

72 VeriSM is a flexible service management approach that integrates various frameworks, methodologies and technologies to help organisations deliver value-driven, customer-focused IT and digital services while adapting to evolving business needs.

DEPLOYMENT APPROACHES AND DEVOPS

DevOps (see Chapter 4) is not itself a deployment approach, but is integral to all deployment approaches. It bridges the gap between development (Dev) and IT operations (Ops), streamlining software delivery through practices such as CI, CD, automation, collaboration and rapid feedback. These practices greatly enhance the speed, consistency and reliability of software deployments. Every deployment approach benefits from DevOps through increased automation, accelerated release cycles, reduced complexity and stronger collaboration between development and operations teams. Containerised, cloud and serverless deployments particularly align with DevOps due to their inherent flexibility, automation and programmability.

Continuous integration and continuous deployment

Continuous integration involves regularly merging code changes – often multiple times per day – into a central repository, triggering automated builds and tests to promptly identify and fix integration problems. This ensures the codebase remains stable and functional. Continuous deployment builds on CI by automatically releasing tested and validated code changes directly to production environments without manual steps, enabling quicker and more reliable deployments.

CI and CD together create a cohesive pipeline: CI maintains code quality and stability through frequent automated testing, while CD automates delivering these verified updates. This unified approach accelerates software delivery, provides rapid feedback and improves reliability, consistency and efficiency across all deployment methods. The specific ways CI/CD practices are applied vary according to the unique characteristics and demands of each deployment approach, as outlined below:

- **On-premises deployment**: CI/CD enhances traditional on-premises deployments by automating software builds, testing and deployments within internal data centres, improving reliability and consistency and reducing manual intervention, though constrained by physical infrastructure limitations.

- **Cloud deployment**: CI/CD seamlessly integrates with cloud platforms to enable scalable, flexible and rapid software updates. Automated provisioning (setting up and configuring IT infrastructure and resources) and infrastructure as code facilitate quicker deployments, increased agility and easier rollback capabilities.

- **Hybrid deployment**: CI/CD simplifies the complexity of hybrid setups (combining cloud and on-premises resources), facilitating consistent software delivery across mixed environments. Automated pipelines ensure synchronised deployments, reducing discrepancies between environments.

- **Containerised deployment**: CI/CD pipelines support containerised applications by automating container builds, testing and tagging,[73] and deployments to orchestration platforms such as Kubernetes or Docker Swarm. This ensures rapid, consistent and portable application releases across diverse environments.

---

[73] Tagging refers to assigning version labels or identifiers to container images, helping to track and manage different builds for deployment and rollback purposes.

- **Serverless deployment**: CI/CD effectively manages frequent deployments of microservices or functions in serverless environments, enabling automated testing, packaging, versioning and deployment directly into provider-managed infrastructure, such as AWS Lambda and Azure Functions. This facilitates rapid, iterative development without infrastructure overhead.

- **Edge computing**: CI/CD helps to manage the complexity of distributed edge deployments by automating updates and deployments to devices and edge nodes. This ensures consistent, reliable software releases across decentralised locations, despite limited connectivity or varying infrastructure conditions.

9 PREPARING FOR DEPLOYMENT

INTRODUCTION

Preparing for the deployment of a new digital solution requires careful planning to ensure a smooth transition to live operation. This transition goes beyond technical implementation (the focus of the previous chapter) and encompasses the people, processes and organisational elements (e.g. capabilities, resources and culture) that are essential to a smooth transition.

This chapter introduces a process for successful deployment and explores each stage from planning to post-deployment support, review and optimisation.

THE DEPLOYMENT PROCESS

The process shown in Figure 9.1 offers a structured framework for transitioning to a new or updated digital solution. It ensures the solution is properly prepared, thoroughly tested and effectively adopted by users, while minimising disruption to business operations and aiding the realisation of business goals and benefits.

Figure 9.1 The digital solution deployment process

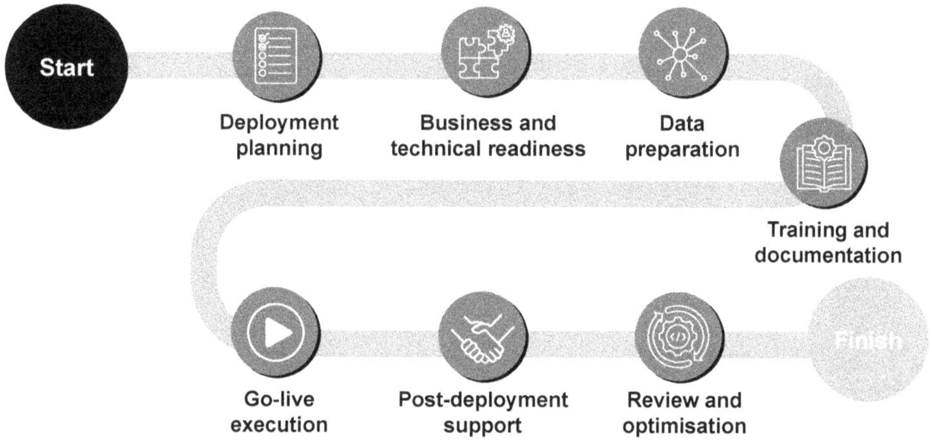

Start

Deployment planning

Business and technical readiness

Data preparation

Training and documentation

Go-live execution

Post-deployment support

Review and optimisation

Finish

Deployment planning	Deployment planning involves defining clear goals, timelines, resources and responsibilities, while also establishing risk management and rollback strategies. It includes coordinating stakeholders to align expectations and ensure the organisation is prepared for the upcoming changes.
Business and technical readiness	**Business readiness** Business readiness ensures that people, processes and organisational resources are effectively aligned to support the transition to a new digital solution. This involves updating business processes to align with the new system, defining and developing appropriate training provision for stakeholders, clearly communicating changes and ensuring that support and governance structures are firmly in place. **Technical readiness** Technical readiness involves setting up and verifying infrastructure and environments, configuring systems and integrations and conducting security checks, compliance reviews and final testing to ensure the solution is stable and ready for deployment.
Data preparation	Data preparation involves creating essential system data such as user profiles and configuration settings, migrating relevant information from legacy systems and validating all data for accuracy, completeness and consistency.
Training and documentation	This stage involves delivering role-specific training to users and support teams, along with preparing documentation and support resources to ensure effective use and adoption of the digital solution.
Go-live execution	This stage involves finalising data migration – potentially including a data freeze – deploying the solution to the production environment and closely monitoring system performance and user activity to ensure a smooth transition.
Post-deployment support	This penultimate stage includes the provision of a helpdesk and technical assistance, monitoring system performance, resolving issues and gathering user feedback to make any necessary improvements.
Review and optimisation	The final stage of the process focuses on evaluating the success of the deployment against its objectives, identifying lessons learned and areas for improvement, and planning for ongoing updates, support and continued user engagement.

Deployment planning

Deployment planning involves clearly defining the goals, timelines, resources and responsibilities required to deliver a digital solution. A well-structured plan not only supports a smooth transition to live operations, but also includes rollback strategies to address any unexpected issues, helping to minimise disruption and support successful adoption. It should outline key activities, assign the necessary resources and set realistic timelines to ensure effective implementation.

Typical components of a deployment plan include:

1. Introduction and objectives:
   - purpose of the deployment plan;
   - scope and key objectives;
   - expected benefits and success criteria.

2. Deployment strategy:
   - deployment approach (see Chapter 8);
   - changeover strategy (see Chapter 10);
   - key deployment milestones and timelines;
   - deployment locations and affected business areas.

3. Roles and responsibilities:
   - deployment team members and their roles;
   - key stakeholders and decision-makers;
   - responsibilities for execution, monitoring and issue resolution.

4. Infrastructure and technical readiness:
   - hardware, software and network requirements;
   - system compatibility and integrations;
   - data migration and backup plans.

5. Testing and validation:
   - pre-deployment testing (unit, integration, system and UAT);
   - performance testing and security checks;
   - post-deployment validation and monitoring.

6. Business readiness and training:
   - the People, Organisation, Processes, Information, and Technology (POPIT), Customer Product Process Organisation Location Data Application Technology (CPPOLDAT) and McKinsey's 7S models described below provide useful frameworks for undertaking a business readiness assessment as part of a business change initiative;
   - training plans for end-users and support teams;

- change management strategies (e.g. Kurt Lewin's model – see Chapter 10);
- user guides, documentation and knowledge transfer.

7. Risk management and contingency plans:
   - identification of potential risks and impact assessment;
   - mitigation strategies and contingency planning;
   - rollback strategy in case of deployment failure.

8. Communication plan:
   - internal and external communication strategies;
   - stakeholder engagement and updates;
   - escalation process for issues and decision-making.

9. Post-deployment support and maintenance:
   - monitoring and performance evaluation;
   - incident management and troubleshooting;
   - ongoing support and solution enhancements.

10. Success metrics and review:
    - key performance indicators to measure success;
    - feedback collection and lessons learned;
    - plan for continual improvements.

Business readiness

Business readiness refers to an organisation's ability to successfully adopt and operate a new digital solution by aligning people, processes, information and other organisational resources to support the change. This includes training users, updating business processes, communicating changes effectively and establishing appropriate support and governance structures. Ensuring business readiness is crucial to maximise user adoption, minimise disruption and realise the expected benefits of the solution.

Prior to deployment, a business readiness assessment should be conducted to evaluate the organisation's preparedness for adopting the new solution. This assessment identifies potential gaps and actions needed for a smooth transition, examining factors such as stakeholder alignment, workforce readiness, process modifications, change management strategies and operational capacity. It also considers governance, risk and compliance to help anticipate challenges and support successful implementation. Ultimately, the goal is to ensure that the organisation is fully prepared – technically, operationally and culturally – to maximise the effectiveness and long-term success of the digital solution.

There are a range of business analysis frameworks that can help to consider business readiness in a holistic way. Three such frameworks are briefly described below. Further details, and additional techniques that can be used during business change deployment, can be obtained from the BCS book *Business Analysis Techniques: 123 Essentials Tools for Success* (Cadle et al., 2021).

POPIT model

The POPIT model (introduced in *Defining Digital Solutions* and reproduced in Figure 9.2) helps to assess business readiness for implementing a new digital solution by providing a holistic view of the key factors that influence successful adoption. Each element of the model highlights specific areas (discussed below) that must be evaluated to ensure a smooth transition. By systematically addressing each element of the POPIT model, organisations can identify risks, resolve gaps and build a comprehensive readiness strategy that ensures a smooth and successful transition to the new digital solution.

Figure 9.2 The POPIT model (© Assist Knowledge Development Ltd)

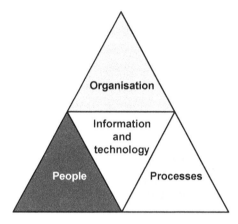

People	People-related considerations include user adoption, skills gaps, training needs and resistance to change. Organisations must assess whether employees and stakeholders have the necessary knowledge and engagement to use the new solution effectively, identifying areas where training and support are required. Effective change management is crucial to addressing concerns, promoting engagement and ensuring a positive transition. Employees may experience a range of emotions during organisational change, and failing to acknowledge this can increase resistance and undermine the initiative, potentially leading to failure. Assessing workload impact, clear communication, leadership support and stakeholder involvement help to set expectations and ease the transition.
Organisation	Organisational considerations include leadership alignment, governance structures, cultural readiness and regulatory compliance. Strong leadership support is essential to drive adoption, set expectations and allocate resources. Organisations must ensure that existing policies, decision-making frameworks and compliance requirements align with the new solution to mitigate risks. Cultural readiness plays a crucial role, as resistance to change can hinder implementation. Clearly defining roles, responsibilities and accountability facilitates a structured transition, while assessing the organisation's capacity to manage change ensures the necessary support structures are in place for successful integration.

Processes   Process-related considerations involve assessing the impact of a new digital solution on existing workflows and ensuring any necessary changes align with business objectives. Organisations must evaluate whether current processes can integrate with the new solution or whether they require optimisation to improve efficiency. While automation is often a key driver for digital transformation, it is crucial to ensure that the new solution enhances processes without introducing new challenges, such as bottlenecks. Managing process dependencies effectively can also help to minimise disruptions during the transition.

                     Clear documentation and well-defined standard operating procedures promote consistency and user adoption, and ensure employees understand and adapt to revised workflows, which is essential for a smooth transition and long-term operational success.

Information   Information-related considerations focus on the data and information captured, recorded and used by the organisation, and include data quality, security, accessibility and compliance. Organisations must ensure their data is accurate, well-structured and compatible with the new solution for seamless integration. A carefully planned data migration strategy helps to prevent loss, duplication or corruption during the transition. Security measures such as encryption and access controls are essential for protecting sensitive information and meeting regulatory requirements. Additionally, organisations should assess how data is stored, shared and managed to support business processes, while ensuring users have reliable, up-to-date information. Aligning with existing information management frameworks helps to maintain consistency and compliance.

Technology   Technology-related considerations include system compatibility, infrastructure needs, scalability, security and ongoing maintenance. These issues were discussed in the previous chapter as factors influencing the choice of deployment approach.

                     Organisations must determine whether the new solution integrates with existing IT systems and if upgrades or additional resources are necessary. Ensuring scalability is essential for supporting future growth and evolving business needs. Security measures, such as data protection, access controls and cybersecurity protocols, must be in place to mitigate risks. Additionally, organisations should evaluate their IT support capabilities for deployment, monitoring and maintenance to ensure the long-term stability and performance of the solution.

McKinsey 7S model

The McKinsey 7S model (Waterman et al., 1980; Peters and Waterman, 1982) is a strategic framework that helps organisations to assess and align key internal factors for effective change management and business performance. It consists of seven interrelated elements that identify areas to consider when preparing for change: strategy, structure, systems, shared values, skills, style and staff. These are categorised into hard elements (strategy, structure, systems) and soft elements (shared values, skills, style, staff). The lines that connect the elements represent interconnections that also need to be considered.

By analysing these seven elements, organisations can identify misalignments and make necessary adjustments to improve performance, drive change and achieve strategic goals. Where there is misalignment between areas, such as strategy and skills, the change programme is likely to be adversely affected.

Figure 9.3 shows an updated version of the original model that identifies 'shared values' as the central element – the original version identified this as 'superordinate goals'.

Figure 9.3 7S model (Source: After Waterman et al., 1980)

| Shared values | Shared values, also known as superordinate goals, form the fundamental principles, concepts, values and beliefs that unify, drive and motivate the organisation or business area. They influence decision-making, employee behaviour and corporate identity. Strong shared values promote a positive work environment, alignment with business goals and commitment to organisational success. |

| Strategy | Strategy refers to an organisation's long-term plan to achieve its business objectives and gain a competitive advantage – the approach to be taken by the organisation or business area to achieve its stated mission and objectives over the medium to longer term. It defines the direction, priorities and key initiatives needed for success, ensuring alignment with market trends, customer needs and internal capabilities. A well-crafted strategy guides decision-making and resource allocation while responding to changes in the external environment or internal business drivers. Organisations develop and refine their strategy to strengthen their market position and adapt to evolving challenges and opportunities. |

Structure   Structure represents the organisational hierarchy, roles and reporting relationships. It defines how authority and responsibilities are distributed, whether through a centralised, decentralised or matrix model. An effective structure ensures clear communication, efficient workflows and effective coordination between teams.

Systems   Systems encompass the processes, procedures, data and technologies that define an organisation's working practices and support its daily operations. This includes IT infrastructure, performance measurement tools and operational workflows. Well-designed systems improve efficiency, facilitate automation and ensure the successful execution of business strategies.

Style   Style refers to the leadership approach and management culture within an organisation, shaping decision-making, employee motivation and team collaboration. The leadership style adopted by senior managers plays a crucial role in influencing employee engagement, promoting innovation and shaping the overall corporate environment.

Staff   Staff refers to the employees within an organisation, including their roles, development and overall workforce management. This encompasses hiring, training, performance evaluation and succession planning to ensure the right people are in place to support business objectives. A well-structured workforce strategy enhances productivity, promotes growth and ensures long-term business sustainability.

Skills   Skills encompass the collective expertise, capabilities and competencies of the workforce. Organisations must evaluate whether their employees have the necessary skills to execute business strategies and adopt new digital solutions effectively. Investing in upskilling, training and talent development is crucial for maintaining a competitive edge and adapting to evolving business needs. This element also considers the broader organisational capabilities required for sustained success.

CPPOLDAT

An alternative to the POPIT and McKinsey 7S models is the CPPOLDAT framework, which similarly supports organisations in assessing key factors that influence the successful implementation and adoption of business change. By examining its eight key elements, organisations can identify gaps, mitigate risks and develop a comprehensive readiness plan to ensure a smooth transition and maximise the success of digital transformation initiatives. Some of the key considerations for each element are:

Customer   Have the customers been identified and have relevant communications been made to them?

Product   Is the product ready for deployment? How will it be deployed (e.g. incrementally or in a 'big bang')?

Process   Does the change align with the organisation's processes and have changed processes been documented and communicated?

Organisation   Is reorganisation or changes in people's roles required?

Location   Are employees working on-site, remotely or in a hybrid setup, and how should the change approach reflect that? Are teams in one location or spread across regions or time zones, and how will this impact coordination and communication? Does each location have the infrastructure needed to support the change? What cultural differences might affect how the change is received? Are there local laws or compliance requirements that must be addressed?

Data   Is the organisation's data in a fit state for migration and/or have arrangements been made for initial data capture?

Application   Do the changes align with the organisation's applications architecture? Are any alterations required to that?

Technology   Is the change in line with the infrastructure architecture and is the required technology available?

Critical activities in preparing an organisation for deployment

The following activities help to ensure that an organisation is informed, equipped and ready to adopt a new digital solution:

- **Change impact assessment**: Identifying how the new solution will impact roles, workflows and responsibilities across the organisation is essential for managing change effectively. Understanding these effects early enables organisations to plan targeted communication, training and support, helping to ease the transition, reduce resistance and support successful adoption of the solution.

- **Risk assessment**: Identifying potential issues that could impact the success of a digital solution deployment – such as system failures, user resistance or data security threats – is essential for effective risk management. By evaluating the likelihood and impact of technical, operational and business risks, and putting in place effective mitigation, contingency and rollback plans, organisations can minimise disruptions, enable a smoother deployment and improve overall readiness and resilience.

- **Process alignment**: Reviewing and updating business processes to align with the capabilities and workflows of the new digital solution is essential for a smooth deployment. This ensures that operations run efficiently, minimises disruptions and helps the organisation to realise the full value of the solution.

- **Readiness reviews**: Readiness reviews are formal checkpoints conducted before deploying a digital solution to confirm that all technical, business and operational components are fully prepared. They help to ensure that environments are correctly set up, teams are trained, processes are aligned and risks are managed. These reviews are essential for confirming that both the digital solution and the organisation are prepared for a smooth transition to new ways of working.

- **Stakeholder engagement**: It is crucial to engage key individuals and groups – those affected by or influential in the deployment of a digital solution – early in the process. Involving stakeholders from the start helps to build support, address concerns, gather valuable feedback and ensure alignment with business objectives. This collaborative approach enhances buy-in, reduces resistance to change and contributes to a smoother and more successful deployment.

- **Communication and coordination**: Clearly communicating the solution's purpose, benefits and impact helps to manage expectations, reduce uncertainty and build support across the organisation. At the same time, strong coordination ensures that tasks are well-organised, responsibilities are understood and teams – including business stakeholders, developers and operations – are aligned and working together.

- **Training and documentation**: Providing training sessions, user guides and helpdesk support equips users with the knowledge and skills needed to use the new digital solution effectively. Well-designed training builds confidence, reduces errors and supports user adoption. Clear, accessible documentation provides ongoing guidance and reference, helping users to adapt more easily. Together, training and documentation play a key role in ensuring a smooth and successful transition to the new solution. See below for further details.

- **User acceptance testing (UAT)**: UAT involves engaging end-users to test the digital solution with real-world scenarios to ensure it meets their needs, and performs as expected. This process helps to confirm the solution is fit for purpose, builds user confidence and identifies any remaining issues before deployment.

- **Post-implementation support**: Ensuring users have the necessary help and resources once a digital solution is live is essential for a smooth transition. Post-implementation support includes technical assistance, troubleshooting and ongoing guidance to resolve issues, answer user questions and maintain system performance. This support helps users to adapt, encourages continued adoption and contributes to the long-term success of the solution.

Technical readiness

Technical readiness ensures that all systems, infrastructure, environments and tools are fully prepared and operating as expected before deployment begins. It is a vital part of any deployment strategy, helping to reduce the risk of failures, minimise downtime and enable a smooth transition to live operational use – ultimately supporting a successful and stable rollout.

Typical technical readiness activities include:

- **Infrastructure setup and verification**: Preparing and validating the necessary hardware, software, network components and cloud resources is an essential part of technical readiness prior to deploying a digital solution. This involves provisioning servers, configuring networks, setting up databases and confirming that all components meet the required specifications. A well-prepared infrastructure ensures the deployment environment is stable, secure and capable of supporting the solution's performance, availability and scalability needs. Thorough setup and verification help to minimise the risk of technical issues during deployment.

- **Automated provisioning**: Infrastructure-as-code (IaC) tools or scripts enable the automatic deployment of infrastructure and the configuration and management of resources, ensuring a consistent and reliable setup.

- **Configuration management**: Managing infrastructure and application configurations with standardised settings and version control ensures consistency across environments, supporting a reliable and uniform deployment process.

- **Code freeze and final builds**: Locking down code changes and generating final, production-ready builds or packages helps to ensure a stable and predictable deployment. Freezing the codebase enables teams to test and validate a fixed version of the software, reducing the risk of last-minute defects or inconsistencies. Producing a final build also guarantees that the version being deployed has been thoroughly tested and approved, and is fully prepared for production. This minimises the chance of unexpected issues during deployment and confirms that all quality, security and performance standards have been met, enabling a smooth and controlled transition to the live environment.

- **Security and compliance checks**: Conducting vulnerability scans, access control audits and compliance checks helps to ensure the digital solution is secure and meets legal, regulatory and organisational standards before it goes live.

- **Data migration and validation**: Preparing and verifying data migration processes, ensuring accuracy and integrity. Data creation and migration are discussed further below.

- **Testing and validation**: Verifying that the digital solution integrates seamlessly with existing systems and services is a key part of testing and validation (see Chapter 6). This process ensures the solution functions correctly, performs as expected and meets quality, security and compliance standards. It involves a combination of automated and manual testing – including functional, integration, performance, security and acceptance tests – to identify and resolve issues before deployment and ensure the solution is ready for production.

- **Backup and recovery planning**: Configuring data backups and establishing clear rollback or recovery strategies helps to ensure that critical data and system settings can be restored if a failure occurs during or after deployment. This is vital for minimising downtime, preventing data loss and enabling rapid recovery, all of which contribute to the stability and resilience of the digital solution.

- **Monitoring and logging setup**: Implementing tools for real-time monitoring, logging and alerting during and after deployment is crucial for quickly identifying and resolving issues, ensuring system performance and maintaining visibility into the health and behaviour of the digital solution. These tools help teams to respond proactively to problems, minimise downtime and support ongoing stability and reliability.

- **User access and permissions configuration**: Setting up user access and permissions before deployment ensures that each user has the access to systems, data and features required to conduct their role effectively. Effective access management (which includes advising users about passwords, multifactor authentication and ensuring any necessary security software is installed) enhances security, prevents unauthorised access, reduces the risk of data breaches and supports smooth operations after deployment by enabling users to work efficiently without unnecessary restrictions or exposure.

Data preparation

Data preparation is a critical stage in the digital solution deployment process, ensuring the new system is populated with accurate, complete and well-structured data to enable effective operation from day one. It involves both creating essential new data and migrating existing data from legacy systems to support a smooth and reliable transition.

Data creation

Data creation involves generating or inputting the foundational data a digital solution needs to operate effectively from the moment it goes live. Without this essential data, the solution may not function as intended, potentially causing operational errors, delays, a poor user experience or even software failures.

Data creation typically includes:

- **setting up user accounts** with appropriate roles and permissions;
- **configuring system settings** such as workflows, preferences or defaults;
- **entering reference data** such as product lists, service categories or organisational structures; and
- **creating content or templates** needed for the system to operate (e.g. emails, forms or dashboards).

A critical factor in successful data creation is timing. Effective timing of data creation is essential. It should occur after the system is stable enough to support it, but early enough to enable thorough testing and user training – striking the right balance to support a smooth and successful deployment. Key considerations include:

- **Creating data too early**: If data is created too far in advance, it may become outdated or misaligned with evolving system configurations or business requirements. Early creation increases the risk of duplicate or inconsistent data if updates occur before the go-live date.

- **Creating data too late**: Delayed data creation can cause deployment bottlenecks, reduce time for testing and validation, and potentially delay the go-live date. It may leave insufficient time for training users with real or representative data.

- **Coordination with system configuration**: Data creation should align with the completion of system setup and configuration to ensure compatibility and avoid re-work.

- **Impact on testing**: Timing must allow for data to be available during UAT so users can validate functionality with real scenarios.

- **Phased or incremental creation**: In some cases, data can be created in phases, starting with essential elements and adding more as the deployment progresses, reducing risk and improving accuracy.

Data creation is typically carried out through a combination of manual entry, automated tools and system configuration processes. The specific approach depends on the nature of the data, the complexity of the system and the deployment strategy.

- **Manual entry** is used for small volumes of data or highly specific, organisation-defined content. It often applies to configuration settings, user roles, reference data or initial records, and requires careful planning and validation to avoid errors.

- **Automated scripts or tools** are commonly used to handle large or repetitive datasets. These scripts – often written in SQL, Python or platform-specific languages – automate the creation of records such as user accounts, departments or configuration templates. This approach helps to ensure consistency, reduces manual effort and saves time, particularly in large-scale deployments.

- **System configuration interfaces** are often included in set-up wizards or admin portals for entering foundational data. These enable administrators to input data directly into the system through user-friendly interfaces.

- **Templates and import functions**, often provided as comma separated values (CSV) or Excel files with the solution, enable users to enter data in a structured format and import it directly into the system. This approach is commonly used to load information such as user accounts, configuration settings and product lists efficiently and accurately.

- **Automated data take-on** may be achievable when the digital solution integrates with existing systems. In such cases, data can be automatically retrieved from or synchronised with these connected systems, helping to reduce duplication and maintain consistency across systems.

Regardless of the method, created data should be tested in staging or test environments to ensure it works as expected, prior to the go-live date.

Additional considerations include:

- **Relevance and accuracy**: It is essential that all created data is accurate, complete and relevant to the solution's intended use and business processes.

- **Data structure and format**: Data should be aligned with the required formats, fields and relationships defined within the data design for the new solution, to avoid compatibility issues.

- **Scalability and future use**: Consideration should be given to how the created data will support future growth or system updates to avoid limitations down the line.

- **Testing and validation**: The created data should be validated to ensure that it supports intended functionality, and that the functionality behaves correctly using the data.

- **Documentation**: Records should be maintained of how and why data was created, including sources and standards used, to support governance and troubleshooting.

- **Security and compliance**: Sensitive or regulated data should be managed carefully, ensuring compliance with data protection and privacy regulations.

- **Alignment with business processes**: Data should be created to align with and support updated business processes, facilitating smooth user adoption.

Data migration

Data migration involves transferring existing data from legacy systems or other sources into the new solution. This includes extracting, cleaning, transforming and loading data to ensure it is accurate and compatible. Effective data migration maintains business continuity and ensures that historical data remains accessible and usable.

As with data creation, timing is critical when migrating data from legacy systems to a new digital solution. Careful planning and scheduling help to ensure data integrity and accuracy while minimising disruption. By managing the timing effectively, organisations can reduce risks and support a smooth and successful transition. Key considerations include:

- **The scope of the migration work**: This involves determining how much data needs to be transferred to the new system, including decisions on which data entities (tables) should be migrated. For example, whether to migrate all customers or just the active ones, or those active in the past six months. Additionally, a decision needs to be made whether full historical data is required to support operational use. For example, whether all historical address changes for a customer are needed or just the most recent one.

- **Alignment with deployment schedule**: Data migration should be timed to align with technical readiness and go-live plans, ensuring that the new solution is populated with current and validated data before launch.

- **System availability**: Data migration should be scheduled during periods of low activity or planned downtime to minimise the impact on ongoing business operations and reduce the risk of data loss or corruption.

- **Data freeze period**: Implementing a data freeze shortly before migration helps to prevent changes in the legacy system, which can lead to inconsistencies between the old and new environments.

- **User acceptance testing (UAT)**: Data migration must be timed so that the migrated data is available during UAT to enable end-users to validate the solution using realistic and meaningful data.

- **Contingency planning**: It is prudent to allow time in the schedule for unexpected delays, re-work or a rollback to the legacy system if issues arise during or after migration.

- **Incremental versus full migration**: When planning a data migration, it is important to decide whether to use a phased (incremental) approach or a single full migration. This choice should be guided by factors such as system complexity, the volume of data and the specific needs of the business.

- **Testing and validation**: It is essential to allocate sufficient time prior to go-live to test and validate the data in the new system for accuracy, completeness and compatibility. In practice, the testing often takes place as part of migration trials. The actual final migration event usually needs to keep within strict timescales and so validation based on criteria defined in advance should be all that is needed to approve the data for go-live. Validation could take the form of reports comparing new data values with legacy data values to ensure accuracy of all key data attributes.

Transferring data from legacy systems to a new digital solution requires a structured, multi-step process that typically uses a mix of automated tools, scripts and manual checks. Figure 9.4 shows a logical process that ensures a controlled, consistent and secure transition of data, enabling the new digital solution to operate effectively from day one.

Planning and assessment	The process starts by defining the scope, goals, timeline and resources needed for the data migration. This stage also involves identifying the data sources, types, volumes and dependencies and reviewing the source data for quality and compatibility with the new system.
Data mapping and design	During this stage, source data fields are mapped to their corresponding fields in the target system, and transformation rules are established for formatting, cleaning and restructuring the data. It is also important to design the migration architecture at this point, including the extract–transform–load (ETL) processes and the tools that will be used.
Data extraction	In this stage, data is extracted from the source systems using queries, scripts or export tools, ensuring it is retrieved securely and in the correct format for the next stages of the migration process.
Data cleaning and transformation	After extraction, the data is cleaned by removing duplicates, correcting errors and filling in missing values. It is then transformed to ensure it aligns with the structure and requirements of the target system. Cleansing may also take place in the legacy system ahead of extraction. This saves time during the go-live migration, where timescales are usually very tightly controlled.
Data loading	The transformed data is loaded into the target system, either all at once or in phases, using import tools, APIs or automated scripts to ensure accuracy and efficiency.
Testing and validation	Once loaded into the target system, the migrated data should be validated for accuracy, completeness and consistency. Functional testing and UAT should be carried out using the migrated data to ensure it performs as expected in the new environment.
Data freeze and final migration	Before performing the final migration prior to go-live execution (see later in this chapter), the source data should be frozen to prevent any changes. If needed, a final round of ETL should be carried out to ensure the most current data is accurately migrated.
Documentation and backup	In this penultimate stage, the entire process is documented, covering data mapping, transformation rules and procedures. Additionally, the source and migrated data is backed up to support recovery and audit requirements.

Figure 9.4 Data migration process

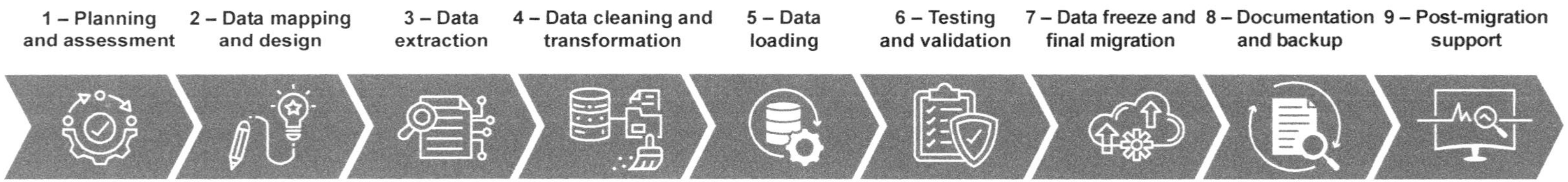

1 – Planning and assessment

2 – Data mapping and design

3 – Data extraction

4 – Data cleaning and transformation

5 – Data loading

6 – Testing and validation

7 – Data freeze and final migration

8 – Documentation and backup

9 – Post-migration support

Post-migration support

In the final stage of the data migration process, system performance and data integrity are monitored after go-live, and user support is provided to resolve any migration-related issues. This helps to ensure a smooth transition to the new digital solution and supports its continued reliability.

Not all stages shown in Figure 9.4 occur as separate, sequential steps. In practice, the process often begins with planning, followed by the development and documentation of ETL routines, testing of both the process and the data, and finally, the actual migration – which involves a data freeze and execution of the ETL. ETL routines are typically developed iteratively, with adjustments made as errors are identified, feedback is received or new business processes and data needs arise. Trial migrations help test the entire end-to-end process and are distinct from validating data quality. Once the data is frozen, a full ETL is performed. If the migration is undertaken in phases, each phase should include its own data freeze before the ETL is executed.

Training

Training plays a vital role in the successful deployment of a new digital solution. It ensures that users and key stakeholders are confident, capable and fully prepared to adopt the solution from day one. Well-planned training reduces resistance to change, minimises errors and supports a smooth organisational transition. By building user confidence and competence, training promotes quicker adoption of new tools and workflows and helps to ensure the long-term success and sustainability of the solution.

Various groups within the organisation need role-specific training tailored to their responsibilities:

- **End-users** need training to use the system effectively in their day-to-day tasks, with a focus on navigation, key features and how business processes are carried out in the new system, including any changes to existing workflows.

- **System administrators** need training in how to manage and maintain the system, focusing on configuration, user access management and troubleshooting.

- **Managers and supervisors** need training in how to support team adoption and monitor performance, with a focus on reporting tools, dashboards and overseeing and coaching their teams.

- **IT support staff** need training in how to provide technical assistance and resolve issues, focusing on system architecture, troubleshooting and escalation procedures.

- **Project and change management teams** need training in how to lead the transition and manage organisational change, with a focus on user engagement, communication and support planning.

- **Trainers** need training to deliver training to others (train the trainer), focusing on effective training delivery methods, user scenarios and system functionality.

A range of training methods are commonly used during the deployment of a new digital solution to support different learning needs and roles. These include:

- **Instructor-led training**: Classroom or virtual sessions led by a trainer to guide users through system features and tasks.

- **Hands-on workshops**: Interactive sessions where users practice real tasks in a test environment.

- **E-learning modules**: Self-paced online tutorials, videos or courses accessible at any time for flexible, independent study.

- **Quick reference guides**: Concise documents that provide step-by-step instructions for common tasks.

- **Webinars and live demos**: Online presentations to introduce system functions and answer user questions in real time.

Training is not only provided before go-live, but also reinforced with refresher and follow-up sessions after go-live to support learning, answer user questions and introduce any updates or changes.

Documentation

During the deployment of a new digital solution, various types of documentation are created to assist users, administrators and support teams. These materials help to ensure a clear and consistent understanding of the system, provide ongoing guidance and promote effective use. Common examples of documentation produced during the deployment stage of the digital solution life cycle include:

- **User guides** offer clear step-by-step instructions to help users navigate the system and make effective use of its key features.

- **Quick reference sheets** provide concise summaries of common tasks or processes for easy access.

- **Technical manuals** provide detailed guidance for system administrators and IT staff on system configuration, maintenance and troubleshooting.

- **Process documentation** explains how business processes are executed using the new system, highlighting any changes from previous workflows.

- **Frequently asked questions (FAQs)** provide answers to common user queries and are designed to address recurring concerns or issues effectively.

- **Training materials** include slide decks, handouts and e-learning content used to support training sessions. See *Training* above.

- **Release notes** are shared with users to summarise system updates, enhancements and bug fixes, keeping them informed about changes and ongoing improvements to the digital solution.

Go-live execution

Go-live execution is the point in the deployment process when the digital solution is released into the production environment for live, operational use, often through incremental or phased rollouts. It marks the shift from preparation to active operation and involves a series of carefully coordinated steps to ensure a smooth and successful launch:

- **Final data migration**: All data not already migrated must be transferred from the legacy systems to the new solution. This typically involves a data freeze beforehand to prevent further changes in the source systems and ensure the final dataset is accurate and up to date. If the data is likely to change right up to go-live, it's often simpler to migrate everything in one step rather than creating routines to handle only the delta (the data not yet migrated).

- **System deployment**: The solution is deployed to the production environment (see *Migrating software to a production environment* below), making it accessible to end-users. This may be done all at once or in phases, depending on the changeover strategy being adopted (see Chapter 10).

- **Monitoring and support**: During and immediately after go-live, the system is closely monitored to ensure it performs as expected. Key metrics such as system stability, performance and user activity are tracked.

- **Issue resolution**: A support team (sometimes referred to as 'floor walkers') is on standby to quickly respond to any issues that arise. This ensures minimal disruption to business operations and provides reassurance to users.

- **Communication and coordination**: Clear communication with users, stakeholders and support teams is essential to guide them through the transition and ensure everyone knows what to expect.

The success of the go-live stage depends on thorough planning, technical readiness, user training and strong coordination. A well-executed go-live ensures the solution is launched effectively and sets the stage for confident adoption and long-term success.

Migrating software to a production environment
During go-live execution, migrating software components to the production environment involves moving the final, tested version of the digital solution from the development or staging (pre-production) environment to the production environment, for live operational use. This ensures all components are correctly installed, configured and ready for end-users. The specific method used will vary depending on the chosen deployment approach (see Chapter 8), but typically includes the following steps:

1. **Final build packaging**: The latest version of the software – known as the production build – is packaged for deployment. This includes application files, media files, databases, configuration settings and any supporting services or libraries.

2. **Transfer to production environment**: The packaged components are deployed to production servers or cloud infrastructure using automated tools (e.g. CI/CD pipelines), deployment scripts or manual processes, depending on the organisation's setup. IaC may be used to ensure consistent environment setup.

3. **Configuration and integration**: Components are configured to match the production environment's settings, including database connections, service endpoints, authentication and security controls. Integrations with other systems (e.g. APIs, data feeds) are established and verified.

4. **Data synchronisation**: Any required data, such as configuration data or migrated legacy data, is loaded into the system. Legacy data migration can be carried out in phases, with a final migration typically scheduled during planned downtime or following a data freeze, to ensure consistency and accuracy.

5. **Validation and smoke testing**: After deployment, quick validation or 'smoke tests' are run to ensure key components are functioning correctly in the production environment.

6. **Activation and monitoring**: The system is activated for users, and performance is closely monitored to detect any issues early. Logging and alerting tools track errors, load and user activity.

Post-deployment support

Post-deployment support is a key stage in the digital solution deployment process that takes place after the solution goes live. It focuses on maintaining stability, resolving issues and providing ongoing user assistance. This stage is essential for ensuring a smooth transition from implementation to day-to-day operation, building user confidence and supporting the adoption and long-term success of the digital solution.

Key activities include:

- **Monitoring**: Actively tracking system performance, availability and usage to detect and address any technical issues early.

- **Helpdesk and technical support**: Providing timely assistance to users, troubleshooting problems and answering questions as they arise.

- **Issue resolution**: Identifying, prioritising and resolving any defects, configuration errors or integration issues that may emerge after deployment.

- **Obtaining user feedback**: Engaging with users to identify usability concerns, improvement opportunities or training gaps.

- **Updates and adjustments**: Making minor refinements or updates based on real-world use and feedback to enhance functionality, performance or user experience.

Review and optimisation

The final stage of the digital solution deployment process focuses on evaluating the success of the deployment and identifying opportunities for improvement. This stage ensures the solution realises business benefits and evolves to meet changing business needs.

Key activities include:

- **Performance evaluation**: Assessing whether the deployment met its original objectives, timelines and user expectations.

- **User and stakeholder feedback**: Collecting input from users and stakeholders to understand their experiences and identify any ongoing challenges or areas for enhancement.

- **Post-project review**: This is a structured evaluation of a digital solution development project to assess its success, capture lessons learned and identify areas for improvement. It considers factors such as objectives, outcomes, timelines, budget and stakeholder satisfaction. The insights gained support continual improvement and help to guide future projects or system updates.

- **Benefits review**: This is where the benefits predicted in the business case (produced during the inception stage of the digital solution life cycle) are reviewed to see if they have been realised and to determine if additional actions are needed to ensure realisation occurs. Some benefits are measured immediately whereas others may require an extended period before they can be evaluated.

- **Optimisation planning**: Making adjustments to improve functionality, user experience and performance based on real-world use and feedback.

- **Ongoing support and updates**: Establishing plans for regular maintenance, support, training and future system enhancements.

By reflecting on the deployment process and acting on insights gained, this stage helps to ensure the digital solution continues to support business goals and realises sustained value over time.

RELEASE MANAGEMENT

Release management is the ITSM practice responsible for planning, scheduling, coordinating and controlling the deployment of new or changed IT services into a live environment. A smooth and successful deployment relies on confirming that all systems, components and teams are fully prepared. To minimise risks and disruptions, release management must validate the technical readiness before the release goes live.

Release management works by guiding a new or changed IT service through a structured and controlled deployment process to ensure it is delivered smoothly, safely and with minimal disruption. By coordinating people, processes and technology, it facilitates predictable and reliable change implementation, acting as a vital link between development and operations – particularly in Agile and DevOps environments.

Key release management activities include:

- **Planning the release**: This involves defining the scope, goals and schedule of the release while identifying what is being deployed – such as software, features or updates. Coordination with change management and technical teams ensures alignment and readiness for the upcoming deployment.

- **Building and testing**: During this activity, the release package – including code, configurations and documentation – is prepared and tested to verify functionality, performance and user acceptance. Technical readiness is confirmed by checking infrastructure, dependencies and rollback plans.

- **Scheduling and approvals**: The release is scheduled to minimise disruption and avoid conflicts with other changes. Necessary approvals are obtained from relevant stakeholders, including change management and operations teams, to confirm readiness for deployment.

- **Deployment**: This activity is where the release is deployed to the live environment using approved methods, either manually or through automation. During rollout, stability and performance are monitored. Rollback procedures are executed if issues are detected.

- **Post-release review**: After deployment, the release is evaluated to ensure it meets its goals. Feedback is collected, performance is reviewed and lessons learned are documented to guide improvements for future releases.

10 CHANGEOVER STRATEGIES

INTRODUCTION

The previous two chapters have focused on the more technical aspects of deploying a new digital solution, and the broad range of activities this involves. This chapter explores a range of strategies used by organisations to effect the transition from an existing way of working (which may or may not involve the use of digital technology) to a new way of working based around a new digital solution. These methods are commonly referred to as changeover strategies and their purpose is to manage the transition in a way that minimises risk, disruption and downtime while ensuring continuity of service and user confidence, resulting in effective adoption of the new solution.

Before examining various changeover strategies, this chapter introduces a long-established business change model that offers a clear and structured approach to managing organisational change. It concludes by exploring key factors that influence the selection of an appropriate changeover strategy.

A MODEL FOR BUSINESS CHANGE

Kurt Lewin, a German–American psychologist, developed his influential change model in the 1940s as part of his broader work on field theory and group dynamics. Influenced by Gestalt psychology, which focuses on understanding the whole rather than its parts, Lewin sought to understand how to effectively initiate and sustain change within organisations and social groups. He introduced the concept that change involves disrupting the status quo, transitioning to a new state and then stabilising that state – an idea that became the foundation of his three-stage model of change (Lewin, 1947).

Lewin's model offers a clear and structured framework that is widely used to manage and guide organisational change. It remains a foundational approach in change theory, valued for its simplicity and effectiveness in helping individuals and groups navigate transformation while reinforcing and sustaining new behaviours and practices.

The three stages in Lewin's model – unfreeze, change and refreeze – are discussed below.

Stage 1: Unfreeze

The unfreeze stage focuses on preparing individuals and the organisation for change by challenging existing attitudes, behaviours and perceptions, and building awareness of why change is needed. This begins with assessing readiness, identifying the need for change through data, feedback or performance issues and clearly communicating that need to create a sense of urgency. Engaging key stakeholders early helps to build support and reduce resistance, while encouraging open conversations about current ways of working helps to break down attachment to the status quo and sets the stage for effective and lasting change.

Stage 2: Change

The change stage, also known as transition, involves individuals and the organisation transitioning from old ways of working to new ones by adopting new processes and adjusting mindsets and behaviours. In addition to implementing updates to IT systems and technologies, this stage may also involve changes to organisational structures and culture. Successful transition depends on clear and consistent communication, as well as the provision of training, coaching and resources to support individuals through the change. Involving staff in the process encourages ownership and reduces resistance, helping to ensure a smoother, more effective changeover.

Stage 3: Refreeze

The refreeze stage, also known simply as freeze, focuses on embedding new behaviours, mindsets and processes into the organisation's operating model and culture to ensure the change is sustained and becomes part of everyday operations. This involves reinforcing the new ways of working through supportive policies, procedures and strong leadership. Recognising and celebrating achievements along the way helps to highlight the value of the change and maintain momentum. Continuous monitoring and evaluation are essential to assess the impact and make any necessary adjustments. Aligning organisational systems such as performance management and reward structures with the new practices further helps to stabilise and solidify the change over the long term.

CHANGEOVER STRATEGIES

Direct changeover

A direct changeover strategy (also known as big bang) is where the old system is completely replaced by the new system at a specific point in time. This means the organisation stops using the existing solution and immediately begins using the new one across all users and processes.

Key characteristics of a direct changeover include:

- **Instant switchover**: The transition happens all at once – the old system is switched off and the new one is switched on, with no overlap in use.

- **High risk**: If the new system fails, there is no fallback, which can lead to major disruptions.

- **Low cost**: It avoids the expense of running two systems simultaneously (as is the case with parallel run).

- **Requires thorough preparation**: Extensive testing and user training must be completed before the switchover to reduce the risk of failure.

Direct changeover is typically chosen when the new system must be launched by a fixed deadline, the old system is no longer viable or the organisation is confident in the reliability of the new solution.

Parallel run

A parallel run is a strategy where both the old and new systems are operated simultaneously for a period of time. During this transition phase, the same inputs are entered into both systems and their outputs are compared to ensure the new system is working correctly before the old one is fully retired.

Key characteristics of a parallel run include:

- **Gradual transition**: The new and existing systems run side by side for a period, enabling the new system to be fully integrated and tested before the old one is deactivated.

- **Low risk**: Since the old system is still operational, it provides a safety net in case any problems arise with the new system. If the new system fails, it can be switched off and the business operation continues with the old system.

- **High cost and effort**: Running and maintaining two systems simultaneously demands extra time, resources and user effort, as both require continuous support, monitoring, data synchronisation and training – essentially doubling the workload during the transition. Additionally, there's considerable operational overhead, since transactions must be entered into both systems instead of just one.

- **Supports validation**: Enables thorough comparison of results, helping to identify discrepancies or problems in the new system during live operational use.

- **User confidence**: Gives users time to become comfortable with the new system while still relying on the old familiar one.

Parallel runs are often used in critical environments (e.g. finance and healthcare) where accuracy and reliability are essential, and system failure would have significant consequences.

Pilot changeover

With a pilot changeover strategy (sometimes referred to as just a pilot), the new system is introduced to a small, controlled group of users or a specific part of the organisation before it is rolled out more widely. This approach enables the organisation to test the system in a real-world (live) setting while limiting the risk of failure.

Key characteristics of a pilot changeover include:

- **Controlled rollout**: By only releasing the new system to a limited group of users or a specific area of the organisation, a pilot changeover facilitates close monitoring and issue resolution before wider implementation.

- **Risk management**: A pilot changeover reduces the risk of disruption to the day-to-day business operation by limiting the initial rollout to a small, selected group. This enables any issues arising from initial use to be contained within a specific area where they are easier to identify and resolve.

- **Real-world feedback**: The pilot group can provide valuable insights by using the new system in a real-world setting, helping to uncover usability issues, unexpected behaviours and areas for improvement that might not appear during testing. These insights can be used to refine the system before full rollout. This is often referred to as **live testing**.

Pilot changeovers are ideal when an organisation wants to test the new system with minimal disruption or when user feedback is essential for fine-tuning the solution before full deployment.

Phased changeover

A phased changeover strategy introduces the new system step by step, implementing and stabilising each module or subset of features before progressing to the next. This gradual transition aligns well with Agile digital solution development, which delivers functionality incrementally for testing and deployment.

Key characteristics of a phased changeover include:

- **Gradual rollout**: The new system is deployed for live, operational use in stages – one component or feature at a time – enabling each part to be implemented, tested and stabilised before moving on to the next, thus reducing pressure on users and support teams.

- **Lower risk**: Any issues arising from initial system use can be isolated and resolved within a specific phase, reducing the chance of widespread disruption across the entire system.

- **Easier training and support**: With a phased changeover, staff can be trained incrementally, focusing on each new feature or process as it is introduced, thus making the process more manageable and less overwhelming.

- **Flexibility**: The pace, order or scope of the rollout can be adapted during the transition in response to feedback, insights from earlier stages, system performance or evolving organisational needs.

Phased changeovers are ideal for complex systems or large organisations where a full switch would be too risky or disruptive, and where different parts of the system can operate independently during the transition.

Blue/green deployment

A blue/green deployment is a software release strategy that reduces downtime and risk by running two identical production environments – blue and green – as follows:

- **Blue environment**: This is the current live (production) version of the application that users are actively using.

- **Green environment**: This is the new version of the application, fully tested and ready to go live.

When ready for release, the new version is deployed to the green environment and thoroughly tested to confirm it functions as expected. Once validated, traffic is redirected from the blue environment (the current live version) to the green environment, typically using a load balancer or Domain Name System (DNS)[74] update. In the event of any issues following the switch, traffic can be promptly reverted to the blue environment, enabling a fast and seamless rollback.

Key characteristics of a blue/green deployment include:

- **Two identical environments**: Maintaining two environments facilitates smooth and safe updates to an application. The new version runs in a separate, identical environment (green), so it can be tested without affecting the live version (blue). Once it is ready, traffic can be quickly switched to the green environment with no downtime. If any issues occur, it is easy to switch back to the blue version.

- **Seamless traffic switching**: Traffic is switched from blue to green using a load balancer or DNS update, enabling a zero-downtime deployment.

- **Low-risk rollback**: If issues occur in the green environment, traffic can be quickly reverted to the blue environment, reducing the negative effects on users and business operations.

- **Full pre-production testing**: The green environment can be fully tested before going live, ensuring it works as expected in a production-like setting.

- **Minimal downtime**: The switch between environments is almost instantaneous, making this strategy ideal for high-availability systems.

- **Improved deployment confidence**: Blue/green deployment enables DevOps teams to release with confidence, knowing there's a clear and immediate rollback path.

- **Supports automation**: Works well with continuous integration/continuous deployment (CI/CD) pipelines, where deployments are automated and frequent.

Blue/green deployments are commonly used in scenarios where minimising downtime, ensuring stability, reducing deployment risk and maintaining reliable and uninterrupted service are priorities. They are particularly valuable in the following situations:

---

74 DNS is the system that translates human-readable domain names (e.g. www.example.com) into IP addresses (e.g. 192.0.2.1) that computers use to identify each other on a network.

- **High-availability requirements**: When applications or services must remain available 24/7 (such as in ecommerce, finance or healthcare) and downtime is costly or unacceptable.

- **Production safety and risk mitigation**: When an organisation needs to test a new software version in a live environment without impacting end-users, having the ability to quickly revert to the previous version is essential for minimising disruption and maintaining uninterrupted service.

- **Complex or high-impact updates**: When making large or critical updates that may introduce defects or incompatibilities, or implementing infrastructure changes that could affect system performance or behaviour.

- **Continuous deployment/delivery pipelines**: When following a DevOps approach where updates are made frequently and must be deployed smoothly and reliably.

- **Need for parallel environments**: When it is necessary to compare different versions or carry out final validation (such as performance checks or A/B testing) before fully switching to the new version.

Canary release

A canary release is a software deployment strategy where a new version of an application is first rolled out to a small subset of users. If no issues are detected, the release is gradually expanded to the wider user base, helping to reduce the risk of widespread problems. The name comes from the idiom 'canary in a coal mine', symbolising an early warning system to detect potential issues before they impact all users.

A canary release and a pilot changeover are very similar, but with some subtle differences that are summarised in Table 10.1. In essence, a canary release is technical- and performance-focused, while a pilot changeover is more user- and feedback-focused. They can be used together in a hybrid strategy for maximum effectiveness.

Key characteristics of a canary release include:

- **Gradual rollout**: The new version is released to a small subset of users first, then gradually expanded to a larger audience, rather than all users at once.

- **Risk mitigation**: By limiting initial access, any defects or performance problems affect only a small portion of users, reducing the risk of widespread disruption.

- **Real-world (live) testing**: The software runs in the actual production environment, enabling teams to observe how it behaves under real user conditions, rather than relying solely on test environments.

- **Monitoring and metrics**: Canary releases rely heavily on monitoring tools to track performance, stability, error rates and user behaviour. These insights help to determine whether to proceed, pause or rollback the release.

- **Rapid rollback capability**: If issues are detected, the system can quickly revert traffic to the previous stable version, helping to maintain service reliability.

- **Automation-friendly**: Canary releases are often integrated into CI/CD pipelines and can be automated using feature flags, deployment tools or traffic routing mechanisms.

- **User segmentation**: The canary group can be chosen based on location, device, account type or randomly, depending on what best suits the testing goals and risk profile.

Table 10.1 Canary release and pilot changeover compared

Feature	Canary release	Pilot changeover
Audience	Small percentage of live users	Specific group (e.g. team or region)
Purpose/focus	System performance and issue detection	Business fit and user feedback
Rollout style	Automated, gradual	Controlled, often manual
Rollback	Fast and automated	Manual or partial

Dark launch

A dark launch is a software deployment strategy in which new features or updates are released to the production environment but remain hidden from users. The functionality runs in the background without being visible or accessible through the user interface, enabling teams to test performance and stability in a live setting. This approach enables safer, more informed releases by enabling the refinement of features before public exposure.

For example, an ecommerce site might dark launch a new recommendation engine. It runs in production, processes real data and logs performance, but users still see the old recommendations until the new system is activated.

Key characteristics of a dark launch include:

- **Feature hiding**: New features are deployed to the production environment but stay hidden from end-users, usually concealed within the user interface and managed using feature flags.

- **Live in production**: The new feature is active in the production environment but accessible only to internal teams. Although hidden from end-users, the feature is fully active in the live environment and interacts with real data and live systems.

- **Controlled activation**: Features can be gradually turned on for specific users or teams (e.g. internal testers) before being fully released to the public.

- **Risk reduction**: By hiding incomplete or untested features from users, dark launches reduce the risk of exposing defects or unfinished functionality.

- **Early testing opportunity**: New features can be tested in the live production environment without being visible to end-users, giving development and operations teams the opportunity to evaluate performance, stability and integration under real-world conditions. This approach enables teams to identify and fix issues early, collect actual usage data and system metrics, and refine features before public release.

- **Supports continuous delivery**: Dark launches are ideal for incremental releases, enabling DevOps teams to deploy code frequently and safely.

- **Data-driven decisions**: Since the feature is active in the live environment, teams can gather real usage data, observe its behaviour and make informed improvements prior to a full release.

Dark launches are particularly beneficial in high-risk, high-complexity or data-sensitive deployments, where early feedback, system safety and seamless user experience are critical. For example:

- **Testing new features without impacting end-users**: When a new feature needs to be evaluated in a live environment, but it is not yet ready for public use, a dark launch enables teams to test functionality, performance and integration without affecting the user experience.

- **Validating back-end changes**: For updates that involve back-end systems – such as new algorithms, databases or infrastructure components – a dark launch helps development teams to ensure stability and correctness before exposing the changes through the UI.

- **Supporting gradual rollouts**: When planning a canary release or A/B testing, a dark launch can act as a preliminary step, ensuring the feature runs correctly behind the scenes before being activated for a small user segment.

- **Performance monitoring and tuning**: Dark launches are useful when there is a need to collect real-world usage data, monitor resource usage or tune performance under actual load, especially for features that could impact system behaviour at scale.

- **Minimising risk in high-stakes releases**: In industries like finance, healthcare or ecommerce, where user-facing errors can be costly or damaging, dark launches enable early detection and correction of issues before full public release.

- **Complex system integration**: When integrating new services or components into an existing system, dark launches facilitate safe, staged validation in the live environment while preserving service continuity.

Hybrid strategies

A hybrid changeover strategy involves combining two or more deployment or transition methods to manage the rollout of new digital solutions, features or updates more effectively. By leveraging the strengths of different approaches, hybrid strategies offer a balance of control, safety and speed. This enables organisations to tailor the change process to their specific needs, system complexity and the potential impact on users. For example, a company might begin with a pilot rollout to a small user group, gradually expand access through a phased or canary release, and maintain the old system in parallel until the new version proves stable.

Hybrid strategies are particularly valuable in complex digital environments where flexibility, risk management and performance assurance are critical for successful implementation, or where a single changeover or deployment method alone may not adequately meet the requirements of the situation. This could be due to:

- **High risk**: A single method may not offer enough control or rollback options.
- **Complexity**: The system or update is too large or varied for one approach to handle effectively.
- **User impact**: A single method might not minimise disruption or enable gradual user exposure.
- **Testing needs**: One method might not support the necessary level of validation before full release.

Examples include:

- large-scale enterprise system upgrades;
- cloud migrations or platform transitions;
- deployments affecting multiple user groups or geographies; and
- high-risk updates.

Some examples of how changeover strategies can work together are described below.

Example 1: blue/green deployment + canary release

A new software version is deployed to a separate environment (green), as in blue/green deployment, and then traffic is gradually shifted using a canary release strategy. For example, 5 per cent of users are directed to the green environment initially, then 25 per cent, and so on. This enables staged validation with rollback capability, combining the safety of blue/green with the control of canary testing.

Example 2: pilot changeover + phased changeover

A pilot group of users (e.g. a single department or region) receives an initial release of a new digital solution containing a subset of the final feature set. When this initial release has been proven with the pilot group it is deployed to the rest of the user base. The pilot group then receive the next release of features and the process repeats until the entire solution has been deployed to the entire user base.

Example 3: dark launch + parallel run

A dark launch rolls out a new feature or system in the background (without exposing it to users), while the current system continues to operate through a parallel run. The organisation monitors the new system's performance and collects data before officially enabling it for users.

Example 4: phased changeover + direct changeover

A phased rollout may be used for non-critical components to gradually introduce changes, followed by a direct cutover for a core module once stability and readiness are confirmed in earlier phases. This offers agility while preserving risk control.

LEWIN'S MODEL AND CHANGEOVER STRATEGIES

The connection between Lewin's change model and the changeover strategies discussed in this chapter lies in their shared goal of managing change effectively while minimising disruption. Lewin's three-stage model – unfreeze, change, refreeze – offers a high-level framework for understanding and guiding the human and organisational side of change, while changeover strategies provide the technical and operational methods for carrying out that change in practice. Each strategy can be aligned with a stage of Lewin's model:

- **Unfreeze** involves preparing people and systems for change. Strategies such as pilot changeover, parallel run and dark launch support this phase by enabling change teams to test, gather feedback and build readiness before full implementation.

- **Change** is the stage where the new solution is rolled out. Approaches such as direct changeover, blue/green deployment and canary release help to manage how and when users experience the new system, balancing speed with control.

- **Refreeze** focuses on embedding the new behaviours, processes or systems to ensure the change becomes permanent. This aligns with the final steps of the changeover strategies, where the new system is fully adopted, feedback is incorporated, performance validated and the organisation updates its policies, training and culture to support the new way of working.

Together, Lewin's model and the changeover strategies offer a comprehensive approach to change, blending psychological readiness with operational execution.

FACTORS AFFECTING THE CHOICE OF CHANGEOVER STRATEGY

Choosing the most suitable changeover strategy is a vital part of deploying a new digital solution and can have a major impact on the overall success of the transition. Each strategy outlined earlier comes with its own set of benefits and risks, and the decision involves evaluating various factors – such as system complexity, organisational risk tolerance, resource availability and the need for testing and rollback. The goal is to strike a balance that supports business objectives while reducing disruption and risk. By integrating these strategies into the change management life cycle, organisations can respond more effectively to unexpected issues and maintain operational resilience.

The key considerations that influence the choice of appropriate changeover strategy for a given context include:

- **Risk tolerance**: The level of uncertainty an organisation is willing to accept in the event of failure or disruption strongly influences its choice of changeover strategy. Cautious organisations tend to prefer safer, more controlled approaches – such as phased or parallel changeovers, canary releases or blue/green deployments – to minimise disruption. Organisations more comfortable with risk may choose quicker options such as direct changeovers or dark launches, prioritising speed or cost efficiency. Aligning the strategy with the organisation's appetite for risk helps to ensure a suitable balance between control and progress.

- **System criticality**: The importance of a system to core business functions or customer services affects the choice of changeover strategy. Critical systems typically require high-reliability approaches – such as parallel or phased changeovers, canary releases or blue/green deployments – to reduce downtime and operational risk. Less critical systems may tolerate more rapid transitions, making direct changeovers or dark launches more feasible.

- **User impact**: The extent to which a changeover affects users – through usability, accessibility or potential disruption – shapes the changeover strategy. If the change could lead to confusion or downtime, gradual methods like phased changeovers, canary releases or dark launches provide smoother transitions and better user support. When the impact is minimal, direct changeovers can be more appropriate. Considering user experience helps to preserve trust and continuity.

- **Complexity of the change**: The scope and technical complexity of the change – including the number of systems, processes or teams involved – can determine the most effective changeover strategy. More complex changes benefit from controlled, testable approaches such as phased or parallel changeovers, canary releases or blue/green deployments. More straightforward changes may be implemented more efficiently with a direct changeover.

- **Speed of deployment**: The urgency of the transition also influences the choice of changeover strategy. For time-sensitive changes, faster methods like direct changeovers, blue/green deployments or dark launches may be necessary, even if they carry more risk. If there is more flexibility, phased or canary-based strategies offer a slower, safer rollout. The chosen approach should balance speed with acceptable risk levels.

- **Size and diversity of user base**: The number and variety of users impacted by the change can shape the changeover strategy. Large or diverse user groups – differing in location, roles or technical skill – may benefit from phased changeovers, canary releases or pilot deployments, enabling staged rollouts and tailored support. Smaller or more uniform user groups can typically manage faster strategies such as direct changeovers with less risk.

- **Compliance and regulatory requirements**: The need for the organisation to comply with legislation and industry standards may dictate how changes are implemented, particularly around audit trails, approvals and testing. These constraints often make phased, parallel or blue/green deployments preferable, as they offer greater control and documentation opportunities. Meeting these obligations helps to avoid penalties and ensures a compliant change process.

- **System availability requirements**: If a system must remain available with little to no downtime – as in healthcare, finance and customer-facing services – strategies such as phased or parallel changeovers, blue/green deployments or canary releases are better suited. When brief downtime is acceptable, quicker approaches such as direct changeovers may be used.

- **Availability of resources**: The people, time, tools and budget available to support a changeover affect the choice of changeover strategy. Resource-intensive methods such as phased, parallel, blue/green or canary deployments require more planning, infrastructure and support. When resources are limited, more straightforward approaches like direct changeovers may be more realistic.

- **Data migration needs**: The need to move data from one system to another during changeover can significantly influence the strategy chosen. When dealing with large or complex datasets, blue/green deployments can be beneficial as they allow time for thorough testing and issue resolution. Phased or parallel changeovers introduce complexities and risks not seen in a direct changeover approach, and these challenges grow with the size and complexity of the data. As a result, direct changeovers are often more appropriate for smaller or lower-risk data migrations. In phased migrations, reports and integrations must function across both systems, and it is essential to clearly define which system holds the authoritative data for each data entity (table). If different phases involve migrating parts of the same database, merging the data into the live system requires additional planning and development. For parallel migrations, data can easily fall out of sync unless updates are validated in both systems. These added complexities make phased or parallel approaches potentially riskier than a direct changeover for large-scale migrations. Regardless of the strategy adopted, it is critical to ensure data accuracy, integrity and availability throughout the process.

- **Rollback requirements**: The ability to quickly reverse a change if issues arise is a key consideration when selecting a changeover strategy. Blue/green deployments, parallel changeovers and canary releases provide reliable rollback options by keeping the original system available during the transition. Direct changeovers are more difficult to undo, making them riskier for systems requiring a clear fallback plan.

- **Need for testing and validation**: When thorough testing is required before full deployment – especially under real-world conditions – strategies like phased or parallel changeovers, canary releases, pilot deployments or dark launches are ideal. They enable issues to be identified and resolved while the existing system remains operational. For straightforward, low-risk changes, direct changeovers may still be suitable.

- **Segmentation of the application portfolio**: The ease of dividing the portfolio into distinct segments is an important factor. Phased migration is more practical when the existing system landscape consists of multiple legacy systems with separate datasets that can be transitioned individually, or when different lines of business or geographic regions can be migrated independently.

RISK MITIGATION IN THE EVENT OF A FAILED CHANGEOVER

Even with meticulous planning, changeovers can sometimes fail, introducing unexpected risks to operations, service continuity or customer satisfaction. It is therefore imperative to consider practical strategies for mitigating risks should a changeover not go as planned. By identifying potential failure points in advance and implementing robust contingency plans, organisations can minimise disruption, protect critical assets and maintain stakeholder confidence during periods of uncertainty.

The following strategies can help to mitigate risks and support recovery:

- **Rollback**: This involves reverting a system or service to its previous stable state if a changeover fails. It enables organisations to quickly undo changes and restore normal operations, minimising downtime and disruption. Rollback plans should be carefully prepared, tested in advance and include clear criteria for when to activate them. This strategy is especially useful when the risk of failure is high or the impact of disruption is significant.

- **Fix-forward**: Instead of reverting to the old system after a failed changeover, the fix-forward strategy involves addressing issues directly within the new environment. The goal is to quickly identify and resolve problems to stabilise the updated system. This approach is often used when rolling back is not practical or could lead to greater disruption. It relies on skilled teams, strong monitoring and a clear understanding of the issue to minimise downtime and restore normal operations efficiently.

- **Redundancy and failover systems**: Having backup components or systems ready to take over if the primary system fails during a changeover is a key risk mitigation strategy. These setups help to maintain service availability and minimise downtime by automatically switching to standby or duplicate infrastructure. This is particularly important for critical services that demand high reliability, ensuring operations can continue smoothly while problems are addressed.

- **Incremental deployment**: As described earlier, incremental deployment involves rolling out changes gradually, rather than all at once. By introducing updates in small, controlled stages – such as to a limited group of users or systems – it becomes easier to detect and address issues early. If a problem occurs, the impact is limited, and the change can be paused or adjusted before continuing. This strategy is particularly effective for complex or high-risk environments.

- **Communication protocols**: Establishing clear communication processes and escalation paths is crucial for managing risk during a changeover. In the event of failure, these structures enable a coordinated response, prompt issue resolution and timely updates to stakeholders. This reduces confusion, builds trust and accelerates recovery. Keeping stakeholders informed about potential risks and recovery timelines also helps to manage expectations and ensures a more effective overall response.

- **Predefined contingency procedures**: Planned actions and responses designed for use if a changeover fails help to ensure a swift and organised recovery. These procedures define clear roles, recovery steps, communication plans and user support protocols. When documented and rehearsed in advance, these reduce downtime, minimise confusion and enable quicker restoration of services during unexpected issues.

- **Monitoring and alerting**: Tracking system performance and behaviour in real time during and after a changeover helps to quickly detect issues and respond before they escalate. Automated alerts act as an early warning system, notifying teams the moment something goes wrong. This reduces downtime, limits the impact of failures and supports faster recovery.

- **Post-failure analysis**: Reviewing what went wrong after a failed changeover helps to identify root causes and understand how issues occurred. This insight enables change teams to refine change management processes, improve planning and prevent similar problems in the future. Conducting a thorough post-change review supports continual improvement and strengthens overall change practices.

11 POST-DELIVERY

INTRODUCTION

The successful deployment of a digital solution marks a major milestone – but it is far from the end of the journey. Once the solution is live, a new set of challenges begins. This chapter explores the final stages of the digital solution life cycle, focusing on what happens after delivery: day-to-day operations, ongoing maintenance and eventual decommissioning. It highlights the importance of monitoring performance, applying updates and supporting users to ensure the solution remains effective and continues to realise beneficial outcomes for the organisation and the end-users. By understanding and planning for these post-delivery activities, organisations can maximise the long-term impact of their digital investments.

OPERATING THE SOLUTION

Operating a new digital solution involves several key practices to ensure the solution performs reliably, continues to meet user needs and delivers beneficial outcomes throughout its active life. This is typically where the discipline of digital solution development hands off to the discipline of IT service management (ITSM).

ITSM was introduced in Chapter 1, where it was described as:

> A set of tools and practices used by IT teams to keep services stable, useful and continually improving for users.

As new technologies such as the cloud and AI are introduced, ITSM helps to manage them by ensuring quality and compliance, providing visibility through reports and service catalogues and enabling smoother updates through DevOps integration. It also gathers valuable data from incident patterns, user feedback and performance metrics, which supports the continual improvement of future solutions in terms of design, usability and alignment with business needs.

ITSM and ITIL

The Information Technology Infrastructure Library (ITIL) is the most widely used ITSM framework. It provides best practices for delivering high-quality IT services that align with business objectives, while promoting efficiency, consistency and reliability. ITIL v4 (AXELOS, 2019) defines an IT service as:

A means of enabling value co-creation by facilitating outcomes that customers want to achieve, without the customer having to manage specific costs and risks.

Core to this definition are the following elements:

- **Value co-creation**: IT services are designed not just to realise value but to work collaboratively with customers to co-create it.
- **Facilitating outcomes**: The focus is on helping customers to achieve their desired results.
- **Abstracting complexity**: IT services remove the need for customers to manage the underlying technology, costs or risks themselves.

ITIL v4 introduces several core concepts (explored in the following sections) that form the foundation of modern ITSM. These concepts reflect a shift towards a more flexible, value-driven and holistic approach to managing IT services.

The Four Dimensions Model

To ensure a balanced approach to service management, ITIL v4 identifies four dimensions that must be considered in every service:

- organisations and people;
- information and technology;
- partners and suppliers; and
- value streams and processes.

These dimensions influence how services are delivered and maintained, ensuring alignment with business goals.

The ITIL Service Value System

The Service Value System (SVS) (Figure 11.1) was introduced in ITIL v4, and replaced the service life cycle model from ITIL v3. The SVS provides a structured framework that ensures all organisational components work together to co-create value through effective and efficient service management. This aligns service management with other key business change methodologies such as Agile, DevOps and Lean.

The SVS provides a comprehensive view of how all components and activities of an organisation work together to create value through IT-enabled services. The key elements of the SVS are described below.

Figure 11.1 ITIL v4 Service Value System (Source: AXELOS, 2019)

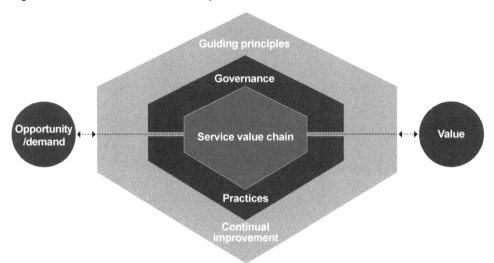

| Guiding principles | The guiding principles are a set of universal recommendations that support decision-making and actions across all levels of the organisation. They encourage a consistent, values-driven approach to ITSM, promoting practices such as focusing on value, building on existing successes, nurturing collaboration and maintaining transparency. Adapted from earlier ITIL guidance and influenced by frameworks like Agile, Lean and DevOps, these principles help organisations to apply ITIL in a flexible and adaptable way. |

The seven principles are:

1. Focus on value.

2. Start where you are.

3. Progress iteratively with feedback.

4. Collaborate and promote visibility.

5. Think and work holistically.

6. Keep it simple and practical.

7. Optimise and automate.

| Governance | Governance provides the structure for directing and controlling the organisation through clearly defined policies, roles and responsibilities. It ensures accountability and oversight, helping service management activities align with strategic objectives, comply with regulations and adhere to internal standards. |

Service value chain	The service value chain is the core of the Service Value System, providing a flexible operating model that outlines the key activities needed to convert demand into value. It consists of six interconnected activities, each contributing to the creation and delivery of valuable services:

- plan;
- improve;
- engage;
- design and transition;
- obtain/build; and
- deliver and support.

These activities can be adapted to fit different contexts, enabling organisations to respond effectively to changing needs while maintaining a consistent approach to service management.

Practices	Practices (explored further below) are sets of organisational resources designed to perform work or achieve specific objectives in support of effective service management. In ITIL v4 'practices' replaced 'processes' from ITIL v3.
Continual improvement	Continual improvement is a structured, ongoing effort to assess and enhance services, processes and practices, ensuring they stay effective, efficient and aligned with changing business needs. It encourages a culture of reflection and iterative progress throughout the organisation.

Co-creation of value

ITIL v4 emphasises collaboration between service providers and consumers. Value is not delivered *to* customers – it is co-created *with* customers through active engagement and shared goals.

Key practices to support the operation of digital solutions

In ITIL v4, the term practices replaces the more rigid concept of processes (as per ITIL v3), offering a more flexible and holistic approach to service management. Practices are sets of organisational resources and capabilities used to perform tasks or achieve specific objectives. ITIL v4 defines 34 management practices, grouped into three categories (see the following sections), which provide flexible, adaptable ways to manage services and align with modern operating models.

General management practices

ITIL v4 identifies 14 general management practices (see Table 11.1) that help to create a strong foundation for effective service management by aligning IT services with broader organisational goals and capabilities. These originate from business management disciplines and are adopted and adapted for service management. They support the overall operation and governance of the organisation, not just IT services.

Table 11.1 ITIL v4 general management practices

Practice	Description
1. Architecture management	Ensures the logical structure and alignment of systems and processes with business goals
2. Continual improvement	A structured approach to evaluating and enhancing services and processes over time
3. Information security management	Protects information and services against security threats and vulnerabilities
4. Knowledge management	Ensures valuable information is captured, shared and used effectively
5. Measurement and reporting	Supports data-driven decision-making through consistent metrics and reporting
6. Organisational change management	Prepares and supports individuals and teams during change initiatives
7. Portfolio management	Manages the organisation's projects, programmes and services as strategic investments
8. Project management	Plans and delivers specific initiatives within defined scope, time and cost constraints
9. Relationship management	Builds and maintains strong relationships with stakeholders
10. Risk management	Identifies, assesses and controls risks to business operations and services
11. Service financial management	Manages budgeting, accounting and charging for services to ensure financial transparency
12. Strategy management	Defines and maintains the organisation's direction and goals
13. Supplier management	Manages supplier relationships and performance to ensure value delivery
14. Workforce and talent management	Ensures the organisation attracts, develops and retains the necessary skills and talent

Service management practices

Service management practices focus on delivering and supporting IT services effectively. These practices are central to ITSM and ensure that services meet the needs of users and the organisation. ITIL v4 defines 17 service management practices (see Table 11.2). These practices are essential for managing the full life cycle of IT services, from design and transition to operation and continual improvement.

Table 11.2 ITIL v4 service management practices

Practice	Description
1. Availability management	Ensures services deliver agreed availability levels to meet business needs
2. Business analysis	Identifies business needs and recommends solutions that offer value (provide beneficial outcomes) to users and customers
3. Capacity and performance management	Ensures services and infrastructure can meet current and future performance demands
4. Change enablement (formerly change management)	Ensures changes are assessed, authorised and implemented with minimal risk
5. Incident management	Restores normal service operation as quickly as possible after an interruption
6. IT asset management	Tracks and manages IT assets throughout their lives to maximise value
7. Monitoring and event management	Observes systems and services to identify and respond to events and issues
8. Problem management	Identifies and addresses root causes of incidents to prevent recurrence
9. Release management	Plans and controls the release of new or changed services into the live environment
10. Service catalogue management	Provides a single source of consistent information about all live services
11. Service configuration management	Maintains accurate information about service components and their relationships
12. Service continuity management	Ensures critical services can continue or be recovered after a disruption
13. Service design	Designs services that meet business objectives and user needs
14. Service desk	Acts as a single point of contact for users to report issues and request help
15. Service level management	Defines and manages service quality through service level agreements (SLAs)
16. Service request management	Handles routine user requests such as access, information or small changes
17. Service validation and testing	Ensures new or changed services meet requirements and perform as expected

Technical management practices

Technical management practices focus on maintaining and supporting the underlying technology that enables IT services. They provide the expertise needed to keep infrastructure and platforms stable, reliable and scalable, ensuring they can support high-quality service delivery. ITIL v4 defines three technical management practices (see Table 11.3).

Table 11.3 ITIL v4 technical management practices

Practice	Description
1. Deployment management	Manages the deployment of new or modified hardware, software, documentation, processes or any other service components into live environments. This includes planning, testing and executing deployments to ensure they are carried out smoothly and with minimal disruption.
2. Infrastructure and platform management	Oversees the management of physical and virtual infrastructure and platforms that support the delivery of IT services. This includes tasks related to provisioning, configuration, monitoring and ongoing maintenance.
3. Software development and management	Involves the design, development and maintenance of software applications to meet business requirements. This practice supports modern software delivery methods, including Agile and DevOps.

MAINTAINING THE SOLUTION

Maintenance refers to the ongoing practices needed to keep a digital solution functional, secure and aligned with business needs after it has been deployed. This includes tasks such as fixing defects, applying updates, optimising performance, addressing security vulnerabilities and adapting the solution to changing requirements or environments. Effective maintenance ensures that the solution remains reliable, efficient and compliant, continuing to support users and deliver beneficial outcomes throughout its operational life.

Types of maintenance

In practice, maintaining a digital solution involves much more than just fixing defects – it is a continuous effort to keep the solution reliable, secure and aligned with evolving business goals. There are four main types of maintenance (explored below), each playing a distinct role in ensuring the solution remains effective and adaptable. While these categories often overlap in practice, all are vital to ensuring the long-term success and sustainability of the solution.

Corrective maintenance

Corrective maintenance involves fixing defects that are discovered after the solution has been deployed. These defects may affect functionality, performance, security or user experience and typically arise from problems not detected during initial development or testing.

The goal of corrective maintenance is to restore the solution to its intended state, ensuring it continues to operate reliably and meet user and business expectations. This type of maintenance is reactive, often triggered by user reports, monitoring alerts or incident management processes.

Typical examples of corrective maintenance include:

- fixing a defect that causes an application to crash when a user submits a form;
- correcting a calculation error in a financial report;
- repairing broken links or missing images in a web application; and
- resolving a login failure due to incorrect session handling.

Adaptive maintenance

Adaptive maintenance involves updating the solution to ensure it remains compatible with changes in its environment (such as new versions of operating systems, hardware, networks or third-party services), and compliant with new or updated legislation or regulatory requirements. Changes may also be made to address new business requirements that come to light during live, operational use.

The goal of adaptive maintenance is to ensure the digital solution continues to function effectively as external conditions change and new business requirements come to light. It helps to maintain the solution's relevance and proactively prevents issues that could arise from changes to the environment within which it operates.

Typical examples of adaptive maintenance include:

- updating an application to support a new version of a mobile operating system;
- modifying the integration of an application with a third-party API that has changed;
- modifying security features to comply with new data protection legislation;
- migrating the application to a new cloud platform or hosting environment; and
- adding new functionality as a result of the organisation offering additional services.

Perfective maintenance

Perfective maintenance involves enhancing the performance, efficiency, usability or overall effectiveness of a digital solution based on user feedback, recurring service desk issues, performance metrics or observed usage patterns. Rather than fixing errors or altering core functionality, it focuses on optimising the solution to meet evolving user needs and expectations.

The goal of perfective maintenance is to ensure that the solution remains effective and user-friendly, and continues to deliver beneficial outcomes.

Typical examples of perfective maintenance include:

- enhancing the user interface of an application to improve the user experience;

- optimising database queries to load pages more quickly;

- adding a search filter to help users find content more easily; and

- streamlining navigation based on user behaviour analytics.

Preventive maintenance

Preventive maintenance involves proactively improving a system's stability, performance and maintainability to reduce the risk of future issues. Rather than waiting for problems to occur, it focuses on identifying and addressing potential risks, inefficiencies or technical debt early.

The goal of preventive maintenance is to minimise unplanned disruptions, extend the solution's lifespan and ensure reliable, long-term operation.

Typical examples of preventive maintenance include:

- refactoring complex or outdated code to improve maintainability;

- applying periodic security patches to reduce evolving cyber vulnerabilities;

- upgrading an old version of a JavaScript framework to a newer, supported version; and

- archiving or purging outdated data from large tables to reduce storage usage and improve query efficiency.

Maintenance in practice

Effective maintenance requires careful consideration of a range of factors, including:

- **Stability versus change**: Maintaining a digital solution involves striking the right balance between stability – keeping the system reliable and consistent – and change, such as implementing updates, enhancements or adapting to new requirements. Excessive change can introduce risk, while too little change may result in stagnation or misalignment with business objectives. Effective maintenance manages this balance through structured change processes and thorough testing.

- **Security and compliance**: Maintaining the security and compliance of a digital solution is a continuous responsibility. This includes addressing vulnerabilities, applying patches and updating configurations to defend against evolving threats. It also requires staying up to date with changing legal and regulatory requirements. Neglecting these tasks can lead to data breaches, reputational damage and legal consequences. Ongoing maintenance helps to ensure the solution remains secure and compliant over time.

- **User satisfaction**: To remain effective, a digital solution must continue to meet user expectations and evolving needs. This involves addressing usability issues, incorporating feedback and maintaining consistent performance. Regular updates informed by user insights help to boost engagement and support ongoing adoption. Prioritising user satisfaction during maintenance ensures the solution stays relevant and continues to deliver beneficial outcomes.

- **Scalability and performance**: As user demand increases or shifts, the solution must be able to scale effectively while maintaining strong performance. Maintenance activities such as monitoring performance, optimising infrastructure and adjusting capacity help to ensure the system remains responsive and reliable under changing loads. Regularly assessing performance ensures the solution continues to meet expectations, as poor scalability or slow response times can negatively affect user experience and business operations.

- **Cost efficiency**: Maintenance should be carried out in a way that maximises value while controlling costs. This involves optimising the use of infrastructure, licences and other resources, automating routine tasks and avoiding unnecessary upgrades. Cost efficiency also means making smart decisions about when to extend, improve or retire parts of the solution to prevent overspending on outdated or underused components.

In addition to software modifications, maintenance activities also encompass the following tasks, many of which align with the ITIL practices discussed earlier:

- **Monitoring and reporting** involves leveraging real-time tools and analytics to monitor system performance, availability, usage and errors – enabling early issue detection, informed decision-making and consistent service quality. Regular reporting provides valuable insights into system behaviour and emerging risks, supporting proactive maintenance and continual improvement.

- **Patching and updates** involves applying patches[75] to a digital solution's software or components to deliver fixes, improvements and new features. Activities may include correcting defects, closing security vulnerabilities, boosting performance and introducing additional functionality.

- **Incident and problem management** involves addressing unexpected issues that disrupt normal operations and identifying their root causes to prevent them from happening again. This activity helps to restore services quickly, minimise downtime and enhance the long-term stability and reliability of the digital solution.

- **Configuration and change management** involves maintaining up-to-date records of a digital solution's components and following structured processes to implement changes. This approach minimises risk, ensures updates are applied smoothly, preserves system stability and clearly documents the impact of each change.

- **Backup and recovery** involves routinely creating secure copies of critical data and system configurations, along with maintaining tested procedures for restoring them in the event of data loss, corruption or system failure. This helps to ensure business continuity and minimises downtime in the event of unexpected disruptions.

---

75 A patch is a small update applied to an existing program to fix defects, close security vulnerabilities or make minor improvements without replacing the entire system or application.

- **Security management** involves safeguarding a digital solution against threats by conducting vulnerability assessments, applying security patches, enforcing access controls, monitoring for suspicious activity and performing regular audits. The goal is to protect data, preserve system integrity and maintain compliance with security standards and regulations.

- **Licence and asset management** involves tracking software licences, hardware and related assets throughout their lives to ensure compliance, optimise usage and control costs. This helps to prevent overspending, supports audit readiness and ensures effective use of the organisation's digital resources.

- **User support and training** involves delivering helpdesk services, self-service tools and training resources to assist users in effectively using a digital solution. This includes offering guidance, resolving issues and providing updated materials to promote confident and efficient system use.

Several best practices have emerged relating to the maintenance of digital solutions, including:

- **Proactive maintenance**: Schedule regular health checks and updates to avoid issues before they arise.

- **Automation**: Use tools to automate routine tasks like patching, monitoring and backups.

- **DevOps practices**: Integrate maintenance into continuous integration and deployment pipelines for faster and safer updates.

- **Continual improvement**: Use feedback and performance data to identify areas for enhancement over time.

- **Service level management**: Ensure maintenance activities support agreed service levels (SLAs).

DECOMMISSIONING THE SOLUTION

Decommissioning marks the final stage of the digital solution life cycle. It is a structured process for retiring a digital solution, software application or platform that is no longer needed, supported or cost-effective. The goal is to safely remove the solution from operation while minimising disruption, ensuring compliance with legal, security and data retention requirements, and preserving any necessary records or knowledge. This process helps to reduce costs, mitigate risks and maintain a streamlined and secure digital environment.

Figure 11.2 provides an overview of the decommissioning process, with each stage described below. Figure 11.3 offers a decommissioning checklist.

Figure 11.2 Process for decommissioning a digital solution

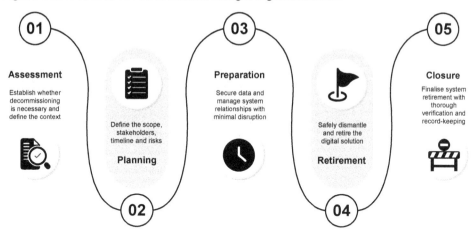

Phase 1: Assessment	The assessment phase establishes the rationale and context for decommissioning a digital solution. It begins by confirming whether the solution is obsolete, redundant or being replaced. This involves identifying key stakeholders (e.g. the business and technical owners), mapping system dependencies and evaluating legal, regulatory or compliance requirements. A business case is then produced to support the decision to proceed with decommissioning.
Phase 2: Planning	In the planning phase, the foundation for decommissioning is set by defining the project scope, timeline, stakeholders and associated risks. It includes taking a full inventory of all components involved – hardware, software, data and integrations. A detailed project plan is developed with key milestones, responsibilities are assigned and a risk assessment is conducted to anticipate and prepare for potential issues.
Phase 3: Preparation	This phase focuses on securing data and managing dependencies to ensure a smooth transition. Activities include categorising data for archiving, migration or destruction, and executing these actions securely. It also involves validating data integrity, storing archived data properly and removing unnecessary information. Dependencies are managed by identifying all system integrations, informing impacted stakeholders, disabling relevant connections and ensuring users receive clear communications and support resources related to the decommissioning plan.
Phase 4: Retirement	The retirement phase is where the actual dismantling of the digital solution takes place. This involves creating a final backup (if needed), revoking access, disabling authentication methods and shutting down services and infrastructure. Licences and configurations are removed or terminated, and any related hardware is either disposed of or repurposed according to organisational policy.

Phase 5:
Closure

The closure phase finalises the decommissioning process through thorough verification and documentation. It includes confirming the complete shutdown of the solution, validating that no access or vulnerabilities remain, and updating records such as asset inventories and configuration management databases. An audit or review is conducted, and formal sign-off is obtained. Lessons learned are documented, and all plans, logs and key information are archived securely for future reference.

Figure 11.3 Checklist for decommissioning a digital solution

1. Preliminary Assessment
☐ Confirm the solution is no longer required or is being replaced.
☐ Identify business owner and technical owner.
☐ Review dependencies (systems, users, processes).
☐ Determine regulatory, compliance or legal obligations.
☐ Conduct a cost–benefit analysis of keeping vs. decommissioning.

2. Planning
☐ Define scope and objectives of the decommissioning project.
☐ Identify all components (software, hardware, data, integrations).
☐ Create a decommissioning plan with timelines and milestones.
☐ Assign roles and responsibilities.
☐ Conduct risk assessment and mitigation planning.

3. Data Management
☐ Identify what data needs to be: archived, migrated, destroyed.
☐ Validate data migration (if applicable).
☐ Ensure archived data is stored securely and remains accessible.
☐ Confirm data destruction follows security/compliance standards.

4. Dependencies and Integrations
☐ List all integrations and interfaces with other systems.
☐ Notify impacted systems or teams.
☐ Disable or redirect integrations as needed.
☐ Remove any scheduled jobs, data feeds or automated processes.

5. Communication and Notifications
☐ Notify all users well in advance.
☐ Communicate changes to internal/external stakeholders.
☐ Provide guidance or support materials (e.g. FAQs, new system access).
☐ Coordinate with IT support and service desks.

6. System Decommissioning
☐ Backup final system state (if needed).
☐ Disable user access and authentication.
☐ Shut down servers/services.
☐ Remove software, licences and configurations.
☐ Return, repurpose or dispose of hardware (if any).

7. Validation and Closure
☐ Verify system and services are fully decommissioned.
☐ Validate no unauthorised access remains.
☐ Update asset inventories and documentation.
☐ Conduct a post-decommission review or audit.
☐ Capture lessons learned for future decommissioning efforts.
☐ Archive decommissioning plan and related artefacts.
☐ Log key decisions, outcomes and approvals.
☐ Record data retention details and system retirement metadata.

12 SOFTWARE TOOLS TO SUPPORT DIGITAL SOLUTION DELIVERY

INTRODUCTION

In the rapidly evolving landscape of digital innovation, the success of delivering impactful solutions hinges not only on visionary ideas and Agile methodologies but also on the effective use of software tools. This chapter explores the diverse range of tools that support the development, testing, deployment and maintenance of digital solutions, providing a brief description of each category of tool with a summary of their key features and example products. Not all tools provide all the features of their category and the list of specific tools is not exhaustive.

The main tools can be grouped as follows, with some overlap across categories:

* collaboration tools;
* backlog management tools;
* document management tools;
* risk management and security tools;
* documentation tools;
* computer-aided requirements engineering (CARE) tools;
* computer-aided software engineering (CASE) tools;
* computer-aided software testing (CAST) tools;
* programming languages;
* integrated development environments;
* standalone development tools;
* web development platforms;
* model-driven architecture (MDA), no-code and low-code platforms;
* configuration management tools;
* data management tools (including database management systems and ETL (extract–transform–load) tools);
* deployment tools;
* ITSM tools;
* DevOps tools; and
* AI-driven development tools.

Some of the tools explored in this chapter are common to defining and designing digital solutions, and have been reproduced from Books 1 and 2 for completeness.

COLLABORATION TOOLS

Collaboration tools play a vital role in promoting effective teamwork by enabling seamless communication, coordination and idea sharing among team members. Designed to boost productivity and innovation, these tools empower remote and in-office teams to collaborate smoothly and efficiently, ensuring everyone remains informed and aligned.

Typical features provided by collaboration tools include:

- real-time messaging and video conferencing;
- digital whiteboards for brainstorming;
- file sharing and integration with other tools; and
- task tracking and commenting for collaborative work.

Typical examples of collaboration tools include: Microsoft Teams, Slack, Miro, Mural, Google Workspace, Dropbox, Asana and Notion.

BACKLOG MANAGEMENT TOOLS

Backlog management tools assist teams in effectively organising, prioritising and tracking tasks or features throughout the development process. These tools provide a centralised platform to manage requirements, user stories and defects, ensuring transparency and clear visibility of what needs attention. By ranking tasks based on urgency or value, they help designers and developers to focus on critical work that aligns with project objectives. Additionally, they promote collaboration by enabling team members to update progress, share feedback and assign responsibilities in real time, thereby enhancing productivity, minimising miscommunication and ensuring the final solution meets user and stakeholder expectations.

Typical features provided by backlog management tools include:

- Agile and Kanban boards for visualisation and prioritisation of tasks and features;
- backlog refinement and dependency tracking;
- integration with development workflows and tools; and
- iteration planning and burndown charts for monitoring team progress.

Typical examples of backlog management tools include: Jira, Trello, Azure DevOps, Wrike and ClickUp.

DOCUMENT MANAGEMENT TOOLS

Document management tools are essential for centralising, organising and securely managing digital documents. They facilitate efficient document retrieval and collaboration, helping development teams to streamline workflows, maintain compliance and reduce dependence on paper-based processes.

Typical features provided by document management tools include:

- version control;
- role-based access;
- advanced search and metadata tagging;
- collaboration with commenting and real-time updates; and
- compliance with regulatory standards.

Typical examples of document management tools include: SharePoint, Google Workspace, Box, Alfresco, M-Files, Notion and DocuWare.

RISK MANAGEMENT AND SECURITY TOOLS

Risk management and security tools help to identify, assess and mitigate potential risks while ensuring robust protection against security threats. These tools enable teams to conduct vulnerability assessments, monitor for breaches and enforce compliance with security standards and regulations. By integrating features like threat detection, risk scoring and real-time alerts, they enable designers and developers to address vulnerabilities early in the design process. This proactive approach ensures that digital solutions are not only secure and resilient, but also align with user trust and organisational requirements for data protection and risk minimisation.

Typical examples of risk management and security tools include: ProjectManager, StandardFusion, RSA Archer and LogicManager.

DOCUMENTATION TOOLS

Documentation tools facilitate the creation, organisation and sharing of technical and project-related information. There are various sub-categories of documentation tools, identified below.

Generic documentation

Typical examples of general documentation tools include: Confluence (a collaborative workspace for creating, sharing and organising project documentation, meeting notes and knowledge bases), Notion (a flexible all-in-one workspace for documentation, wikis and task management, popular for both technical and non-technical teams), Microsoft OneNote (for capturing project notes, ideas and meeting minutes in a structured, searchable format) and Google Docs (enables real-time collaboration on documents, often used for drafting and sharing specifications, plans and reports).

API and developer documentation

Typical examples of API and developer documentation tools include: Swagger/OpenAPI (defining and documenting APIs), PostMan (testing and monitoring APIs throughout the development process) and Read the Docs (hosts documentation built from code repositories – commonly used for open-source or developer-centric projects).

Code documentation

Typical examples of code documentation tools include: Doxygen (generates documentation from annotated C++, C, Java and other source code files), Javadoc (for generating API documentation in HTML format from Java source code comments) and Sphinx (widely used in the Python ecosystem to create intelligent and structured documentation from reStructuredText sources).

System and process documentation

Typical examples of system and process documentation tools include: Lucidchart (a visual collaboration tool for drawing diagrams such as flowcharts, architecture diagrams and process maps), Diagrams.net (a free diagramming tool for creating system models, workflows and technical architecture diagrams; formerly Draw.io) and Markdown (with GitHub/GitLab wikis; a lightweight markup language used to document code, projects and processes directly in repositories).

CARE TOOLS

CARE tools are specialised software applications that assist in the various tasks associated with the discipline of Requirements Engineering. These tasks include eliciting, analysing, documenting, validating and managing requirements. CARE tools play a crucial role in ensuring that requirements are well defined, consistent, comprehensive and traceable throughout the entire development life cycle. By leveraging these tools, development teams can minimise misunderstandings, enhance collaboration with stakeholders and significantly improve the likelihood of delivering a digital solution that aligns with user expectations and business objectives.

Typical features provided by CARE tools include:

- **Requirements elicitation support**: Tools for capturing stakeholder needs, such as interview templates, surveys or collaboration platforms.
- **Modelling and visualisation**: Support for creating diagrams such as use cases, class diagrams and wireframes.
- **Requirements documentation**: Support for maintaining a repository of requirements definitions (e.g. a requirements catalogue or solution backlog). See also *Backlog management tools*.

- **Traceability management**: Linking requirements to design elements, test cases and implementation artefacts.

- **Version control and change tracking**: Managing revisions and tracking changes to requirements over time.

Typical examples of CARE tools include: IBM Engineering Requirements Management DOORS (formerly IBM Rational DOORS), Jama Connect, ReqView and Modern Requirements4DevOps.

CASE TOOLS

CASE tools streamline and automate essential stages of the software development life cycle (SDLC). While they were once at the core of development workflows, many CASE tools have since been incorporated into more extensive and specialised software ecosystems. These tools support system design, modelling, code generation and testing, enhancing efficiency and shortening development timelines. Designed to integrate seamlessly into contemporary workflows, CASE tools enable teams to develop high-quality software systems with greater accuracy and reduced error rates.

Typical features provided by CASE tools include:

- support for modelling and design (such as Unified Modeling Language (UML) diagrams and entity–relationship diagrams);

- code generation (forward engineering) and reverse engineering;

- integration with testing, debugging and deployment tools; and

- workflow automation for SDLC phases.

Typical examples of CASE tools include: IBM Rational Rose, IBM Engineering Workflow Management (formerly Rational Team Concert), Enterprise Architect, Visual Paradigm, ArgoUML, StarUML, MagicDraw and Modelio.

CAST TOOLS

CAST tools are software applications designed to automate or support various aspects of the software testing process. These tools enhance the efficiency, accuracy and coverage of testing activities, helping teams to identify defects, verify functionality and ensure the quality and reliability of digital solutions.

Typical features provided by CAST tools include:

- automating repetitive tests (such as running test cases automatically) to reduce manual effort and increase speed;

- managing test cases by organising, documenting and executing test scenarios in a structured way;

- tracking defects through identifying, logging and monitoring bugs or issues found during testing;

- performance testing by simulating load, stress or scalability conditions to evaluate system behaviour;

- support for regression testing by automatically running suites of regression tests to ensure that new changes don't break existing functionality; and

- continuous testing through integration with CI/CD pipelines to enable frequent and consistent testing throughout development.

Typical examples of CAST tools include:

- TestRail and Zephyr (test management), Selenium and Katalon Studio (automated functional testing);

- JMeter, LoadRunner and Selenium (performance testing);

- JUnit, NUnit, Pytest and Mocha (unit testing frameworks);

- JUnit, TestNG and Spring (integration testing);

- GitHub Actions and Jenkins with test plugins (continuous testing);

- SonarQube (static analysis: cyclomatic complexity, lines of code, code coverage, Halstead metrics, technical debt, maintainability index); and

- GitHub Pull Requests, GitLab Merge Requests, Crucible and Phabricator (code reviews).

Many CAST tools specifically support Agile testing, such as:

- Selenium (for automating web browser interactions);

- JUnit/PyTest/NUnit (for unit testing across different languages – Java, Python, .NET);

- Cucumber (for behaviour-driven development, enabling business stakeholders to write tests in natural language);

- Jenkins (a CI/CD tool for automating test execution within build pipelines); and

- TestRail (for managing and tracking test cases and results).

PROGRAMMING LANGUAGES

Programming languages are formal languages used to communicate instructions to a computer, enabling developers to create digital solutions. Each language has its own syntax, structure and use cases, enabling developers to express logic (algorithms), control hardware, process data and build user interfaces. From general-purpose languages like Python and Java to specialised ones like HTML or SQL, programming languages form the foundation of all digital solutions, translating human ideas into executable commands that drive technology.

A wide range of programming languages are used to develop digital solutions, each with its own strengths and typical use cases. Some of the more popular languages are described briefly here:

- **JavaScript**: A core language for front-end web development, JavaScript enables dynamic and interactive elements on websites. With environments such as Node.js, it is also widely used for back-end development.
- **Python**: Known for its readability and versatility, Python is used in web development (e.g. with Django or Flask), data science, machine learning, automation and scripting.
- **Java**: A statically typed, object-oriented language often used for enterprise applications, Android development and large-scale systems. It is known for portability and scalability.
- **C#**: Developed by Microsoft, C# is widely used for developing Windows applications, enterprise software and games (via Unity).
- **PHP**: A server-side scripting language commonly used for web development and content management systems such as WordPress. Frameworks like Laravel have modernised PHP-based development.
- **Ruby**: Known for its elegant syntax, Ruby is primarily used with the Ruby on Rails framework for building web applications quickly and efficiently.
- **TypeScript**: A superset of JavaScript that adds static typing, TypeScript improves code maintainability and is widely adopted in large-scale web applications.
- **Go (Golang)**: Developed by Google, Go is known for its simplicity and performance, often used in cloud computing, networking and microservices.
- **Swift**: A powerful language developed by Apple for building iOS, macOS and other Apple ecosystem applications, known for safety and performance.
- **Kotlin**: A modern, concise language that is fully interoperable with Java, Kotlin is now the preferred language for Android app development.
- **Structured Query Language (SQL)**: A specialised programming language used for managing, querying and manipulating data in relational databases.
- **HyperText Markup Language (HTML)**: A markup language[76] used to structure and present content on the web by defining elements such as text, images, links and multimedia.

These languages form the backbone of modern software development, and the choice of language depends on the project's requirements, platform targets and developer preferences.

---

76 A markup language is a system for annotating text in a way that defines its structure and presentation, often using tags to format and organise content for display in browsers or other media.

INTEGRATED DEVELOPMENT ENVIRONMENTS

IDEs are software applications that provide a comprehensive set of tools for software development within a single user interface. They are designed to streamline and support the coding process by combining a range of individual tools and features that developers typically use during the software engineering cycle (see Chapter 2). IDEs improve productivity by reducing the need to switch between separate tools and by offering smart code suggestions, quick navigation and built-in tools that help to detect and resolve issues more efficiently.

Typical features provided by IDEs include:

- **Source code editor**: A text editor tailored to specific programming languages, offering features such as syntax highlighting and validation, automatic formatting, intelligent code completion and real-time error detection.

- **Compiler or interpreter**: An integrated tool that translates source code into executable software. It enables developers to test code as it is written, identifying compilation errors early in the development process. A compiler translates the entire source code into executable machine code before the program runs, while an interpreter executes the code line by line at runtime without producing a separate executable file.

- **Debugger**: Helps developers to identify and fix issues by running code line by line and inspecting the runtime environment (e.g. the value of variables and object properties).

- **Build automation**: A built-in tool that automates routine tasks involved in creating executable software, such as compiling, linking, packaging code and running tests. See also *DevOps tools*.

- **Version control integration**: Supports systems like Git for managing code changes and collaboration (such as checking code in and out).

- **Project and file management**: Organises code files, libraries and configurations in a structured workspace.

- **Console and UI simulator**: Enables developers to view program output and interact with a simulated user interface, enabling real-time testing and debugging of applications.

- **Emulators for operating systems, devices and browsers**: Software that enables developers to test and debug applications in virtual environments that replicate real-world platforms and conditions.

- **Static testing and code quality metrics**: These are used to analyse source code without executing it to identify potential errors, enforce coding standards and assess maintainability and overall code quality.

- **Integration with unit testing frameworks**: Enables developers to write, execute and manage automated tests directly within the IDE, ensuring individual components function correctly and supporting test-driven development.

Typical examples of IDEs include:

- Visual Studio (for .NET, C++ and other languages);

- IntelliJ IDEA (for Java, Kotlin and other languages);

- Eclipse (for Java, C/C++ and other languages);

- PyCharm (for Python);

- Xcode (for iOS/macOS app development); and

- Android Studio (for Android app development).

STANDALONE DEVELOPMENT TOOLS

While IDEs offer a comprehensive suite of features within a single interface, many developers also rely on standalone development tools that serve specific purposes outside an IDE. These tools are often more lightweight, modular or specialised, providing flexibility and control over various aspects of the development workflow. Examples include dedicated code editors, version control systems (VCSs), compilers, debuggers, build tools and linters.[77] Unlike IDEs, which bundle these features together, standalone tools enable developers to tailor their environments to their specific needs, often integrating them through command-line interfaces or configuration files.

Some of the most commonly used standalone development tools are explored below.

Front-end development tools

Front-end development tools are software applications and frameworks that assist developers in designing and building the visual and interactive elements of websites and web applications – the parts users see and interact with. These tools include code editors (like VS Code), frameworks (such as React, Angular or Vue.js), cascading style sheets (CSS) pre-processors (such as Sass or LESS) and build tools (such as Webpack or Vite) that streamline the coding process. They help to manage layout, styling, responsiveness and user interactions while improving code efficiency, maintainability and performance. Front-end tools also often include debugging utilities, browser developer tools and component libraries that accelerate development and ensure a consistent user experience across devices and platforms.

Back-end development tools

Back-end development tools are software solutions and frameworks used to build and manage the server-side logic, databases and application architecture that power web and mobile applications behind the scenes. These tools handle functions such as data processing, authentication, API creation and server configuration. Common back-end languages like Python, Java, Node.js, PHP and Ruby are supported by frameworks such

---

77 A linter is a code analysis tool that automatically checks source code for syntax errors, defects and stylistic issues, helping developers to improve code quality and maintain consistency.

as Django, Express.js, Spring Boot and Laravel, which help to streamline development by providing reusable components and structure. Back-end development tools also include database management systems, version control and DevOps/infrastructure tools (see below), all of which contribute to building scalable, secure and efficient applications.

Code optimisation tools

Code optimisation tools are software utilities designed to improve the performance, efficiency and maintainability of source code. These tools analyse code to detect issues such as redundancy, inefficient algorithms, memory leaks or unnecessary complexity, and often provide suggestions or automated fixes. They help to streamline execution by reducing load times, minimising resource consumption and improving overall responsiveness. Common examples include linters (e.g. ESLint, Pylint), profilers[78] (like Valgrind, VisualVM) and minifiers[79] (such as UglifyJS or CSSNano) that compress files for faster delivery. By identifying bottlenecks and enforcing best practices, code optimisation tools play a crucial role in enhancing software performance and ensuring a smoother user experience.

Version control tools

Version control tools are software utilities that help developers to manage and track changes to code throughout a digital solution development project. They maintain a full history of edits, making it easy to go back to earlier versions, fix conflicts and enable multiple people to work on the same code without overwriting each other's changes. Key features include change tracking, branching, merging and rollback, which support collaboration and well-organised development. Tools such as Git, Subversion and Mercurial, along with platforms including GitHub, GitLab and Bitbucket, also offer cloud storage and team features, making version control a vital part of producing high-quality software.

Build automation tools

Build automation tools are software utilities that automate the process of compiling source code into executable programs, packaging applications and managing dependencies. These tools streamline repetitive tasks such as compiling code, executing tests, creating builds and deploying applications, helping developers to ensure consistency and efficiency across development and production environments. They are essential in CI and CI/CD pipelines, reducing human error and saving time. Common examples include Apache Maven (for Java), Gradle, Make and npm scripts, all of which help to standardise the build process and improve overall productivity in software development.

---

78 A profiler is a performance analysis tool that monitors a program's execution to identify resource-intensive functions, memory usage and bottlenecks, helping developers to optimise code efficiency.

79 A minifier is a code optimisation tool that reduces file size by eliminating unnecessary characters – such as whitespace, comments and line breaks – without changing the code's functionality, helping to improve load times and overall performance.

Mocking frameworks

Mocking frameworks are standalone libraries that integrate smoothly with test environments to simulate the behaviour of real objects or components, enabling developers to test code in isolation without relying on external systems such as databases, APIs or services. Using mocking frameworks, developers can define how dependencies should behave during tests and verify interactions, making unit tests more reliable, faster and easier to write. For example, in C#, the **Moq** framework can mock an interface like `iUserService` to return a specific user without needing the real implementation. In Java, **Mockito** enables developers to create mock objects and specify expected method calls, while in Python, **unittest.mock** can replace parts of an application during test execution.

Code documentation tools

Code documentation tools enable developers to generate and manage clear, consistent documentation directly from source code by leveraging comments, annotations or structured markup. These tools automate the creation of references, usage guides and developer notes, reducing manual effort while improving accuracy and consistency. They play a key role in enhancing collaboration, accelerating onboarding and ensuring long-term project maintainability by keeping technical information organised and accessible. Common examples include Javadoc (for Java), Doxygen (for C/C++) and Sphinx (for Python).

Complementing these tools, markdown editors (such as Obsidian, StackEdit, Mark Text and Atom) enable users to write and format lightweight, structured documents using Markdown syntax, which can be easily converted into styled HTML for web-based documentation.

Evolutionary prototyping tools

Evolutionary prototyping tools support a development approach where a functional prototype is built early and continuously refined based on user feedback, evolving into the final product. This method is particularly useful when requirements are not fully understood from the outset, enabling developers to implement known features first and iteratively add new ones as they become clearer. Tools like Axure, Proto.io and Adobe XD facilitate this process by enabling designers to create interactive prototypes that can be incrementally updated. These platforms support the integration of new features and adjustments without the need to rebuild from scratch, making them ideal for projects that benefit from ongoing user input and iterative development. IDEs and no-code/low-code tools are also suitable for supporting evolutionary prototyping, as well as languages such as JavaScript/HTML/CSS and SwiftUI (for iOS apps).

Remote pair programming tools

Introduced in Chapter 4, pair programming is a collaborative technique where two developers work together on the same code, with one writing (the driver) and the other reviewing and guiding (the navigator), regularly switching roles to improve code quality and share knowledge.

Remote pair programming tools extend this practice across different locations, enabling real-time collaboration and communication. These tools typically offer features such as shared code editing, video/audio chat and collaborative debugging within IDEs, effectively replicating the experience of in-person pairing. Popular tools include Visual Studio Live Share for real-time collaboration in VS Code, CodeTogether for cross-IDE coding, Tuple for low-latency pairing, GitHub Codespaces and CodeSandbox Live for browser-based live sessions. By using these tools, distributed development teams can stay connected, productive and aligned, regardless of where they work.

Behaviour-driven development tools

Behaviour-driven development (BDD) tools support a collaborative software development process that encourages communication between developers, testers and business stakeholders by using natural language descriptions of desired system behaviour. These tools enable teams to write test scenarios using the Gherkin language (Given–When–Then structure) – which serves as both documentation and automated acceptance tests. BDD tools bridge the gap between technical and non-technical team members, ensuring shared understanding of requirements. Popular BDD tools include Cucumber (a widely used BDD framework that supports the automation of tests written in Gherkin syntax to create feature files[80]), SpecFlow (for .NET), Behave (for Python) and JBehave (for Java). By integrating with testing frameworks and CI/CD pipelines, BDD tools help to ensure that applications meet business expectations while promoting test-driven and collaborative development practices.

WEB DEVELOPMENT PLATFORMS

Web development platforms are software environments or services that provide the tools and frameworks needed to build, deploy and manage websites and web applications. Designed to accommodate users of all skill levels, these platforms range from intuitive website builders for beginners to advanced full stack environments and application frameworks for experienced developers. By streamlining the development and launch process, they make it easier for individuals and teams to create functional, scalable web solutions tailored to a variety of technical needs and project requirements.

Typical features provided by web development platforms include the following:

- **Pre-built components** are ready-made interface elements or code modules – such as forms, buttons and navigation menus – that help users to quickly assemble and customise websites or applications without the need to develop each element manually.

- **Customisable templates** are pre-designed website layouts that users can easily modify in terms of content, style and structure to match their specific branding and functional needs.

---

80 A feature file in is a plain-text document that contains one or more scenarios typically written in the Gherkin language to describe the desired behaviour of a software feature.

- **Visual website builders** provide an intuitive drag-and-drop interface that enables users to design and edit web pages by visually arranging elements in real time, making it easy to customise layouts and content without the need to write code.

- **Code editors** enable developers to write, edit and manage source code with features such as syntax highlighting, auto-completion and error detection to enhance productivity and code accuracy.

- **Hosting and domain management** enable users to publish their websites online and manage domain names directly within the platform, streamlining deployment and ensuring seamless access for visitors.

- **Search engine optimisation (SEO) tools and analytics** help users to optimise their websites for search engines and track performance metrics such as traffic, user behaviour and engagement, enabling data-driven improvements and increased online visibility.

- **Integration with third-party services** enables web development platforms to connect seamlessly with external tools (such as payment gateways, marketing platforms, CRM systems and social media), enhancing website functionality and the user experience.

There are a variety of different types of web development platforms, including the following:

- **No-code/low-code platforms** enable users to build websites and applications with minimal or no programming, using visual interfaces and pre-built components to streamline the development process. Typical examples include Microsoft PowerApps, Wix, Squarespace, Webflow and Bubble.

- **Content management systems (CMSs)** enable users to create, manage and publish digital content on websites without needing to write code, using customisable templates and user-friendly interfaces. Typical examples include WordPress, Joomla and Drupal.

- **Full stack development platforms** offer a comprehensive set of tools and services for both front-end and back-end development, often incorporating features such as version control, testing and deployment to support the entire SDLC within a unified environment. Typical examples include Visual Studio Code + Node.js, Firebase and Netlify.

- **Ecommerce platforms** provide specialised tools and features for building and managing online stores, including product catalogues, shopping carts, payment gateways, inventory tracking and customer management, all within a single platform. Typical examples include Shopify, BigCommerce and Magento.

- **Framework-based platforms** offer structured environments and reusable components that streamline the development of custom web applications, supporting best practices, scalability and rapid development. Typical examples include Django, Ruby on Rails and Laravel.

MDA, NO-CODE AND LOW-CODE PLATFORMS

Model-driven architecture, no-code and low-code platforms represent a modern approach to software development that emphasises speed, automation and accessibility. These platforms reduce or eliminate the need for manual coding by enabling users to build applications through visual models, pre-built components and drag-and-drop interfaces. While MDA focuses on generating application code from high-level models using defined standards, no-code platforms cater primarily to non-technical users by offering fully visual development environments. Low-code platforms strike a balance between the two, enabling developers to accelerate application delivery while retaining the flexibility to add custom code when needed. Together, these approaches empower a broader range of users to participate in digital solution delivery.

Typical features provided by MDA platforms include the following:

- **Model-based design tools** support the creation of high-level visual models (e.g. UML) to define application structure and behaviour.

- **Automatic code generation** creates application code from models using transformation engines.

- **Platform independence** means design models can be transformed into applications for different target platforms.

- **Standards-based architecture** enables the use of Object Management Group standards like UML, Meta-Object Facility (MOF) and XML Metadata Interchange (XMI) for model consistency.

- **Traceability and version control** maintains links between models, code and documentation for life cycle management.

Typical features provided by no-code platforms include the following:

- **Drag-and-drop interface** enables users to build UIs and workflows visually with no coding required.

- **Pre-built templates and components** provide ready-to-use modules for forms, pages, reports and logic.

- **Workflow automation** using tools to define and automate business processes and logic.

- **Real-time previews** with instant feedback on changes made during app design.

- **Built-in deployment** with one-click publishing and hosting of applications.

Typical features provided by low-code platforms include the following:

- **Visual development environment** that combines graphical tools with the ability to add custom code when needed.

- **Reusable components** such as drag-and-drop widgets, connectors and logic blocks for faster app creation.

- **Integration capabilities** using APIs and connectors to link with third-party systems and databases.

- **Version control and collaboration tools** support team-based development and deployment.

- **Scalable deployment options** so apps can be deployed across environments such as cloud, on-premises or hybrid.

Typical examples of MDA, no-code and low-code platforms include: OutSystems (MDA and low-code), Mendix (MDA and low-code), Sparx Systems Enterprise Architect (MDA), GeneXus (MDA), Visual Paradigm (MDA), Wix (no-code), Squarespace (no-code), Bubble. io (no-code and low-code), Appian (low-code), Microsoft Power Apps (low-code).

CONFIGURATION MANAGEMENT TOOLS

Configuration management tools are essential for automating the setup, deployment and maintenance of infrastructure across development, testing and production environments. These tools ensure consistency, reliability and standardisation by defining system configurations as code – enabling version control, auditing and reusability. A core element of configuration management is the identification and tracking of **configuration items** – such as servers, software components, network devices and documentation – which are recorded in a **configuration management database**. The configuration management database serves as a central repository that stores information about each configuration item and its relationships with other configuration items, helping teams to understand system architecture and inter-dependencies, assess the impact of changes and maintain compliance. Common features of configuration management tools include provisioning, dependency management and rollback capabilities. Popular tools such as Ansible, Chef, Puppet and Terraform help to manage large-scale IT environments efficiently, reduce manual errors and support modern DevOps and CD practices by promoting infrastructure as code (IAC).

DATA MANAGEMENT TOOLS

Data management tools are software solutions designed to help organisations collect, store, organise, protect and utilise data efficiently. These tools support a wide range of functions, including:

- metadata management;

- data governance;

- database management;

- data integration;

- data quality assurance;

- data security; and

- data analytics and visualisation.

By centralising control over data assets, data management tools enable consistent data access, reduce redundancy, ensure compliance with regulations and improve decision-making across departments.

Popular tools that support these functions are discussed below.

Metadata management tools

Metadata management tools are software solutions that help organisations to systematically capture, organise and maintain metadata – information about data such as its origin, structure, meaning, usage and relationships. These tools provide a centralised repository for metadata, enabling users to understand the context and lineage[81] of data assets across systems and the organisation as a whole. By supporting features such as data cataloguing, lineage tracking, impact analysis and business glossaries, these tools enhance data governance, improve data quality and facilitate compliance with regulations. Commonly used tools include Collibra, Alation, Informatica Enterprise Data Catalog and IBM Watson Knowledge Catalog.

Data governance tools

Data governance tools are software solutions designed to help organisations define, implement and enforce policies and procedures for managing data assets responsibly and effectively. These tools provide frameworks for data ownership, access control, policy enforcement, compliance tracking and data stewardship (responsible management and oversight of the organisation's data assets to ensure their controlled use across the enterprise), ensuring that data is accurate, secure and used in alignment with regulatory requirements and business objectives. They often include features such as role-based permissions, audit trails, data quality monitoring and integration with metadata management systems. Popular data governance tools include Collibra, Alation, Informatica Axon and IBM Data Governance.

Database management systems

Database management systems (DBMSs) are software applications that enable users to efficiently create, store, retrieve, update and manage data in structured formats. They provide an interface between end-users or applications and the underlying data, ensuring data integrity, security and consistency across multiple operations. DBMSs support various data structures, with **relational databases** (e.g. MySQL, PostgreSQL, Microsoft SQL Server, IBM DB2 and Oracle Database) being the most common, while **NoSQL databases** (e.g. MongoDB and Cassandra) are suited for unstructured or large-scale data. Key features include query processing, transaction management, access control, backup and recovery and data concurrency.

---

81 Data lineage is the process of tracing the flow of data from its original source through various transformations to its final destination, helping to ensure transparency, accuracy and regulatory compliance.

Data integration tools

Data integration tools are software solutions that enable organisations to combine data from multiple, often disparate, sources into a unified and consistent view, making it easier to analyse and derive insights. These tools support the extraction, transformation and loading (ETL) of data (see *ETL tools* below), as well as real-time and batch integration methods, ensuring that data is synchronised, accurate and readily accessible across systems. Key features often include connectors for various data sources, data mapping, cleaning and workflow automation.

ETL tools

ETL tools are a specialised type of data integration software that helps to transfer and prepare data from multiple sources for use in centralised repositories such as data warehouses or data lakes. The **extract** phase involves gathering data from sources such as databases, APIs, spreadsheets and files. During the **transform** phase, the data is cleaned, formatted and restructured to align with business needs. Finally, in the **load** phase, the processed data is transferred into the target system for analysis and reporting. ETL tools are vital for building reliable data pipelines enabling seamless data flow, and also play a key role in data migration, especially when preparing to launch new digital solutions. These tools support automation, scheduling, error handling and data quality checks, ensuring that workflows are efficient, accurate and repeatable. Popular examples include Talend, Apache Nifi, Informatica, Microsoft SQL Server Integration Services and Apache Airflow.

Data quality assurance tools

Data quality assurance tools are software solutions designed to assess, monitor and improve the accuracy, completeness, consistency and reliability of data across an organisation. These tools help to identify and correct errors, standardise data formats, eliminate duplicates and validate data against defined business rules. They often include features such as data profiling, cleaning, validation checks, real-time monitoring and dashboards for tracking data quality metrics. Popular tools include Informatica Data Quality, Talend Data Quality, SAP Information Steward and Ataccama, which support both automated and manual data quality processes.

Data security tools

Data security tools are software solutions designed to protect digital information from unauthorised access, corruption, theft or loss. They employ various techniques, including encryption, access controls, data masking, data loss prevention, monitoring and backup and recovery to ensure the confidentiality, integrity and availability of data. They are essential for organisations to maintain data privacy, comply with regulations such as General Data Protection Regulation (GDPR) and protect against cyber threats. Popular data security tools include Symantec Data Loss Prevention, McAfee Total Protection for Data Loss Prevention, Varonis Data Security Platform and Digital Guardian.

Data analytics and visualisation tools

Data analytics and visualisation tools are software applications that empower organisations to collect, process, analyse and visually represent data to uncover insights and support informed decision-making. These tools facilitate the transformation of raw data into interactive dashboards, charts and graphs, making complex information more accessible and understandable for both technical and non-technical users. Prominent examples include Tableau, Microsoft Power BI, Qlik Sense, Looker Studio and IBM Cognos Analytics, which offer features like real-time data integration, customisable visualisations and advanced analytics capabilities. Additionally, platforms such as KNIME provide a visual workflow interface for data analysis, catering to users with varying levels of programming expertise.

DEPLOYMENT TOOLS

Deployment tools are software solutions that automate and manage the release of applications and updates across different environments, such as testing, staging and production. They streamline the transition from development to live deployment by handling key tasks like version control, configuration, packaging, distribution and rollout strategies, including blue/green and canary deployments. By automating these processes, deployment tools help to reduce downtime, minimise human error and accelerate the delivery of new features and bug fixes. They are essential for ensuring consistent, repeatable and high-quality releases, and often integrate with CI/CD pipelines to support Agile and DevOps workflows (see *DevOps tools* below). Common deployment tools include AWS CodeDeploy, Octopus Deploy, Ansible, Spinnaker, Jenkins and Azure Pipelines.

ITSM TOOLS

IT service management tools are software solutions that enable IT teams to plan, deliver, operate and manage IT services effectively in alignment with business needs. They streamline processes such as handling service requests, incidents, problems, changes and asset management using standardised workflows and ITIL-based best practices. Common features include service desk ticketing, self-service portals, knowledge bases, automation and reporting dashboards. By enhancing visibility, accountability and response times, ITSM tools improve user satisfaction and operational performance. Widely used platforms such as ServiceNow, BMC Helix, Ivanti, Freshservice and Jira Service Management play a vital role in delivering consistent, high-quality and compliant IT services across organisations.

DEVOPS TOOLS

DevOps tools comprise a unified ecosystem that automates and streamlines software development, testing, deployment and operations throughout the entire delivery life cycle. By reducing manual effort, enhancing collaboration and accelerating release cycles, these tools enable teams to deliver high-quality software more reliably and efficiently.

In the planning phase, tools like Jira, Trello, Asana and Azure DevOps Boards help to manage tasks and track progress. For coding and version control, developers use Git, GitHub, GitLab, Bitbucket and IDEs such as Visual Studio Code and IntelliJ IDEA. Build automation is handled by tools such as Jenkins, Maven, Gradle and Apache Ant, which compile and package code.

Testing is a key part of the DevOps process, with tools including Selenium for browser automation, JUnit, PyTest and NUnit for unit testing, Cucumber for BDD, Apache JMeter for performance testing, and OWASP ZAP for integrating security tests into CI/CD pipelines.

CI tools – such as Jenkins, CircleCI, GitLab CI/CD and Azure Pipelines – automate the integration of code changes into a shared repository, running builds and tests with each commit[82] to catch issues early and maintain code stability. CD tools then automatically release validated code to production, eliminating manual steps, reducing errors and enabling faster delivery of updates.

During the release and deployment stages, tools such as Jenkins, GitLab CI/CD, CircleCI, Travis CI, AWS CodeDeploy, Azure Pipelines, Docker, Kubernetes, Ansible and Helm automate delivery and infrastructure provisioning. IaC is managed with tools including Terraform and AWS CloudFormation, while configuration management is supported by Ansible, Chef and Puppet.

In the monitoring and operations phase, tools such as Prometheus, Grafana, New Relic, Splunk and the ELK Stack (Elasticsearch, Logstash, Kibana) offer insights into system performance, health and usage through real-time metrics and log analysis.

Together, these tools support a seamless DevOps workflow, from planning and coding to deployment and monitoring.

AI-DRIVEN DEVELOPMENT TOOLS

AI-driven tools play a transformative role in the delivery of digital solutions by applying AI and machine learning (ML) across the SDLC to boost productivity, precision and responsiveness. These tools streamline tasks such as code generation, automated testing, defect detection and deployment, while also enabling predictive analytics, data-driven insights and anomaly detection for smarter decision-making.

In project management, AI helps to optimise scheduling, resource allocation and risk forecasting, while in operations it supports intelligent monitoring, proactive troubleshooting and even self-healing systems (software or infrastructure that can automatically detect, diagnose and fix issues or failures without human intervention). For example, GitHub Copilot and Tabnine assist developers by generating code suggestions and enhancing coding speed and accuracy. Testim.io and Applitools use AI for automated UI, regression and functional testing, ensuring higher software quality. Tools like Dynatrace and New Relic apply AI to monitor performance, identify issues and recommend improvements in real time. Finally, platforms such as TensorFlow, PyTorch and Google Vertex AI empower teams to build and embed custom AI models into their applications.

By integrating AI-driven tools, development teams can accelerate delivery, reduce manual errors and create more adaptive, efficient and resilient digital solutions.

---

82 A commit is the action of saving a set of code changes to a VCS, creating a snapshot that records what was changed, by whom and why. In CI, each commit triggers automated processes including building and testing the application.

AFTERWORD

The *Digital Solutions* series takes readers on a complete journey through the life cycle of digital solutions, from initial concept to operational reality. Book 1 (*Defining Digital Solutions*) introduces how digital solutions are conceived and procured in response to business needs, emphasising the importance of strategic alignment, effective Requirements Engineering and informed acquisition decisions. It highlights the foundational role of clear, well-managed requirements and robust modelling practices in setting up digital initiatives for success.

In Book 2 (*Designing Digital Solutions*), the focus shifts to shaping business needs into structured, practical designs. The book explores the design of system inputs and outputs, processes, data structures, controls (including cybersecurity) and architecture, illustrating how strong design principles underpin scalable, secure and user-centred solutions. It demonstrates how thoughtful design acts as a bridge between business aspirations and technical realisation, ensuring solutions are functional, resilient and adaptable.

Book 3 (*Delivering Digital Solutions*) completes the journey by examining the disciplines and practices that transform solution design into operational systems. It covers essential activities such as software engineering, testing, deployment, change management and post-delivery support, offering practical guidance on sustaining the long-term value of digital solutions in a constantly evolving business environment.

Together, the three books offer a comprehensive framework for professionals involved in digital business change, including analysts, designers, developers, managers and business stakeholders. In an era of rapid technological evolution, the ability to define, design and deliver digital solutions effectively is crucial. The series aims to equip readers with the knowledge, techniques and confidence to drive successful digital transformation within their organisations.

LOOKING TO THE FUTURE OF DIGITAL SOLUTIONS

In today's fast-paced technological landscape, digital solutions are transforming how businesses, governments and individuals interact with the world. Developments in AI, cloud computing, low-code platforms and the Internet of Things are driving new levels of efficiency, personalisation and connectivity. Organisations are embracing digital-first strategies to meet rising customer expectations, streamline operations and stay competitive in a global market. Meanwhile, advances in cybersecurity, data analytics and automation are creating smarter, more resilient ecosystems that not only enhance existing processes but also fundamentally reshape industries and societies.

As digital technologies continue to evolve, emerging fields such as quantum computing,[83] augmented reality[84] and autonomous systems[85] are set to push the boundaries of what is possible. Businesses and societies must look beyond adapting to current trends and proactively prepare for the next wave of transformation. Future-ready strategies will prioritise agility, ethical innovation and sustainable growth, ensuring that digital solutions continue to drive progress while addressing complex global challenges.

While nobody has a crystal ball to see into the future, the following areas of innovation are likely to dominate in digital solutions of the future:

- **Hyper-automation**: Future digital solutions are likely to combine AI, robotic process automation, low-code platforms and advanced analytics to automate increasingly complex business and IT processes end-to-end.

- **AI-generated solutions**: Generative AI models are likely to play a larger role in designing, developing and optimising digital solutions, from creating code to designing user interfaces, testing and even creating documentation automatically.

- **Quantum computing integration**: As quantum computing matures, it will open new possibilities for solving complex optimisation, encryption and data analysis problems at speeds unattainable with classical computing, leading to a new generation of digital solutions.

- **Ethical and sustainable digital design**: Future digital solutions will almost certainly place greater emphasis on ethical considerations – such as fairness, transparency and bias mitigation – and on designing for environmental sustainability, including optimised energy usage and carbon footprint reduction.

- **Decentralised architectures**: Solutions leveraging blockchain and decentralised architectures are likely to become more common in areas such as finance, supply chain, digital identity and contract management, offering transparency, trust and reduced dependency on central authorities.

- **Augmented and virtual reality (AR/VR)**: Digital solutions will increasingly incorporate AR and VR technologies to create immersive, interactive experiences for training, education, healthcare, retail and more.

- **Composable architecture**: Future solutions will increasingly be developed using modular, interchangeable components, enabling organisations to quickly adapt and reconfigure their systems in response to emerging opportunities and challenges, without the need for extensive redevelopment.

Thank you for joining me on this journey through the evolving world of digital solutions – may the insights shared in this book and its siblings in the *Digital Solutions Collection* inspire you to shape the future with innovation, purpose and confidence.

---

83 Quantum computing uses quantum bits (qubits) and the principles of quantum mechanics to perform complex calculations much faster than classical computers.

84 Augmented reality is a technology that enhances the real world by overlaying digital content – such as images, sounds or information – in real time, while virtual reality offers a fully immersive experience by placing users in a completely digital environment.

85 Autonomous systems are self-directed technologies that can perform tasks or make decisions without human intervention, often using sensors, algorithms and artificial intelligence.

REFERENCES

AXELOS (2019) *ITIL® Foundation: ITIL 4 Edition*. London: The Stationery Office.

Beck, K. (2003) *Test-Driven Development: By Example*. Boston, MA: Addison-Wesley.

Cadle, J., Paul, D., Hunsley, J., et al. (2021) *Business Analysis Techniques: 123 Essentials Tools for Success* (3rd edition). Swindon: BCS, The Chartered Institute for IT.

Carrie, S. (2024) *Secure Software Design: Safeguarding Your Code Against Cyber Threats*. Self-published.

Cohn, M. (2009) *Succeeding with Agile: Software Development Using Scrum*. Boston, MA: Addison-Wesley.

Crispin, L. and Gregory, J. (2009) *Agile Testing: A Practical Guide for Testers and Agile Teams*. Boston, MA: Addison-Wesley.

Debois, P. (2011) *DevOps from a sysadmin perspective*. Available from: usenix.org/system/files/login/articles/105516-Debois.pdf

De Voil, N. (2020) *User Experience Foundations*. Swindon: BCS, The Chartered Institute for IT.

Fishpool, B. and Fishpool, M. (2020) *Software Development in Practice*. Swindon: BCS, The Chartered Institute for IT.

Flexera (2024) *Flexera 2024 state of the cloud report*. Available from: flexera.com/stateofthecloud

Fraser, G. (2024) *CrowdStrike: What was the impact of the global IT outage*. BBC News. Available from: bbc.co.uk/news/articles/cr54m92ermgo

Gamma, E., Helm, R., Johnson, R. and Vlissides, J. (1994) *Design Patterns: Elements of Reusable Object-Oriented Software*. Boston, MA: Addison-Wesley.

International Organization for Standardization (2019) *ISO 9241-210:2019. Ergonomics of human–system interaction – Part 210: Human-centred design for interactive systems*. Available from: iso.org/standard/77520.html

International Organization for Standardization (2023a) *ISO/IEC 25010:2023. Systems and software engineering – Systems and software quality requirements and evaluation (SQuaRE) – Product quality model*. Available from: iso.org/standard/78176.html

International Organization for Standardization (2023b) *ISO/IEC 25019:2023. Systems and software engineering – Systems and software quality requirements and evaluation (SQuaRE) – Quality-in-use model*. Available from: iso.org/standard/78177.html

International Organization for Standardization, IEC and IEEE (2017) *24765:2017. Systems and software engineering – Vocabulary*. Available from: iso.org/standard/71952.html

International Software Testing Qualifications Board (ISTQB) (2023) *Certified Tester Foundation Level (CTFL) v4.0*. Syllabus.

Leapwork (2024) *The testing pyramid: what is it & how to use it in 2024*. Available from: leapwork.com/blog/testing-pyramid

Lewin, K. (1947) 'Frontiers in group dynamics: concept, method and reality in social science; social equilibria and social change'. *Human Relations*, 1(1). 5–41.

Martin, R.C. (2000) *Design Principles and Design Patterns*. Gurnee, IL: Object Mentor.

Nielsen, J. (1993) *Usability Engineering*. New York: Academic Press.

North, D. (2006) *Introducing BDD*. Available from: dannorth.net/introducing-bdd

Peters, T. and Waterman, R. (1982) *In Search of Excellence: Lessons from America's Best-Run Companies*. New York: Harper & Row.

Thompson, G., Morgan, P., Samaroo, A., et al. (2024) *Software Testing: An ISTQB-BCS Certified Tester Foundation Level guide (CTFL v4.0)* (5th edition). Swindon: BCS, The Chartered Institute for IT.

Waterman Jr, R., Peters, T. and Phillips, J.R. (1980) 'Structure is not organisation in business'. *McKinsey Quarterly*, 80(3). 2–20.

FURTHER READING

Agutter, C., van Hove, S. and Major-Goldsmith, M. (2018) *VeriSM™: Unwrapped and Applied*. Zaltbommel: Van Haren Publishing.

Beck, K. (1999) *Extreme Programming Explained: Embrace Change*. Boston, MA: Addison-Wesley.

Beck, K., Beedle, M., van Bennekum, A., et al. (2001) *The Agile Manifesto*. Dallas, TX: Agile Alliance.

Brennan, K.J., Godwin, S. and Hendrickx, F. (2022) *Digital Product Management*. Swindon: BCS, The Chartered Institute for IT.

Burnett, S. (2024) *AI in Business: Towards the Autonomous Enterprise*. Swindon: BCS, The Chartered Institute for IT.

Cohn, M. (2004) *User Stories Applied for Agile Software Development*. Boston, MA: Addison-Wesley.

Cohn, M. (2005) *Agile Estimating and Planning*. Harlow: Pearson Education.

DAMA International (2017) *DAMA-DMBOK: Data Management Body of Knowledge* (2nd edition). Basking Ridge, NJ: Technics Publications.

European Commission (2019) *Ethics guidelines for trustworthy AI. European Commission High-Level Expert Group on Artificial Intelligence*. Available from: ec.europa.eu/digital-strategy/en/news/ethics-guidelines-trustworthy-ai

European Commission (2021) *Ethics by design and ethics of use approaches for artificial intelligence*. Available from: ec.europa.eu/info/funding-tenders/opportunities/docs/2021-2027/horizon/guidance/ethics-by-design-and-ethics-of-use-approaches-for-artificial-intelligence_he_en.pdf

Evans, N.D. (2017) *Mastering Digital Business: How Powerful Combinations of Disruptive Technologies Are Enabling the Next Wave of Digital Transformation*. Swindon: BCS, The Chartered Institute for IT.

Farley, D. (2021) *Modern Software Engineering: Doing What Works to Build Better Software Faster*. Boston, MA: Addison-Wesley.

Fowler, M. (2003) *UML Distilled: A Brief Guide to the Standard Object Modeling Language* (3rd edition). Boston, MA: Addison-Wesley.

Fry, H. (2018) *Hello World: How to be Human in the Age of the Machine*. New York: W.W. Norton.

Girvan, L. and Girvan, S. (2022) *Agile from First Principles*. Swindon: BCS, The Chartered Institute for IT.

History of Data Science (n.d.) *Margaret Hamilton: The first software engineer*. Available from: historyofdatascience.com/margaret-hamilton-the-first-software-engineer

IEEE (1990) *IEEE 610.12-1990. IEEE Standard glossary of software engineering terminology*. Available from: https://standards.ieee.org/ieee/610.12/855

International Organization for Standardization (2004) *ISO/IEC 13335-1:2004. Information technology – Security techniques – Management of information and communications technology security – Part 1: Concepts and models for information and communications technology security management*. Available from: iso.org/standard/39066.html

International Organization for Standardization (2022) *ISO/IEC 22989:2022. Information technology – Artificial intelligence – Artificial intelligence concepts and terminology*. Available from: iso.org/standard/74296.html

International Organization for Standardization (2022) *ISO/IEC 23053:2022. Framework for artificial intelligence (AI) systems using machine learning (ML)*. Available from: iso.org/standard/74438.html

International Organization for Standardization (2022) *ISO/IEC 27001:2022. Information security, cybersecurity, and privacy protection – Information security management systems – Requirements*. Available from: iso.org/standard/82875.html

International Organization for Standardization (2022) *ISO/IEC 27005:2022. Information security, cybersecurity and privacy protection – Information security risk management*. Available from: iso.org/standard/82803.html

International Organization for Standardization and IEC (1994) *ISO/IEC 7498-1:1994. Information technology – Open Systems Interconnection – Basic reference model: The basic model*. Available from: iso.org/standard/20269.html

Kim, G., Debois, P., Willis, J., et al. (2022) *The DevOps Handbook: How to Create World-Class Agility, Reliability, & Security in Technology Organizations* (2nd edition). Portland, OR: IT Revolution Press.

Kim, G., Behr, K. and Spafford, G. (2024) *The Phoenix Project: A Novel About IT, DevOps, and Helping Your Business Win* (4th edition). Portland, OR: IT Revolution Press.

Kimball, R. and Ross, M. (2013) *The Data Warehouse Toolkit: The Definitive Guide to Dimensional Modeling* (3rd edition). Chichester: Wiley.

Longbottom, C. (2017) *The Evolution of Cloud Computing: How to Plan for Change*. Swindon: BCS, The Chartered Institute for IT.

Lovatt, M. (2021) *Solution Architecture Foundations*. Swindon: BCS, The Chartered Institute for IT.

Mellor, S. and Balcer, M.J. (2022) *Executable UML: A Foundation for Model-Driven Architecture*. Reading, MA: Addison-Wesley.

Mitchell, M. (2019) *Artificial Intelligence: A Guide for Thinking Humans*. New York: Farrar, Straus and Giroux.

Morris, J. (2020) *Practical Data Migration* (3rd edition). Swindon: BCS, The Chartered Institute for IT.

National Cyber Security Centre (2023) *Guidelines for secure AI system development*. Available from: ncsc.gov.uk/collection/guidelines-secure-ai-system-development

National Cyber Security Centre (2024) *AI and cyber security: what you need to know*. Available from: ncsc.gov.uk/guidance/ai-and-cyber-security-what-you-need-to-know

National Institute of Standards and Technology (2022) *Secure Software Development Framework (SSDF) Version 1.1: Recommendations for Mitigating the Risk of Software Vulnerabilities*. Gaithersburg, MD: National Institute of Standards and Technology.

National Institute of Standards and Technology (2024) *The NIST Cybersecurity Framework (CSF) 2.0* (NIST CSWP 29). Gaithersburg, MD: National Institute of Standards and Technology.

OWASP Foundation (2021) *OWASP Top 10:2021: The Ten Most Critical Web Application Security Risk*s. Wilmington, DE: OWASP Foundation.

Paul, D. and Cadle, J. (2020) *Business Analysis* (4th edition). Swindon: BCS, The Chartered Institute for IT.

Richards, M. and Ford, N. (2020) *Fundamentals of Software Architecture: An Engineering Approach*. Sebastopol, CA: O'Reilly Media.

Ries, E. (2011) *The Lean Startup: How Constant Innovation Creates Radically Successful Businesses*. London: Portfolio Penguin.

Ross, J., Beath, C. and Mocker, M. (2019) *Designed for Digital: How to Architect Your Business for Sustained Success*. Cambridge, MA: MIT Press.

Rumbaugh, J., Jacobson, I. and Booch, G. (2005) *The Unified Modeling Language Reference Manual* (2nd edition). Reading, MA: Addison-Wesley.

Schwaber, K. and Sutherland, J. (2020) *The Scrum Guide: the definitive guide to scrum: the rules of the game*. Available from: www.scrum.org

Skelton, M. and Pais, M. (2019) *Team Topologies: Organizing Business and Technology Teams for Fast Flow*. Portland, OR: IT Revolution Press.

Sutton, D. (2022) *Cyber Security: The Complete Guide to Cyber Threats and Protection* (2nd edition). Swindon: BCS, The Chartered Institute for IT.

UK Government (2018). Data Protection Act 2018, c. 12. Available from: legislation.gov.uk/ukpga/2018/12/contents

World Wide Web Consortium (W3C) (2018) *Web content accessibility guidelines (WCAG) 2.1*. Available from: w3.org/TR/WCAG21

INDEX

Figures and tables are given in italics.

www.ingramcontent.com/pod-product-compliance
Lightning Source LLC
Chambersburg PA
CBHW041554080326
40690CB00060B/5293